Stevan L. Davies

New Testament Fundamentals

Revised Edition

Polebridge Press   *Sonoma, CA*

For
Sally, Michael, and Meredith

Library of Congress Cataloging-in-Publication Data

Davies, Stevan L., 1948–
    New Testament fundamentals / Stevan L. Davies – Rev. ed.
      p.   cm.
    Rev. ed. of: New Testament : a contemporary introduction. c1988.
    Includes bibliographical references.
    ISBN 0-944344-41-0 : $17.95
    1. Bible. 2. N.T.–Textbooks. I. Davies, Stevan L., 1948- New
Testament. II. Title.
BS2330.2.D346   1994
225.6'1—dc20   93-48825
                                                CIP

Printed in the United States of America

10   9   8   7   6   5   4   3   2   1

Contents

One

Analytical Study
of the New Testament

All Christian churches use a collection of short books called the Bible as the foundation of their teaching. They believe that the Bible contains revelation from God and that it may be relied upon as a guide to moral and theological truths. Commonly, in Christian church services, passages from the Bible are read aloud and the minister of the church delivers a commentary called a sermon or homily on the passages. The purpose of a sermon or homily is to point out ways the passages read aloud might beneficially be applied to everyday life. The Bible as used in churches is, therefore, not just a collection of written texts but a resource for religious instruction.

Basic information

The Bible is divided by Christians into two parts. The first part is commonly called the Old Testament and the last part the New Testament. The Old Testament is written in Hebrew and is made up of separate texts called "books." The New Testament is written in Greek and is made up of twenty-seven "books." Protestant churches recognize thirty-nine Old Testament books; the Roman Catholic church recognizes forty-six. The books about which there is disagreement are called, by Protestants, the Apocrypha and are recognized by Protestants as historically important although not divinely inspired. Jewish people regard the Old Testament as revelation and use it in their services (particularly the first five books); they do not recognize the New Testament as revelation. The term *Old Testament* is offensive to Jewish people because it implies the revelations they value are secondary in importance to "new" revelations not contained in their Scriptures. Therefore, in scholarly writing, the term *Hebrew Bible* is now being used as a synonym for Old Testament, and it will be used that way in this book.

For similiar reasons we shall use C.E. (Common Era) for A.D. (Anno Domini = Year of Our Lord) and B.C.E. (Before the Common Era) for B.C.; these abbreviations are now commonly used by scholars.

The Hebrew Bible is important to the New Testament and the authors of the New Testament made repeated references to it. They quoted passages from it, constructed arguments based on it, believed they were writing about matters implied in it. They did this because they, like Christian and Jewish people now, believed it to be revelation from God. Throughout this book, therefore, we will refer to passages in the Hebrew Bible.

1

The twenty-seven New Testament books can be put into several categories. There are four Gospels: Matthew, Mark, Luke, and John. Gospels are accounts of the life of Jesus of Nazareth written in biographical form. The four Gospels that appear in the New Testament contain sayings attributed to Jesus, stories of miracles he is said to have performed, a general narrative of his life story at least from the time of his baptism to the time of his burial, and extensive narrative about the last few days of his life. Luke, in Acts 10:34–43, wrote a very brief summary of the essential information conveyed by such a gospel. The Gospels appear to be biographies, but they are not historical biographies in the twentieth-century sense; they are primarily intended to convey information about the religious meaning and theological significance of Jesus' life. To approach them as books of simple factual history is to miss their authors' intentions entirely.

The Acts of the Apostles (more commonly and simply known as Acts) follows the four Gospels. Its placement is unfortunate, for it was written by the author of the Gospel of Luke and is a continuation of that Gospel. Separated by the Gospel of John, Luke and Acts falsely appear to be two entirely different books. Acts tells of the activities of Jesus' disciples after his crucifixion, focusing first on his disciple Peter and later on Paul. Acts is both a history of the early church and a theological interpretation of that history.

After the four Gospels and Acts come a series of letters (a synonym for letters is *Epistles*) attributed to Paul, mainly in order of length, and then a series of short letters attributed to other important figures of the early Christian movement: James, Peter, John, and Jude. Several of them were real letters written by an individual to other individuals. Others, such as Hebrews and 1 John, are more like essays or sermons than letters.

The last book of the New Testament is Revelation. It is an account of visions seen by a man named John. This is probably not the same man who wrote the Gospel of John or the Letters of John. The visions in Revelation purport to reveal what will happen in the time just before the end of this world and its replacement by the Kingdom of God.

The twenty-seven books of the New Testament are, therefore, of various literary types: interpretive biography (the Gospels), interpretive history (Acts), letters, essays (Hebrews, 1 John), and a visionary account (Revelation).

Learning the story

Throughout this book I shall be making recommendations for reading the New Testament. My first recommendation is this: if you want to get a feel for the subject, to learn the basic stories and become acquainted with fundamental ideas, *Read the Gospel of Luke and the Acts of the Apostles.*

These two books were written by the same person as a continuous story. Luke intended to write an interesting and exciting narrative not a document to be studied line by line, phrase by phrase, so try to read this two-part book as nearly straight through as possible. If you feel at a loss concerning the New Testament, if you are not a Christian or if you are a Christian but do not feel very knowledgeable, one reading of Luke's Gospel and Acts will enable you to catch up in knowledge of the basic New Testament stories with all but the most well educated Christian people. To emphasize this point again, if you read The Gospel of Luke and the Acts of the Apostles you will become generally conversant with the basic facts, themes, and stories that will appear in the study of the New Testament. Please do so soon.

Analytical study of the New Testament

Analytical study (also called critical study) of the New Testament requires you to adopt a certain kind of approach to the New Testament, one that may be new to you. It does not need to be your only kind of approach. People are quite capable of understanding the same texts from different perspectives. The New Testament may be understood at the same time from the perspective of a church and from the perspective of analytical study. One must think in different ways in different contexts and circumstances. This book is not intended to defend an analytical perspective against a church perspective; it is intended to make the analytical perspective clear so it will be available to any person wishing to use it.

The New Testament as a single entity does not exist. Some believe the New Testament is a unit, a single book with various chapters containing essentially the same information. Analytical scholars, on the other hand, regard the New Testament as a collection of diverse letters and pamphlets bound together within a single cover. Looked at in this way, the New Testament is more of a library than a book, and it makes little sense to ask, for example, "What does the New Testament teach about the Law of Moses?" than to ask "What does the library teach about philosophy?" Each book on the subject in the library will approach philosophy somewhat differently. Each author in the New Testament approaches the Law of Moses somewhat differently. To study the New Testament is to study a collection of different works by different people with various views. There are no hard and fast conclusions from analytical study that say, "This is what the New Testament teaches about X." At best we can conclude, "This is what Matthew or Paul or John teaches about X."

Analytical study of the New Testament is not the study of Jesus. It is, rather, the study of diverse teachings about Jesus: what Matthew taught about Jesus, what Mark taught about Jesus, what Luke taught about Jesus, and so forth. What Jesus himself taught is present in the New Testament documents only indirectly. It is quite difficult to distinguish between the teachings about Jesus and his own teaching, as you shall see as you read this book. It is not impossible to isolate Jesus' own teachings from the Gospel accounts, but it is still a highly uncertain endeavor, and no scholarly consensus exists as to exactly what he taught.

Analytical study and Christian theology

Analytical study does not prove or attempt to prove that the New Testament is divinely inspired. Neither does it prove or attempt to prove that the New Testament is not divinely inspired. It is neutral. What it does do is to add greatly to knowledge of the nature of divine inspiration for those who believe in it. In other words, those believing in divine inspiration will affirm God guided the processes through which the New Testament came into being. Analytical study is in great part the study of those processes. Analytical study can therefore be said to reveal how revelation came into being, and as such it is a valuable tool for theology.

Analytical scholars are occasionally accused of denying the inspiration of the Scriptures. This misconception places an unnecessary stumbling block in the way of some people. Because this stumbling block can be a serious one, we will now turn attention to it in some detail.

Some Christians view those who study the New Testament analytically with suspicion, for they are thought not to approach the New Testament from the perspective of faith. Some may not. Some may. If the New Testament was brought into being through divine inspiration, it is analytical scholarship that seeks to learn how divine inspiration occurred. If the teachings of the New Testament authors contain divine revelation, it is analytical scholarship that seeks to discover clearly and distinctly those teachings in all their diversity. If the New Testament is to be understood on its own basis, within its own context, it is analytical scholarship that seeks most earnestly not to impose contemporary ideas of morality or philosophy or theology on those ancient texts.

The idea of divine inspiration leads logically to the conclusion that the documents of the New Testament teach the truth. It does not, however, lead logically to the conclusion that they teach a particular sort of truth. Therein lies the problem. What sort of truth is in the New Testament? Analytical scholars agree only that the documents of the New Testament express what people of faith in the first century believed to be the truth.

The New Testament books are diverse; differences of opinion are common; different and even contradictory reports of the same event are found; not all the historical statements made are historically accurate; words of people other than Jesus are attributed to Jesus. All these things disturb

Christians who presume divine inspiration would not have brought a diverse and sometimes contradictory New Testament into being.

Divine inspiration proceeds as God wished it to proceed. That seems to be an obvious statement, but it has strong implications for the value of analytical study. One should not declare in advance that God dictated revelation directly or that God used eyewitness disciples to write the New Testament. The New Testament texts themselves say nothing of the sort. One must, rather, seek to discover what happened, and, if it turns out to be the case that complex processes of oral tradition, source revision, and personal commentary combined to produce, say, Matthew's Gospel, then that was the way God intended it to be. What happened was what God intended to happen; that is the underlying thesis of the idea of divine inspiration. To find out what happened is an endeavor unifying theologians of revelation and analytical scholars.

If a Christian wishes to know what sort of revelation God would bring about, he or she must turn to the New Testament and find out; it is as simple as that. He or she should not decide in advance what kind of revelation God would bring about and then require the New Testament to be in accord with that decision. But, some people do this, declaring God would never allow a misstatement of historical fact to occur in inspired books, or that God would never allow contradictions to occur. Such people apply human standards to God. Rather than wishing to know what sort of revelation God brought into being, they insist God must have brought into being the kind of revelation they expect. It is almost as if they say, "If I were God this is what I would do," and then react with indignation when they learn God chose to do things another way.

Nearly all denominations of the Protestant and Catholic branches of the Christian church encourage the reading of the New Testament by faithful people. Those who read it are urged to learn from it, find guidance within it, and draw conclusions about God and the Son of God based on it. Nearly all denominations insist that freedom of conscience should exist and that the understanding one person achieves cannot be identical to the understanding of another. People of faith may differ, do differ, in what they believe to be the truth about Jesus and his teaching.

Analytical scholarship denies none of this and applies the same principle to the authors of the New Testament. Those authors, too, drew conclusions based on what they knew. Being human, they reached different understandings; divine inspiration is never thought to cancel out the humanity of the inspired authors.

Christians wish the New Testament to be made relevant to contemporary life and for its teachings to be made useful for modern spiritual life. That is not the job of analytical scholarship; that is the job of church ministers. Scholars, as best they possibly can, try to confine their attention to what the texts meant to those who wrote them in the context of their own times and situations. While the analytical study of the New Testament is not based on the assumption the New Testament is divinely inspired, it does not in any way contradict that assumption.

The people of faith who wrote the New Testament texts differed in what they believed to be the truth about Jesus and his teachings. The idea of divine inspiration does not logically require them all to understand matters in the same way. Rather, it affirms that divine truth exists in all the various answers they achieved. The idea of truth in diversity is quite acceptable to theology. It underlies the concept of freedom of conscience. What is dubious from a theological perspective is the idea that while Christians today may reach different conclusions, the inspired writers of the New Testament necessarily had to achieve identical conclusions.

"The Lord works in mysterious ways," and only the very arrogant will declare they know how God arranges revelation before they have studied it in all of its diversity. If the New Testament is divinely inspired, as we study it we learn about divine inspiration. If it is not divinely inspired, the New Testament we study still is the most important collection of documents in the history of the Western world.

An outline of New Testament history

At the beginning of his Gospel Luke gives a short account of his method of writing and the sources he used (Luke 1:1–4). Citations such as Luke 1:1–4 are commonly used in writing about biblical matters. Luke is the name of the book; 1:1–4 refers to chapter 1 of Luke and to verses 1 through 4 of chapter one; a citation reading Gal. 3:2–4, 6 would refer to Paul's letter to the Galatians, chapter 3, verses 2 through 4, and then also verse 6. Luke's account, in effect, is a brief summary of New Testament history prior to the writing of Luke's Gospel. The results of modern scholarly investigations are, by and large, in accord with Luke's statements. It is useful, therefore, to use Luke's account in introducing the analytic approach. Two translations follow, the first from the New English Bible, the second from the New American Standard Bible.

1. "The author to Theophilus: Many writers have undertaken to draw up an account of the events that have happened among us, following the traditions handed down to us by the original eyewitnesses and servants of the Gospel. And so I in my turn, your Excellency, as one who has gone over the whole course of these events in detail, have decided to write a connected narrative for you, so as to give you authentic knowledge abut the matters of which you have been informed."

2. "Inasmuch as many have undertaken to compile an account of the

things accomplished among us, just as those who from the beginning were eyewitnesses and servants of the word have handed them down to us, it seemed fitting for me as well, having investigated everything carefully from the beginning, to write it out for you in consecutive order, most excellent Theophilus; so that you might know the exact truth about the things you have been taught."

Luke is writing for Theophilus. The Greek word *Theophilus* is a person's name meaning "lover of God." This probably was the name of an individual, but it could have been a term for any lover of God.

Jesus of Nazareth

The presupposition of Luke's book, as for all New Testament books, is Jesus of Nazareth. Jesus lived, did certain things, said certain things. A very few of those things were eventually written down. Somehow, some of Jesus' words spoken in the Aramaic language around C.E. 30 appear in different form in the Greek language about sixty years later in the Gospel of Luke. The process of transmission took place in several stages.

Eyewitnesses

Luke mentions eyewitnesses. These people included Jesus' disciples. Like Jesus they spoke Aramaic. They remembered the sayings they found most important as best they could and repeated them to others. The process of remembering and then repeating what one hears is called *oral tradition,* which is a somewhat technical term for the process of word-of-mouth transmission. A game almost everyone has played involves one person whispering a sentence into the ear of a second; the second then repeats it to a third, the third to a fourth; and after several more repetitions the final person speaks aloud. What the first person said and what the final persons says are usually different. In oral tradition such changes take place, although the initial saying and the final version are usually recognizably similar. Still, changes take place. Long stories will be made shorter; short sayings may be expanded; details will be altered, especially such seemingly insignificant details as the names of towns and people; explanations will be added to puzzling stories or sayings.

Of the hundreds of thousands of things Jesus said during his life, only a hundred or so remain. Jesus did not decree what people should remember from what he said; the people who heard him made those decisions. This process of choice (what was remembered, what was forgotten) is also part of oral tradition.

Servants of the gospel

Luke mentions servants of the gospel, or servants of the word. The word gospel in Greek is *evangelion,* which means "good news.' In the New

Testament the word gospel usually means the good news about Jesus. The use of the word gospel for a book about Jesus came into being after the New Testament period. Most servants of the gospel were not eyewitnesses. What they heard came to them second-hand or third-hand or fourth. By Luke's time there were thousands of Christians throughout the Mediterranean world speaking various languages.

The most common language, the one most often used for business and literary purposes, was Greek. At some point early in the process of oral transmission, some servants of the gospel began to repeat Jesus' sayings in Greek rather than in his own language. This was an enormous change. Greek and Aramaic are not only different languages, they are languages from entirely different linguistic families. Greek, like Latin, Iranian, Spanish, Sanskrit, and English, is from the Indo-European family of languages; Aramaic, like Syriac, Hebrew, and Arabic, is from the Semitic family of languages. Greek is much closer to English than it is to Aramaic. The Greek language is home to the customs and styles of thought found in the philosophy and culture of Greece. Aramaic is home to the customs and styles of thought found in the philosophy and culture of Judaism.

It might be argued that the shift from Aramaic oral tradition to Greek oral tradition was the most important conceptual change to take place in the history of the Christian movement. And, alas, we have no Aramaic records at all from the first century of Christianity. None. Some scholars make intelligent guesses about the Aramaic originals of the Greek sayings of Jesus, but these remain guesses and are impossible to verify.

Recent archaeological excavations in the town of Sepphoris, which is within easy walking distance of Nazareth, indicates that Sepphoris was a populous growing metropolis and that most of its inhabitants spoke Greek. A local village carpenter would almost surely have found work there. Accordingly, it is entirely possible that Jesus could speak Greek as a second language. However, in his speech to peasant Galileans and Judeans he would have used Aramaic and so it remains unlikely that the sayings we have of his were originally in Greek.

Connected narrative

Eyewitnesses retold Jesus' Aramaic sayings to other Aramaic-speaking people, who then told them to people who spoke Greek, and soon those people told the sayings in Greek to Greek-speaking people, some of whom became servants of the gospel. The next logical step would be for someone to begin writing down Jesus' sayings and stories about him. Luke perhaps hints at this stage of development when he states that he will write a "connected narrative" or a narrative "in consecutive order." This may imply that before Luke wrote his Gospel there existed written accounts that were discon-

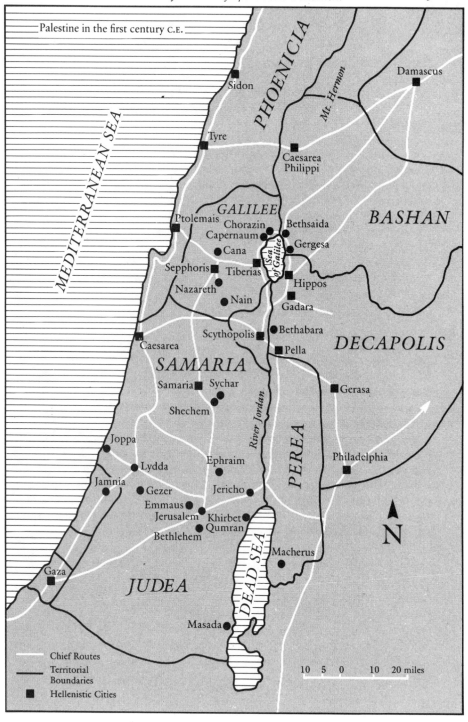

Palestine in the first century C.E.

PHOENICIA

MEDITERRANEAN SEA

Sidon

Damascus

Tyre

Mt. Hermon

Caesarea
Philippi

GALILEE

BASHAN

Ptolemais
Chorazin   Bethsaida
Capernaum
Cana   Gergesa
Sepphoris   Tiberias   *Sea of Galilee*
Nazareth   Hippos
Nain   Gadara

Scythopolis   Bethabara

Caesarea

DECAPOLIS

SAMARIA

Pella

Samaria   Sychar

Shechem

Gerasa

River Jordan

Joppa

PEREA

Ephraim

Lydda

Philadelphia

Jamnia   Gezer   Jericho

Emmaus
Jerusalem   Khirbet
Qumran
Bethlehem

DEAD SEA

Macherus

N

Gaza

JUDEA

Masada

Chief Routes
Territorial
Boundaries
Hellenistic Cities

10   5   0   10   20 miles

nected and not in consecutive order. Scholars do believe such accounts existed. In fact, two kinds of disconnected accounts existed: lists of some of Jesus' sayings, and lists of some of the miracles attributed to him. Neither kind of list was biographical in the sense of presenting a life story of Jesus or of putting the sayings and miracle stories into a biographical context. Rather, sayings and miracle stories were written one after the other and ordered, if at all, by topics.

Although we do not have in our possession ancient copies of the lists of sayings and miracle stories used by the authors of the New Testament, scholars do believe they can be recovered by analysis of New Testament documents. This book has a chapter entitled "Gospel Sources" covering that material. In 1945 a list of sayings attributed to Jesus was found buried in the desert of Egypt. Called the Gospel of Thomas, it contains many ancient and valuable versions of sayings of Jesus found in the New Testament, along with some sayings of his that otherwise are unknown, and other sayings attributed to him that he did not say. The discovery of the Gospel of Thomas has great importance for many reasons, not the least of which is that it confirms the existence of the sort of disconnected lists that scholars believe were used in the writing of the New Testament.

Many writers

"Many writers have undertaken to draw up an account of the events that have happened among us," Luke next writes. This statement points to a fact many overlook: while the New Testament is a valuable source of information about first-century Christianity, and especially about the life of Jesus, for every text it contains, many more have been lost forever. Despite knowing of the accounts of other writers, Luke would not feel the need to provide "Theophilus" with "authentic knowledge" or "the exact truth" unless he found the work of the previous writers to have been inadequate or not authentic enough. Luke carefully took one text, one Gospel by one of the writers who preceded him, and rewrote it eliminating portions, supplementing it substantially, here and there revising passages that he felt did not adequately convey the truth about Jesus. The text he revised is known to us today as the Gospel of Mark; the text he created is the Gospel of Luke. This matter will be discussed in more detail later in this book.

The process by which Luke's Gospel came into being is similar to the process by which other Gospels came into being. While the final author of a Gospel should have credit for it, in a broader sense every Gospel is the product of many people over many years who worked to choose, remember, refine, revise, translate, collect, interpret, and write down the teachings of and the teachings about Jesus.

The names of the gospels

Many people who are beginning to study the New Testament are astonished to discover that Matthew, Mark, Luke, and John had never met Jesus and that Luke, author of Acts, had probably never met Paul. Some people have spent substantial time and effort seeking to prove that the author of the Gospel of John was Jesus' "beloved disciple," that Luke was a physician who traveled with Paul, that Mark was a secretary to Peter, that Matthew was a disciple of Jesus. But they are forced to base their theories on unreliable data from the second and third centuries or even later. It is important to realize that nowhere in their Gospels do Matthew or Mark or Luke or John claim to have known or traveled with Jesus. Nowhere does Luke claim to have known Paul. Only John appeals to eyewitness testimony, and he does so only to validate specific events mentioned at the very end of his Gospel. The idea that the Gospel writers were companions of Jesus is common today, but it is an idea found nowhere in the New Testament.

Most New Testament scholars believe that the names attached to the Gospels were assigned to them in the mid-second century. We simply do not know the names or backgrounds of their authors, except as their backgrounds are revealed through the texts they wrote. But, for convenience, the authors of the Gospels of Matthew, Mark, etc. are still referred to as Matthew and Mark. But what do we know about "Matthew" etc.? Only what the Gospel of that name reveals about him.

Basic tools for research

There are basic reference tools for the study of the New Testament. The best way to become familiar with these tools is to select a passage from the New Testament, go to the library, and, using the following kinds of reference books, write a commentary on that passage.

1. *Textbooks* on the New Testament. While generally agreeing on major themes, each textbook will approach the New Testament differently and will help you understand it, or a specific book in it, in a somewhat different way.
2. *Commentaries* on the New Testament or on specific books of the New Testament. These are quite specific studies of texts and usually will comment on and attempt to explain virtually every significant passage, if not every verse, in a given text. Some commentaries seek to take the historical or analytical approach to the New Testament, but many are written from specific denominational standpoints. In using a commen-

tary you should try to determine the general approach of its author rather than simply to rely upon the author's expertise.

3. *Interlinear translations* of the New Testament take the Greek text and, on every other line, write the equivalent of each Greek word in English. If you become somewhat familiar with the Greek alphabet (which is often given at the beginning of interlinear translations), you will be able to follow the original Greek version more easily than you might think.

4. *Bible dictionaries and encyclopedias* provide detailed information about themes, names, places, and so forth. They usually do not have entries for particular verses.

5. *Concordances* are books locating each word (except such words as *the* or *and*) in the whole Bible or just in the New Testament. They list the passages in which that word occurs, usually with a sentence or a half sentence from those passages so the reader can see the word's context. The best of them use the original Greek words rather than the words of particular English translations. As the Greek words are alphabetized by their most common English language equivalents, people completely ignorant of Greek can use those concordances quite easily.

6. *Gospel parallels* are books that place similar passages from different sources adjacent to one another so that they can easily be compared. Chapter 6 of this book discusses that tool in some detail.

Bibliography

Dunn, J. D. G. *Unity and Diversity in the New Testament*. Philadelphia: Westminster Press, 1977.

Farmer, William R. *Jesus and the Gospel: Tradition, Scripture, and Canon*. Philadelphia: Fortress Press, 1982.

Funk, Robert W., and Roy W. Hoover. *The Five Gospels: The Search for the Authentic Words of Jesus*. New York: Macmillan, 1993.

Grant, Frederick C. *The Gospels: Their Origin and Growth*. New York: Harper & Row, 1957.

Hann, Robert. *The Bible: A User's Manual*. New York: Paulist Press, 1983.

Jeremias, Joachim. *The Central Message of the New Testament*. New York: Scribner's, 1963.

Kee, Howard Clark, *What Can We Know About Jesus?* New York: Cambridge University Press, 1990.

Koester, Helmut. *Introduction to the New Testament*. 2 volumes. Philadelphia: Fortress Press, 1981.

Lohse, Eduard. *The First Christians*. Philadelphia: Fortress Press, 1983.

Moore, Stephen D. *Literary Criticism and the Gospels*. New Haven: Yale Univ. Press, 1989.

Robinson, James M., and Helmut Koester. *Trajectories Through Early Christianity*. Philadelphia: Fortress Press, 1971.

Sanders, E. P. and Davies, Margaret. *Studying the Synoptic Gospels*. Trinity Press International: Valley Forge, PA, 1989.

Two

Judaism and the Roman Empire

Read chapter 12 of the Gospel of Mark from beginning to end. Make a list of every social group and organization mentioned or implied. Do this before you read the following pages. Doing so will help you realize the relevance of historical knowledge to the interpretation of Gospel passages.

Think for a moment about certain obvious facts. The books of the New Testament were written nearly two thousand years ago. Jesus lived and spoke in response to and in reference to the social, economic, religious, and political structures of his own time. These structures were different from those existing today. To understand the New Testament one must therefore understand something of the structures of that ancient time.

People beginning to read the New Testament analytically do not need to know everything about, say, the Pharisees and Sadducees. But certainly when such groups are mentioned, as they frequently are in the Gospels, people should have some basic knowledge of their status and their ideas. In the following pages we will discuss particularly the groups and institutions mentioned in Mark's chapter 12, for nearly all the most important groups and institutions are mentioned or implied there.

Roman empire

Mark 12:13–17 mentions Caesar, the Roman emperor. As an individual the emperor of Rome plays little part in the New Testament, but the empire over which he presided is of great importance. Every person who wrote about or took part in the events narrated in the New Testament lived in the same realm, the Roman Empire. We will consider it first and then turn our attention in more detail to Judaism, a crucial factor for every aspect of the New Testament.

Although Rome had been expanding its territory for several centuries, the birth of the Roman Empire as a fully grown and administratively coherent unit can be dated to the year 27 B.C.E. In that year the reign of Octavius Augustus Caesar began, a reign that was to continue for the next forty-one years. Augustus Caesar was one of those rare political geniuses capable both of conquering territory and of administering it well. The empire established by Augustus lasted for centuries. During the period of the New Testament it was a new empire, and that fact is quite important.

The Roman Empire was not just one more empire, one more conquest of territory. The Roman Empire brought unity to an enormous region containing many different civilizations. By the time of Augustus's death the Roman Empire included the areas now occupied by the Netherlands, Spain, France, Belgium, Switzerland, Austria, Italy, the Balkans, Bulgaria, Romania, Greece, Turkey, Syria, Albania, Morocco, Portugal, Lebanon, Israel, Cyprus, Jordan, Egypt, Libya, Tunisia, and Algeria. For decades after Augustus it expanded, encountering only one opponent capable of holding its own ground—the Parthian Empire in the region now known as Iran. The Roman Empire maintained order through techniques of warfare, administration, and political control. Apart from occasional border skirmishes the great majority of the populace of the empire lived in peace.

It may be convenient to think of the time before the empire as a time of tribalism. The people of Gaul, Palestine, Greece, Carthage, and Rome differed in their codes of law, their religions, their languages, their systems of coinage (if any), the weights and measures they used for commercial purposes. Commerce was difficult in a tribal environment and dangerous in the absence of peace. How many languages must a trader know to sell goods in several regions? How many kinds of coins must a trader carry, how many kinds of law must be obeyed? Who would provide assistance in times of difficulty far from home and family?

During the empire "detribalization" and "urbanization" proceeded at a rapid rate. Ancient local systems of law were terminated in some areas and replaced by Roman law. The Latin language became the language for legal and administrative matters; the Greek language became the language for trade and literature. Roman coins were legal tender throughout the empire, replacing local coinage. Weights and measures were standardized. Roman engineers built a system of roads and aqueducts throughout the empire, constructing it so skillfully that well-preserved remnants exist today in many areas of Europe. The government made sustained efforts to eliminate piracy and banditry. A primitive social welfare system was established in Rome and in some other areas.

The Roman network of roads allowed authors such as Paul regularly to send letters over hundreds of miles. In the Acts of the Apostles we read that the journeys of the apostles, who were Christian missionaries of the first century, took place easily and relatively safely.

The empire brought peace to most and prosperity to many. Stories of the persecution of Christians have led many today to believe the early Christian church and the New Testament texts it produced were opposed to the empire. That is not the case. The four Gospels and the letters of Paul were written by people who supported the authority of the empire, eager to explain as best they could that Christians were loyal inhabitants willing to pay taxes and to obey authority. Paul was a Roman citizen, a status few Jewish people held, and he was proud of that status.

The coming into being of the empire meant the rapid decline of earlier social forms. Widespread travel for purposes of trade (or military service) exposed people to many new influences and new ideas. Truths that seemed certain because one's whole family, whole village, whole tribe agreed seemed less certain hundreds of miles from home in the environs of a different culture with different assumptions. Old tribal laws gave way to new laws, usually Roman; old forms of social organization supported for centuries by custom began to die out in many regions. Many people moved to cities. The empire's great cities were very pluralistic; their inhabitants had to come to grips with changed circumstances while still retaining aspects of their ancestral cultures.

If you imagine Cuba, Mexico, Colombia, Canada, Brazil, Central America and the United States suddenly became one country speaking Portuguese, under Brazilian law, using Brazilian coinage, administered by Brazilian civil and military authority, without the trade or travel barriers now existing between those countries, you may gather some idea of the sort of disorientation that could affect people in the new empire. And yet, despite complaints about heavy taxation, most people were not opposed to the empire. The alternative, they knew, would be a nearly constant state of regional warfare.

Like all conquering powers, the Romans imposed taxes on the inhabitants of their empire. Those who had to pay them resented the obligation, especially in areas such as Palestine where many people desired political independence. Palestine, because of the religious nationalism sustaining its Jewish culture and people, was probably the single most rebellious province in the whole empire.

Mark 12:14–17. The question asked of Jesus, "Are we or are we not permitted to pay taxes to the Roman Emperor" is a clever one, for it is directed to a teacher whose strongest backing came from the people least willing or able to pay such taxes, the peasantry. But Jesus' answer is unambiguous: Yes. "Pay Caesar what is due to Caesar." This answer, and the stories of Jesus dining with and befriending tax collectors, are to show he was not interested in politically revolutionary activity. The second clause in his answer, "and pay God what is due to God," in the context of a question about taxes, means Jesus also expected his followers to pay the temple taxes required under Jewish law. Such taxes were a religious obligation as well as a civil obligation.

Jewish people

The religion of Judaism is not so much a collection of doctrines and practices as it is a community of people. To be born Jewish is to be Jewish and then, as now, Jewish people differed on what exactly they understood the requirements of their religion to be. All agreed on the cardinal principal that there is but one true God. The name of God is Yahweh, but because the name of God is holy it became customary to refer to God indirectly, as Lord (*Adonai* in Hebrew, *Kyrios* in Greek), words that were also used, as Lord is in England, to refer to men in leadership positions. The Lord was believed to have established a covenant with his Jewish people, one dating back to the time of Abraham. A covenant is a contractual relationship between two parties, here the Lord and the Jewish people. Their covenant was believed to establish a special relationship between the parties. God would protect, increase and discipline the people and provide for them the land of Palestine (the "promised land"). The Jewish people would worship God and be obedient to his commandments. The principal form of worship at the time of Jesus took place in Jerusalem at the temple and took the form of the sacrifice of animals and agricultural produce.

Mark 12:1–12. This passage tells the story of a clash between a landlord and tenant farmers. The landlord leaves his land to be farmed by people who would receive some of the produce and provide the rest as rent to the landlord. The landlord sends agents to collect the produce due him; the tenants refuse to provide it and attack the agents. This is no imaginary scenario; it reveals something of the real nature of the Palestinian economy in the early first century. Much land, perhaps most of the prime agricultural land, was owned by absentee landlords who did not work the land or live on it but who lived comfortably in major cities. In Palestine the wealthy usually had homes in Jerusalem, and people in the surrounding countryside resented Jerusalem. Other landlords, like the person mentioned in this passage, lived abroad.

The tensions between tenant farmers and landlords are easily understandable; those who did all the work and who still lived in poverty resented their legal obligation to provide much of what they produced to the owner of the land. They also resented their obligation under Jewish law to tithe, or pay 10 percent of their produce to the priests of the temple in Jerusalem. On top of all this, they had to pay taxes to Rome.

Jesus' audiences were composed primarily of people in the same social class as the tenant farmers. Poor agricultural workers, shepherds, builders, fishermen, were looked down on as crude, illiterate, ignorant, and (literally) unwashed by the wealthy and educated classes. Their adherence to the stricter requirements of Judaism was seriously doubted by religious leaders, and with good reason. Farmers under Jewish law were expected to pay 10 percent (a "tithe") of their produce to the priesthood. Tenant farmers especially and small farmers generally tried to avoid this tax if possible.

Their untithed food, therefore, was technically "impure" under the Law, and strict adherents of the Law would not eat it.

Palestinian peasants lived in an overpopulated country with land owner-ship concentrated in the hands of a few who lived in urban areas. There was very little social mobility. One famous saying of Jesus comments on these bleak economic conditions: "The man who has will always be given more; but the man who has not will forfeit even what he has" (Luke 19:26). In more prosaic terms, "the rich get richer and the poor get poorer." Jesus appears to have spoken to the peasants and identified with them; when he spoke to the rich it was usually to tell them to cease being rich and give all their wealth to the poor. The poor were Jesus' main supporters. Mark 12:12 indicates Jesus' more wealthy opponents were "afraid of the people" and therefore unwilling publicly to arrest him.

Mark 12:1. The landlord who lives abroad is representative of the majority of the Jewish people in Jesus' time. Modern legend has it that nearly all Jews were resident in Palestine until driven out by force. In fact, by the beginning of the first century the majority of Jews had chosen to live outside Palestine. Major cities such as Alexandria, Egypt; Antioch, Syria; and Rome, Italy, had substantial Jewish minorities. Sometimes these mi-norities lived under Jewish Law while the remainder of the city population lived under Roman law or their own customary law. There was frequent conflict between the two segments of the population. Such conflict may have been acceptable to Rome, as it was in Rome's interest to have subject populations fighting among themselves rather than rebelling against the empire.

Jewish traders, merchants, and artisans lived and worked throughout the empire. In every city of moderate size Jewish communities existed. There were Jewish farmers in many regions. As far as we know, most remained loyal to their traditional religion, tried, casually, to keep Jewish Law, paid a small tax to the priesthood for the upkeep of the Jerusalem temple, and felt themselves at home in whatever region they lived. No evidence exists that Jews outside of Palestine desired to settle in Palestine. Jews living outside Palestine were often strongly influenced by the culture surrounding them and were therefore regarded by the Palestinian Jewish leadership with some suspicion.

The Law
Mark 12:18–25 raises the question of what is or is not allowed in Law. Mark's chapter 12 repeatedly raises questions of Law, both religious and secular. Anyone who wishes to understand the New Testament must under-stand the role of Law in first-century Judaism. Notice the word *Law* is capitalized here. That is a reminder that Jewish Law was not thought to

come from courts, congress, or legal officials; Jewish Law was thought to come directly from God. The Law was said to have been given to Moses on Mount Sinai and to have been written down in the first five books of the Hebrew Scriptures: Genesis, Exodus, Leviticus, Numbers, and Deuteronomy. These five "books of Moses" collectively are called *Torah;* the word *Torah* means both the books themselves and the Law contained within the books. We shall often use the term *Torah Law* rather than *Jewish Law,* to emphasize that from the Jewish perspective their Law did not come from the officials of their particular ethnic group but from God. Genesis and Exodus contain narratives with which you are probably familiar: the stories of creation, Adam and Eve, Noah, Abraham, Moses leading his people from bondage in Egypt into the desert toward the Promised Land. Leviticus, Numbers, and Deuteronomy are primarily, but not entirely, books of Law. They too contain narrative. Since Torah is both story and Law code, the term can be used quite flexibly. In Galatians 4:21 Paul uses the term as both story and as Law code in the same sentence.

Many Christians assume that the Law of Moses (which is another way of saying Torah) is the Ten Commandments. This is not true. The Law contains the ten commandments and more than six hundred other specific commandments, along with much interpretation and detailed requirements for temple sacrifice and for formal festivals such as Passover. The fact that the Law is concerned with even small details of daily life is crucial to understanding New Testament authors' serious concern with the Law. Christians today may have no interest in that Law (although many Jewish people still seek to follow it carefully), but if they wish to understand Paul and the evangelists they must pay attention to their interests. The Law was of interest to them all.

Read Leviticus chapters 11, 12 and 23, 24. These passages are a small part of the Torah Law. It is only by reading some of the Law that you can come to understand the range of matters covered and the amount of detail contained.

You will notice a particular concern with purity and impurity (or, clean and unclean). Purity and impurity are not moral categories but ritual categories. God is said to expect his priests, or perhaps all of his "holy" people, to maintain purity and, should they become impure, to regain purity by ritual bathing. There is nothing wrong, evil, or wicked about impurity; it is normal at certain times. Similarly, one who is pure is not necessarily good, innocent, or morally perfect. Purity is only the state of not being impure, and vice versa. As it is written in the Torah, much of the Law and especially the requirements for maintaining purity applied to the priesthood and not to ordinary people.

Impurity can be transmitted; purity cannot be. In other words, a person who is impure can touch another person or touch a bowl of food, and render the person or the bowl impure. Whoever eats the food in the bowl will become impure. The Law is not so much against impurity for its own sake as against the transmission of impurity to holy things such as the food offered at the Jerusalem temple.

Gentiles

Gentile is the word commonly used for all people who are not Jewish; virtually everything in the Gentile world is impure. This is not because there is something immoral about Gentiles but because Gentiles, ignorant of purity laws, pay no attention to them. A Jewish person intent upon maintaining purity would rarely associate with Gentiles during meals.

This matter is important to the New Testament because it gave rise to a crucial question: must Gentiles who become Christians keep Laws regarding food? As we shall see, some of the New Testament authors said yes (for example, Matthew), while others said no (for example, Paul), and some offered a compromise (for example, Luke).

Scribes

Mark 12:28, 32, 35, 38. The scribes (or lawyers or doctors of the Law) were Jewish legal officials about whom little is known. They were probably similar to local magistrates or justices of the peace today. Scribes were not the same as the Pharisees (see below), although both groups were concerned with Law. The scribes, whose influence declined greatly toward the end of the first century, had formal authority during Jesus' life. The Pharisees did not, although they had acquired it by the time the Gospels were being written.

The name *scribes* comes from the historical role of scribes in writing the Torah which, in those days, had to be copied by hand. A scribe-copyist would learn to be very exact, for an error could lead to legal complications and would be an offense against God.

The scribes probably adhered only to the written Torah while Pharisees believed there was also an unwritten oral Torah. The scribes, therefore, were probably allied not with Pharisees but with the authorities who found the written Torah sufficient.

Mark 12:13–17. Two Jewish groups are mentioned in this passage: the Pharisees and men of Herod's party.

Pharisees

Pharisees were members of what would soon become an important religious and political movement that would evolve into the Rabbinic Judaism of today. They believed all of the Jewish people should obey all the Law. This sounds like a simple enough thesis, but it contains two substantial changes from traditional understandings.

First, the Law from the Pharisees' perspective does not distinguish between priests and people in regard to purity. Therefore, the Pharisees believed, all people were subject to many regulations previously applied only to priests. This especially applied to the habits and procedures of dining. Priests' food was holy, consecrated to God because it came from the tithes of common people and from sacrifices at the temple. To make impure something that was consecrated and holy was an offense against God and strictly forbidden. Therefore priests were required to be extremely careful not to render their consecrated food impure. Pharisees were well-educated Jews who sought to extend to its maximum the concept of the holy people of God. In their opinion holiness should not be the responsibility of priests alone but of every Jew; every meal should be eaten in an atmosphere of holiness as if it were eaten at the temple, as if the food had been consecrated to God. Thus the stricter priestly codes of purity were applied even to the common people.

Second, the Pharisees believed the Law included not only the Torah, the five books of Moses, but also a body of legal interpretations supposedly given first to Moses and then passed down by word of mouth to the present day. This has been given the name "oral Torah," from the method of its transmission. From the perspective of the common people both the extension of priestly laws of purity to all Jews and the addition of an extensive oral Torah to the written Torah made the attempt to remain obedient much more difficult. Few peasants could even approach the standards set for them by the Pharisees. A religious leader who identified with the peasantry and who suggested they might be acceptable to God without detailed concern for the oral Torah would be opposed by Pharisees; Jesus was one such leader.

To the two meanings of Torah mentioned earlier (the five books of Moses and the Law contained in those books), we must therefore add another: the Oral Law and the extended interpretations of the Pharisees. In reading the New Testament and thinking about it, the various definitions of Law must be kept clear. One might say, for example, that Jesus did teach obedience to Law while at the same time being in conflict with Pharisaic instructors of the Law who accused him of opposition to it. He may have called for obedience to the Law in the books of Moses without expecting peasant followers to obey strict Pharisaic interpretations of it.

During the time of Jesus the Pharisees were somewhat influential, but they were a distinct minority. Despite their being frequently mentioned in the New Testament, and despite the occasional references to them in first century Jewish writings, we really have very little solid information about the Pharisees' ideas and roles in the society of Jesus' time. Their power grew enormously during the first century, and by the end of that century they were the dominant force in Judaism. This happened because their base of power and influence was local synagogues rather than the temple in Jerusalem, as will be discussed below.

Synagogue

Mark 12:39 refers to the synagogue, where scribes or doctors of the Law are said to have had "chief seats," and where they had "places of honor at feasts." This may well have been more true for Mark's time than for the time of Jesus. The synagogue was the meeting place of the Jewish community. If you are at all familiar with synagogues in your own town you already know much of what you need to know about the synagogues of the first century. Although forms, languages, and procedures have changed over the past two thousand years, the basic nature of synagogues and their services have not. Synagogues served both then and now as centers for Jewish community life and as places for community prayer. Every town of substantial size in the Roman Empire had at least one synagogue, and services in all of them were similar. During services the Torah was read aloud and then discussed by experts in the Law. In the first century many of those experts would have been Pharisees; today they are called rabbis.

In addition to reading and interpreting the Torah, synagogue services included prayer and the singing of psalms. Christians familiar with services that include Bible reading, a sermon, prayers, and hymns will find nothing strange in this; their services are the direct historical descendants of synagogue services.

The first-century function of the synagogue as the center of community life should also be familiar to Christians and Jews of the twentieth century. Jews went to the synagogue for conversation, for occasional meals, for celebrations and festivals. Important passages in life—birth, maturity, marriage, and death—were formalized in synagogues. Christian churches today fulfill the same roles for Christians as synagogues did and do for Jews.

The legal authority of the synagogue leadership in the first century is not paralleled today in the Christian churches. Churches do not have judicial powers over their members in twentieth-century America. But under the Roman Empire the Jewish people were sometimes allowed to keep Torah Law. To keep Torah Law meant the establishment of a system of courts and lawyers. The leaders of the community, who were also leaders of the synagogue, were not just religious but also judicial figures and might be recognized as such by both Jewish and Roman authority. By the time the Gospels were written, the Pharisees were first among those community leaders.

Herod Antipas

Mark 12:13. The men of Herod's party who are associated in the passage with the Pharisees were officials loyal to the government of Herod Antipas. At the time of Jesus' crucifixion Herod Antipas had been installed by Rome as the official "puppet" king of the Jewish people. His father, Herod the Great, ruled both Judea and Samaria from 37 B.C.E. to 4 B.C.E.. Herod Antipas, one of Herod the Great's sons, received one-third of that empire, including the region of Galilee. Both Herods were titled King of the Jews, at least officially. Their rule was regarded with suspicion by a substantial number of Jews. For one thing, they were not descendants of David, the originator of the line of Jewish kings, and so they were theoretically ineligible for the kingship. For another, they were not ethnically Jewish but members of a related group, the Idumeans. Finally, they were puppets of Rome without much independent decision-making power. Their policy in regard to Rome came down to this: If you cannot defeat the great power, you had best get along with it.

It is implied in Luke 1:5 that Jesus was born during the reign of Herod the Great. As Herod died in 4 B.C.E., Jesus was born well before the year C.E. 1, which our present calendar implies is his year of birth. King Herod the Great did great things for his people, including massive building projects such as the reconstruction of the temple in Jerusalem. But he never won favor from his people due to the insufficiency of his claims to the kingship and his tactics of violent pressure.

Herod the Great was succeeded by his son, who was known as Herod Antipas. During the reign of Herod Antipas rioting frequently broke out. He became so hated by his subjects that eventually Rome removed him from office. His reign extended from 4 B.C.E. to C.E. 39. Another Herod is mentioned in the book of Acts, Herod Agrippa who ruled the territory of Herod Antipas after 40 C.E. He was responsible for the death of James son of Zebedee and the imprisonment of Peter. He died in 44 C.E.

Sadducees

Mark 12:18–27 describes a controversy between Jesus and Sadducees. The Sadducees were members of the upper classes. They were often from priestly families, and their center of power was the city of Jerusalem. As people of wealth they sought accommodation with their Roman rulers. They tried to maintain harmony between Rome and the Jewish people, to keep Torah Law, and to avoid offending the Romans who controlled their nation. Their wealth and position depended on political stability.

The disagreement mentioned in the passage is a technical, legal one: to whom is a woman married after her resurrection if she has previously been repeatedly widowed? The Sadducees are not interested in a definitive answer. They are attempting to show the logical absurdity of the idea of resurrection. Sadducees thought God's revelation in the Torah was sufficient. The idea of resurrection is not present in Torah, nor is it clearly present anywhere else in the Hebrew Scriptures. Therefore Sadducees did not believe in it.

This is a point on which Pharisees and Sadducees differed: Pharisees did think there would be a resurrection. Since they believed in the new idea of an oral Torah, they were more open to new ideas than Sadducees, who believed only in the written Torah. In this dispute Jesus is on the side of the Pharisees.

Essenes

One significant group of Jewish people is never mentioned in the New Testament: the Essenes. We learn of the Essenes from other sources, the most important of which are Hebrew Bible texts they used and books they wrote. So far as we know, the Essenes were destroyed during the war that took place between Jews and Romans from C.E. 66 to 73. Aware of the danger, the Essenes from a community in Qumran, near the Dead Sea, hid their books (written on scrolls) in caves. Many of these have been recovered during the past several decades and are known as *the Dead Sea scrolls*.

The Essenes believed in such absolutely strict application of Torah Laws of purity that many of them left the more thickly populated areas of Palestine and established self-contained communities in desert regions. One such community was at Qumran. Other Essenes sought to maintain strict lives of purity in the cities of Palestine. The Essenes believed that the Jerusalem temple was under the control of illegitimate priests and had itself been made impure, so they refused to participate in temple ceremonies. Their own ceremonies were focused on their meals; they elevated dinners into ritual occasions where they dined on food and drink of guaranteed purity.

The Essenes regarded the world in black-and-white terms; the human race was composed of children of light and children of darkness and there was no middle ground. They believed God would bring an end to this world in the immediate future, and only children of light like themselves would be saved. During the end times the messiah would come (or perhaps two messiahs, one of the priesthood, one to be king), and the Romans would be driven away forever. A messiah, literally "one who is anointed," is a Jewish king (or sometimes a Jewish priest) whose right to rule comes from God. In times when the legitimacy of Jewish kings was denied many Jewish people expected God to send a new messiah.

There is no good evidence that Jesus was an Essene, but John the Baptist may have been raised in an Essene community. Some Essenes did not marry but adopted and raised other people's children, especially children from priestly families. John's father was a priest, and Luke reports that "as the child grew up he became strong in spirit; he lived out in the wilds until the day when he appeared publicly before Israel" (Luke 1:80), which may mean he lived in a desert Essene community. John's practice of baptism may derive from ritual bathing, which Essenes practiced more strictly than did most other Jews and which they may, like John, have regarded as a token of repentance for sin. In his preaching John quoted a passage from Isaiah about "a voice crying aloud in the wilderness, prepare a way for the Lord; clear a straight path for him" (Luke 3:4), a passage given prominence in important Dead Sea scrolls. John's refusal to eat village food but, rather, to eat "locusts and wild honey" (Mark 1:6), may have stemmed from Essene training, for they believed that villagers' food was impure, while food found in nature was pure. People raised in desert regions regarded some species of locusts as good to eat and the Torah approves of this. If Jesus was influenced by the Essenes, it was probably through John the Baptist.

Some scholars of the New Testament believe Essene practices and beliefs influenced the formation of Christian practice and belief and that formal Essene meals may have given rise to Christian communion meals. The Essene belief in the immediate coming of the end of this world and the coming of the messiah of God is thought sometimes to have influenced Christian teaching of the coming of the end and the arrival of God's kingdom. These and other connections between Essene and early Christian ideas have not yet been proven conclusively, however, and may be overstated because we have so much information about the Essenes from the Dead Sea scrolls and so little information about other Jewish movements of the first century.

Temple

Mark 12:32–44 deals with events that took place in the temple. During Jesus' lifetime the temple in Jerusalem was the formal center of the Jewish religion. Synagogues were not local temples; they were community worship centers with much less formal religious significance. Only at the Jerusalem temple could sacrifices be made to God, and sacrifices performed by priests were the principal means of ritualized worship demanded by the Torah. Priests were born into a special caste. Many were poor farmers who performed sacrifices as seldom as once each year in the temple. John the Baptist's father, Zechariah, was one such priest (Luke 1:8). Other priests, however, were very important individuals, members of both the religious and political elite who lived year round in Jerusalem officiating at temple sacrifices. The High Priest may have been, in the absence of a legitimate king, the single most important Jewish official.

Temple sacrifices, reflected in *Mark 12:33,* were carried on daily. Bulls, sheep, and goats were brought to the temple to be ceremonially killed by members of the priesthood. Having killed the animal, the priests would splash its blood on the alar and divide its body according to specifications written in the Torah for particular sacrifices. Some of the animal might be burned on the altar, other parts might go to the priests for their meals, and the remainder would be returned to the offerer for his own meals. Any animal brought for sacrifice became holy, consecrated to God, and therefore priests who ate that holy food had to be exceptionally careful not to allow it to become ritually impure.

The priests of the temple were allied with the Sadducees, and the two groups overlapped considerably, for many Sadducees were priests. Priests wished not to offend Rome for fear the Romans might interfere with the operation of the temple.

During festival seasons, especially Passover, Jews from all over Palestine and from distant points of the Roman world came to Jerusalem to offer sacrifices. Passover was then and still is today a religious ceremony of remembrance of the beginning of the Jews' exodus from Egypt. At the time of Passover Jerusalem, usually dominated by conservative forces such as the Sadducees, scribes, and priests, filled with common people from the countryside. This led to great uneasiness on the part of the occupying Roman forces, for it might be at such a festival that revolution would break out. Pontius Pilate, the Roman official in charge of the province of Judea, usually did not stay in Jerusalem, but he did come with his troops during the Passover festival to keep order.

Just before Passover Jesus was executed by order of Pilate. This may have occurred after Jesus had been subjected to an inquiry by the Sanhedrin, a supreme religious court dominated by Sadducees and important priests.

Zealots

Mark 12:1–9 implies the possibility of revolution. We discussed this passage previously in terms of tenant farmer-landlord tensions. The tenant farmers mentioned in the passage rebel and attack the agents of the landlord. There was an organized revolutionary group in Palestine during or shortly after Jesus' lifetime, a movement composed of people known as Zealots, many drawn from tenant farmer and peasant ranks. This liberation organization sought through violent activity to drive the Roman armies from the country. During the first century their activities increased until the region exploded into civil war during the years C.E. 66 to 73.

Zealots do not play a prominent role in the Gospels, although it is conceivable Jesus was executed because he was thought, incorrectly, to be a Zealot. The prisoner called Barabbas, who was reportedly under arrest at the same time as Jesus (Mark 15:7), had been convicted of violent revolutionary activity and may have been a Zealot. Luke reports that one of Jesus' disciples was known as Simon the Zealot (Luke 6:15). Jesus was probably not a Zealot; no Zealot would have associated with tax collectors and advocated the payment of Roman taxes as Jesus did. Further, no record exists of Jesus calling for violent expulsion of Roman authority.

Zealots are more important to the New Testament indirectly than directly. Their revolution, their war against Rome, failed completely. Its failure culminated in the physical destruction of the temple in Jerusalem in the year C.E. 70. That year marks a turning point in the history of the Jewish religion that is perhaps the most important single event in Jewish history since the establishment of the kingdom of David.

During Jesus' life, Judaism was focused on the temple. The duty to perform sacrifices at the temple was as much a part of the Law as any other commandments were. The Sadducees and priests owed their positions of authority to their positions in the temple. The High Priest's great authority stemmed directly from his temple responsibilities. The Pharisees and the synagogues, while of some importance, had nothing like the authority of the temple and its officials.

But after C.E. 70, after the temple had been destroyed, everything changed. Three alternatives were available: (1) Judaism could cease to exist. This did not happen. (2) The temple sacrifices could be offered in other places. But the centrality of the temple was so ingrained in Judaism by then that this alternative was not even tried. (3) Judaism might evolve in a different direction, so that the end of sacrifice might be the beginning of something quite different. This is what took place.

After C.E. 70 most of the Jewish groups we have been considering no longer had power.

The priests no longer had an active role to play in the religion. Although honored in theory, in practice their influence rapidly declined.

The Sadducees failed in their attempt to avoid civil war; Roman trust in them vanished. Their temple-based authority was destroyed. The Sadducees ceased to exist as an influential group.

The scribes, whose formal power was related to that of the priestly authorities in Jerusalem, saw their power rapidly decline, and, like the Sadducees, the scribes soon ceased to exist as an influential group.

The Zealots had been thoroughly and soundly defeated by Roman military power. Although there was another civil war (and another total defeat) in C.E. 135, for the rest of the first century the remaining Zealots were little more than groups of bandits.

At about this time the Essenes too ceased to exist as a significant movement. It seems likely the Essenes interpreted the civil war to be the beginning of the messianic age, when God would empower a legitimate king to drive out his enemies and establish his kingdom, and that they went out from their desert settlements to take part in it. Most were probably killed by Roman soldiers.

Of the groups mentioned in Mark 12:1–44, only the Pharisees came through well. They soon began to set down the legal and religious principles that would govern Judaism for the next two thousand years. Those principles were built upon the assumption that all Jewish people should act in obedience to Torah both written and oral. After the destruction of the temple this principle became policy. Synagogues gained immensely in importance, for they replaced the temple in Jerusalem as the focal point of Jewish life.

The destruction of the temple in C.E. 70 had consequences for the New Testament. For example, as we will see, Paul taught about the sacrificial death of Jesus Christ on the cross, while Matthew taught that a central theme of Christianity is the necessity of following Torah Law as interpreted by Jesus Christ. Paul, writing around C.E. 55, before the destruction of the temple, reflects the existence of the temple and its sacrifices; Matthew, writing around C.E. 85, reflects the Pharisaic renewal of Judaism and its focus on obedience to Torah. The Gospels' portrayal of Pharisees as leading authorities of Judaism, and as Jesus' principal rivals, may owe more to the perception of the evangelists writing fifty years later than to the conditions present during Jesus' ministry in or around C.E. 30. It is an interesting fact of history that Christianity and Rabbinic Judaism came into being at almost exactly the same time.

Mark 12:38–39 might reflect the growing influence of the Pharisees in the report of Jesus' attack on those who are arrogant in the synagogues. Criticisms of Pharisees appear in the Gospels, but nowhere do criticisms of the institution of synagogues appear. The social function of synagogues in the first century was unique. No other institution in all of the empire was so comprehensive in the assistance it offered its people. Jews from Palestine could journey to Greece on business or pleasure and find a Jewish community organized around a synagogue to welcome them on their arrival. Jews could expect some assistance from members of a foreign synagogue if they were without food or shelter or clothing or if they were in legal trouble. Jews in legal trouble away from home could turn to the synagogue for assistance. Because synagogues were common, Jews were more at home in the empire as a whole than was any other group, with the exception of the citizens of Rome itself.

Other religious groups

The religions of the Roman Empire were many centuries old, and, as they developed in different cultures with different languages and customs, they were quite diverse. But to make it somewhat easier to think about them, let us divide them into three general categories: hearth religion, mystery religion, and imperial religion.

Hearth religion

Hearth religion was found throughout the empire. It was focused on the heart of the home, the hearth, the homes' center for warmth, light, and food. Particular deities, varying from place to place or even family to family, were thought to be willing to guide, guard, and assist individuals if properly worshiped. In most of the homes of the empire an area was set aside for worship. Regularly, often at the time of the new moon, the family would provide food and flowers and other tokens of respect for their gods. Hearth religion had its base in homes but could extend to larger social groups, so that each village and city had deities thought to be its special protectors. Christian devotion to patron saints is akin to, and may have developed historically from, customs of hearth religion.

Mystery religion

Mystery religion was more formally organized than hearth religion. It is called mystery religion because at the core of its practice were mysteries, sacred rites initiating adherents into the cult. Some mystery religions had several stages of initiation but in all of them the rites were kept secret. Today, while we know something of the mystery religions, our knowledge is very incomplete because their secrets were so well kept. Each mystery religion was separate from the others in terms of its organization, its history, and its specific practices, but they had general features in common. In order to see their common features, we will discuss four specific mystery religions.

The mysteries in Eleusis, a town in Greece, occurred periodically, but individuals were allowed to participate only once during their lives. A procession formed near Athens and, having taken the drug *kykeon*, proceeded to the small town of Eleusis. There the mysteries of Demeter, the goddess of the earth, were enacted. Although scholars are not certain, most believe the rites included the enactment of the story of Kore-Persephone, daughter of Demeter. Kore was carried off by the god of the underworld, Hades-Pluton. Demeter searched frantically for her and, failing to find her, began to fast. The fasting of the earth goddess produced failure of crops until, eventually, Zeus intervened and brought about the release of Kore.

This mythological tale symbolizes the cycle of the year. There is a period of growth and plenty when Kore and Demeter are together, and a period of death and potential famine (winter) when Kore and Demeter are separated. Those who were initiated at Eleusis believed their initiation guaranteed them eternal life.

The mysteries of Isis began to spread throughout the empire at roughly the same time as did Christianity, but the worship of Isis had long been part of the ancient religion of Egypt. Its mythological and ritual emphasis was on the death and rebirth of Osiris, husband of Isis. Osiris, it was said, had been murdered by his antagonist Seth and had been dismembered. Isis searched frantically for him, reassembled him, and he returned to life. Rather than the yearly cycle, the mysteries of Isis symbolized the daily cycle. Osiris, symbol of the sun, rises to the heavens and dies into the underworld. Initiates of the Isis mysteries believed that after their deaths they would live forever with Osiris.

The mysteries of Mithra originated in Persia. Their principal mythology concerns the god Mithra's battle with a great bull. After Mithra killed the bull, its body returned to life as the earth's plants and animals. Mithra ascended to heaven and joined the god of the sun. Mithra's initiates believed that after death they, like Mithra, would ascend to the realm of the sun. Mithra's birthday was celebrated on December 25th, near the time of the winter solstice when days become shortest and begin again to lengthen. The empire-wide celebration of Mithra's birthday is thought by most scholars to have led Christians to celebrate the birth of Jesus on the same date.

The mysteries of Cybele, which developed in Phrygia in Asia Minor, spread rapidly throughout the empire. The cult worshiped the Great Mother of life, Cybele. Her mysteries are based on the story of her lover Attis who was unfaithful to her. Filled with guilt, Attis castrated himself and died. Cybele eventually brought him back to life. As was the case in Eleusis, the mysteries of Cybele ritually depicted the cycle of the seasons, with Attis taking the role of Kore-Persephone.

The four mystery religions mentioned here had certain motifs in common. Each believed in a deity who died and then rose to life again (Kore-Persephone, Osiris, the Mithraic bull, Attis). Each believed that through participation in the mysteries and faith in their teachings, individuals could achieve eternal life with the deities. Very little in the New Testament derives directly from any specific mystery cult, but it is clear that the Christian teaching of the death and resurrection of Jesus Christ the Son of God, faith in which leads to eternal life with God, would not have seemed utterly novel to people of the ancient world.

Imperial religion

Imperial religion in the Roman world was the formal worship of the emperor of Rome. This is not the same as Roman religion, which involved worship of traditional Roman gods such as Mars, Jupiter, and Venus, as well as traditional practices we have called hearth religion. Julius Caesar was declared formally deified, but this did not mean he claimed to be God in the Jewish or Christian sense. It meant, rather, that he deserved respect because his accomplishments indicated he had a divine spirit in him. His successor Octavian took the name Augustus, which is a religious title meaning one worthy of veneration.

One of Augustus's coins, or perhaps a coin of Tiberius who ruled at the time of the crucifixion, is referred to in *Mark 12:16*. Such coins bore a variety of inscriptions. On some of his coins Augustus referred to himself as "son of god," by which he meant little more than that he was the formally adopted son of the deified Julius Caesar. Many Roman coins had on their "tails" side images of various gods or religious ceremonies or altars. Because of these images, and the image of the emperor on the "heads" side, religious Jews sought to reduce the circulation of ordinary Roman coins in their territory. Accordingly, Roman law permitted in Palestine the use of special coins that bore no offensive imagery. For this reason there were money changers in the environs of the Jerusalem temple.

The worship of the emperor in the early empire was more like a civil ceremony than a religious event, more like pledging allegiance to the flag than worshiping God. The emperor of the early first century who seems most sincerely to have believed himself to have been a god, Gaius (known also as Caligula), was regarded even by the Romans as insane.

Jews were legally excused by Roman authority from the requirement that they take part in the ceremonies of emperor worship. Gentiles who became members of Christian churches claimed this privilege as well, but to them it was denied, for only Jews who kept Torah Law could claim exemption from this Roman law. Christians continued to refuse to participate. This led to increasing Roman persecution of Christians, especially in the second and third centuries.

In addition to the varieties of religion discussed above, many other religious and philosophical sects competed for adherents during the early empire. They are a fascinating area for research. One important point must be made: those religions were inferior in their social aspects to synagogue Judaism. Some, such as the cult of Mithra (exclusively for men), were predominantly for one sex or the other, and so family life could play little or no role in them. In the synagogue the family was included. Others, such as the mystery rituals at Eleusis, were once-in-a-lifetime events, which might be revisited but never repeated and so had little regular social significance. Synagogues, by contrast, assembled at least once every week.

The Roman religion had appeal primarily to Romans, and to political officials who wanted to win favor with Roman authorities. No effort at the conversion of other peoples was contemplated.

Judaism, on the other hand, did make an effort to convert other peoples; anyone willing to accept the responsibilities of Judaism, including especially the responsibility for strict obedience to the laws of God found in the Torah, was welcome to join. Those who did not wish to adopt strict obedience were welcome to affiliate with Judaism and received the title *God-fearers*.

People did wish to join. The rapid growth of Christianity is evidence for this, for Christianity (especially as taught by Paul and his followers) offered to Gentiles the possibility of becoming Jewish. Thousands accepted, especially God-fearers. Jewish, in this sense, means the people of God, worshipers of the God revealed in the Torah. It does not, as understood and taught by Paul, include the responsibility for strict obedience to the laws of God found in the Torah, as we shall discuss in this book's chapter on Paul.

The success of Christianity

The fact that Christianity grew rapidly and eventually became dominant in the empire is familiar to most people. But why did people join? What made so many Gentiles eager to adopt this Christian form of Judaism, a form considered inauthentic by the Jews of the synagogues? There are several reasons.

1. In the Roman Empire the old religions had begun to look rather inadequate. With their many gods, their often morally questionable mythologies, their statues of human and animal-headed deities, most of the ancient religions became difficult to defend outside their own locale. In other words, if you were born, lived, and died in a certain region, whatever religion was customary there was probably satisfactory to you. But away from that region, when custom did not provide sufficient evidence for the truth of the religion, traditional religions could prove hard to justify. Philosophers asserted that all of the deities worshiped in the Roman Empire were versions of each other, that, for example, Hermes of Greece and Mercury of Rome and Thoth of Egypt were one and the same. But the evidence of contradictory mythologies, rival priesthoods, and dissimilar rituals made this assertion difficult to maintain seriously.

2. The Torah, the books of Moses, were widely regarded as ancient and were often respected. Although some laws were viewed with suspicion (Sabbath rest was thought sometimes to be laziness), the moral authority of the Torah in general was frequently acknowledged.

3. Judaism offered one God, God of all the world and not of a region or aspect of the world. There were no images of that God, no embarrassing animal-headed images (as were common in Egypt), no human-headed images (reminiscent of the statues of political leaders). Philosophers of Greece and Rome had defended the concept of the one God; the Jews agreed and claimed they alone worshiped that God.

4. Most religions of the empire were ecumenical; that is, members of various religions were willing to admit the general truth of other religions and to identify others' gods with their own. Judaism, however, was quite adamant that its God was the only God. This was an attractive feature to many people. The feeling that one's religious beliefs are wholly true and the religious beliefs of others who hold different views are entirely false is psychologically satisfying to people unable to face uncertainty. Christians adopted form Judaism the belief that their God was the only God and that all other worship was directed to demons, idols, and illusions.

5. The Jewish idea of prophecy, that certain special people might receive the Spirit of God and be transformed so as to be able to speak God's words, was extended in Christianity to include all Christian believers. The story of Pentecost in the book of Acts chapter 2 is the story of the Spirit coming to all of Jesus' followers. Paul in Romans chapter 8 indicates that reception of the Spirit is of critical importance and in his First Corinthian letter, chapters 11 through 14, he describes some of the manifestations of the Spirit in a Christian community. John's gospel promises that the Spirit, there called the Paraclete, will be given to all Christians. The experience of the reception of the Spirit was one of attainment of special supernatural power that was taken to confirm hopes of eternal life. This pleasurable and empowering experience, promised to all who would be Christian, surely motivated many people to enter the Christian movement. Although the idea of the reception of the Spirit derived from the Jewish prophetic model, official Judaism did not accept that God any longer sent prophets. The Judaism of the common people did accept that there were still occasional prophets, but such people were regarded as very rare. In regard to the common availability of the prophetic experience Judaism and Christianity were, therefore, in disagreement.

6. The synagogues were an extremely attractive institution. They were adapted to an empire where travel for purposes of trade, tourism, and

military service was becoming increasingly common. They were adapted to an urban environment and, in the empire, people frequently came from homes in distant rural regions to live and work in strange cities. The synagogues offered social acceptance and social security to any Jewish person in all regions. No other religion or cult had nearly as comprehensive a social organization. The network of Christian churches that grew rapidly in the first century provided Christians with social centers analogous to synagogues.

Judaism was by no means universally respected. Some Gentiles were opposed to Judaism, but many others were not. A substantial number of Gentiles who were sympathetic to Judaism subsequently adopted Judaism in the form of Christianity. To do so was to worship a single universal God, be addressed by the revelations in the Torah, be guided by the moral principles of the Torah, and be members of a worldwide network of supportive social centers.

It was through Paul's influence that the most successful branch of the Christian church of the first century offered Gentiles the opportunity to join this attractive religion without the adoption of such Jewish customs (and also Torah laws), as circumcision of males, avoidance of certain foods (especially pork and shellfish), and concern for the detailed and difficult rules of purity and impurity. The Christian movement offered its members the opportunity to identify themselves with the chosen people of God, to regard the Hebrew Scriptures and especially the Torah as addressed to themselves, to worship the one God, to receive the Spirit of God. These ideas were attractive to many. But it is likely the most attractive element of all was the opportunity to join the Christian network of churches that arose parallel to the Jewish network of synagogues. In both networks members were expected or even required to love one another, to feed their hungry, visit their fellow members in jail, clothe their fellow members who were naked, shelter their fellow members who were homeless. In the time of the early empire, when many people were forced by Roman law, economic change, and social dislocation to reorient their thinking away from their ancestral ways, it is hard to imagine a more attractive option than this network of churches modeled on the synagogues.

Bibliography

Brown, Raymond E. *The Churches the Apostles Left Behind.* New York: Paulist Press, 1984.

Foerster, Werner. *From the Exile to Christ: An Historical Introduction to Palestinian Judaism.* Philadelphia: Fortress Press, 1964.

Gager, John G. *Kingdom and Community*. Englewood Cliffs: Prentice-Hall, 1975.

Grant, Michael. *The World of Rome*. New York: New American Library, 1961.

Kee, Howard C. *Christian Origins in Sociological Perspective*. Philadelphia: Westminster Press, 1977.

Malherbe, Abraham J. *Social Aspects of Early Christianity*. Philadelphia: Fortress Press, 1983.

Meeks, Wayne A. *The First Urban Christians*. New Haven: Yale University Press, 1983.

Neusner, Jacob. *From Politics to Piety*. Englewood Cliffs: Prentice Hall, 1973.

Newsome, James D. *Greeks, Romans, Jews*. Philadelphia: Trinity Press International, 1992.

Nock, Arthur Darby. *Early Gentile Christianity and Its Hellenistic Background*. New York: Harper & Row, 1964.

Pilch, John. *Introducing the Cultural Context of the New Testament*. Mahwah: Paulist Press, 1991.

Riches, John. *The World of Jesus*. New York: Cambridge University Press, 1991.

Robinson, John A. T. *Redating the New Testament*. Philadelphia: Westminster Press, 1976.

Rhoads, David M. *Israel In Revolution: 6–74* C.E.. Philadelphia: Fortress Press, 1976.

Sanders, E. P. *Jesus and Judaism*. Philadelphia: Fortress Press, 1985.

Three

Gospel Sources

The Growth of the New Testament

25 C.E.

50 C.E.

60 C.E.

70 C.E.

80 C.E.

90 C.E.

100 C.E.

110 C.E.

Dashed Lines: Indirect Influence
Double Lines: Oral Transmission
Single Thick Lines: Use of Written Source
Thin Lines: Followers, Admirers & Imitators

Analytical scholars of the New Testament accept neither of two extreme views. They do not believe the Gospels are fictions invented entirely from writers' imaginations and they do not believe the Gospels are precise transcriptions by eyewitnesses. In agreement with the preface to Luke's Gospel, analytical scholars believe the evangelists used a variety of oral and written sources to compose their books. Some of those written sources can be recovered and studied separately from the gospels in which they are included. To study them is to study approaches to an understanding of Jesus that existed before some or all of the Gospels were written. Two important sources are collections of miracle stories and collections of sayings of Jesus. These will be studied in this chapter.

The miracles sources

Mark, Matthew, and Luke begin their accounts of Jesus' ministry in the same way. After his baptism he amazes those he encounters by healing diseased people and driving out demons. Toward the very beginning of his gospel Mark writes, "They brought to him all who were ill or possessed by devils; and the whole town was there, gathered at the door. He healed many who suffered from various diseases, and drove out many devils." Soon, "all through Galilee he went, preaching in the synagogues and casting out the devils" (Mark 1:39). Similarly, Matthew reports that shortly after his baptism "he went round the whole of Galilee, teaching in the synagogues, preaching the gospel of the Kingdom, and curing whatever illness or infirmity there was among the people. His fame reached the whole of Syria; and sufferers from every kind of illness, racked with pain, possessed by devils, epileptic, or paralyzed, were all brought to him, and he cured them. Great crowds also followed him, from Galilee and the Ten Towns, from Jerusalem and Judaea, and from Transjordan" (Matt 4:23–25). Luke also introduces Jesus' activities this way (Luke 4:40), and John writes toward the beginning of his Gospel, "While he was in Jerusalem for Passover many gave their allegiance to him when they saw the signs he performed" (John 2:23).

The evangelists evidently intended to show that the initial perception people had of Jesus was that he was a miracle worker. Throughout the Gospels we are given reports of miracles he did. Mark begins with a report of Jesus healing Simon's mother-in-law who was ill in bed with fever (Mark 1:30), then gives reports of the cure of a leper (Mark 1:42) and of a paralyzed man (Mark 2:4), then of a man with a withered arm (3:1), and so forth. Stories such as the raising of Lazarus from the dead (John 11:1–44), Jesus' feeding multitudes of people with only a few loaves and fishes (Mark 6:43–44), Jesus walking on water (Mark 6:48), and the resuscitation of a widow's dead son (Luke 7:15) are well known.

Where did these stories come from? Early on they were passed from one person to another orally, and, of course, during this process details were dropped and elements were added. That is inevitable in oral transmission. Later some of the stories were written down.

Many scholars believe in addition to oral tradition Mark and John used written texts as sources for the miracle stories in their Gospels. These sources took the form of booklets or sections of scrolls. They circulated among Christian leaders who used them as sources for the preaching they did to convince non-Christians that Jesus was an exceptional, important, and divinely guided person. These short written lists of miracle stories came into the hands of John and of Mark. Mark may have used two such collections, John one longer one. It is impossible to say for certain, but the miracle sources probably were written a few decades after the crucifixion; c.e. 40–60 is as good an approximate date as any. The names of their authors are unknown.

Some early Christians (like some twentieth-century Christians) based their beliefs and their arguments that Jesus was Christ on the evidence of his miracle-working ability. Peter is quoted in Acts as saying, "I speak of Jesus of Nazareth, a man singled out by God and made known to you through miracles, portents, and signs, which God worked among you through him, as you well know" (2:22). Luke's Acts of the Apostles frequently stresses the importance of miracles in establishing the legitimacy of the apostles, and, according to Acts, working miracles was a principal activity of Jesus during his life.

Nature Miracles and Healing Miracles

Stories of Jesus' miracles can be divided into two major categories, nature miracles and healing miracles. Walking on water, stilling storms, and turning water into wine are examples of nature miracles because the laws of nature are, apparently, overcome. Those who are convinced the laws of nature apply to all times and all circumstances do not believe nature miracles can happen. When Jesus is reported to have healed leprosy, cured blindness, enabled crippled people to walk, or cast out demons, he has performed healing miracles. Healing can result from many things, and even though modern medicine may not be able to explain how a cure happens, the fact an explanation is lacking does not prove natural law has been broken. Faith healing occurs today both in religious settings and in doctors' offices; faith in the healer can, by itself, lead to recovery. Therefore nature miracles and healing miracles differ as to whether natural laws have definitely been broken.

Every psychotherapist is, in a sense, a faith healer, for if a client has no faith in the competence and concern of the therapist, the therapist's efforts are doomed to failure. If a mentally disturbed person believes a healer to be divinely empowered, it would not be at all remarkable for symptoms to disappear. They may also reoccur: "When an unclean spirit comes out of a man it wanders over the deserts seeking a resting-place; and if it finds none, it says, 'I will go back to the home I left.' So it returns and finds the house swept clean, and tidy. Off it goes and collects seven other spirits more wicked than itself, and they all come in and settle down; and in the end the man's plight is worse than before" (Luke 11:24–26).

The idea that Jesus was a person who inspired sick or insane people to have faith in his powers as a healer and that he was a forgiver of sins are two closely interrelated ideas. Theological explanations for physical or mental illness in the ancient world were common. It was often thought distress was the result of angering God or the gods. If a person became seriously ill or paralyzed or blind then it was often believed the person (or perhaps the person's parents) had offended God and therefore God was punishing the offense, or "sin," by the illness (John 9:2). If a sick person believed Jesus had the ability to forgive sin, this would lead to the elimination of the manifestation of sin, the sickness.

People often interpreted disease, especially mental illness, as the work of demons. A distant analogy for this is the common modern supposition that disease is caused by germs. We may not know which germ brings a disease (a virus? a bacterium? a protozoan?), and we may not be able to see the germ, but we are reasonably certain some germ is responsible. A physician is a specialist in determining the name of the germ (say, streptococcus or flu virus) and then prescribing the proper cure for that particular organism. In a similar way, ancient healers were expected to identify particular demons by name, know their natures, and design cures (exorcisms) to get rid of the demons. As offenses against God were thought to cause illnesses, the powers of God were thought to cast out demons.

Faith healers or miracle workers were persons thought to have particular access to the powers of God. Today we are more likely to think it was the people's faith in the healer's powers than the powers themselves that brought about cures. If people do not have faith in a healer, his or her success rate will be very low. For example, in Nazareth, where people knew Jesus well, "he could work no miracle there, except that he put his hands on a few sick people and healed them; and he was taken aback by their want of faith" (Mark 6:5–6). A proverb attributed to Jesus is associated with this passage: "A prophet is not acceptable in his own village; a physician does not heal those who know him" (Gospel of Thomas, 31). It indicates that in the first century (as in any century) healers who depended on the faith of those who came to them might expect to find little faith among childhood acquaintances.

Christians in the first century interpreted Jesus' ability to do healing miracles as evidence he had special access to the powers of God. As God had unlimited power, Jesus' access to it meant that his capabilities were immense. This idea led to the development of stories crediting him with performing even nature miracles, miracles outside the realm of historical credibility, such as withering a tree on command, raising the dead, and turning water into wine. The fact that Mark's gospel begins with Jesus' reception of the Holy Spirit indicates that at least in Mark's opinion Jesus' access to the power of God came through the Spirit within him.

To some people, faith in Jesus meant faith in his powers. These people concluded that he was divinely empowered—perhaps a new prophet or an ancient prophet come back to life (Mark 6:15–16, 8:28; John 6:14). This was the central point of view of the miracle sources, and we are now ready to turn our attention to them specifically.

Many scholars agree the author of the Gospel of John used a written list of miracles attributed to Jesus. It began with the water-into-wine miracle at the wedding in Cana in Galilee (John 2:1–11) and continued with the healing of an official's son (John 4:46–54), also reported to have taken place in Cana in Galilee. The two stories are separated in John's Gospel by accounts of Jesus' journey to Jerusalem for Passover and his cleansing of the temple there, a journey through Judea, and a story of his coming to Samaria. Yet the fact that both miracle stories take place in the same village is a solid clue the stories were originally in sequence. In addition, these two little miracle stories, like the others in John's miracle source, share common language that does not reflect the unique ideas and modes of expression of the great majority of other passages in John's Gospel. This is evidence the miracle stories were originally written down by someone other than the final author of the Gospel of John. Significantly, the first story ends, "This deed at Cana in Galilee is the first of the signs by which Jesus revealed his glory and led his disciples to believe in him," and the second story concludes similarly: "This was now the second sign which Jesus performed after coming down from Judaea into Galilee."

The fact the stories are numbered first and second is another clue pointing to their originally being in sequence. Notice the term *sign* is used here instead of *miracle*. For our purposes the terms will be used synonymously. However, because John's Gospel uses the term *signs* scholars frequently call the miracles source in John the "Signs Source."

John's source seems to have systematically numbered the miracles and carefully located them. In addition to the first two stories placed in the tiny village of Cana in Galilee, the collection contained at least five more miracle stories. In writing his Gospel John edited, revised, and commented on the miracle source's accounts. John's chapter 6 is an extensive commentary on the miracle of loaves and fishes; his chapter 9 is an extensively rewritten account of a miracle wherein Jesus gives sight to a blind man; and the original story of the raising of Lazarus in chapter 11 is rewritten with substantial additions of ideas and expressions characteristic of the author of the Gospel of John. Despite John's revisions, enough of the original source can be observed and recovered to make its recreation possible.

The source has to be re-created by you. Here is how: *underline the following passages, or take a magic marker of a pale color used for highlighting and color them in. Read them carefully.* A verse indicated as 4a means only the first part of verse 4, 4b means only the second part.

John 2:-11
John 4:46–54
John 5:1–15
John 6:1–14
John 6:16–21
John 9:1–4, 6–17
John 11:1–3, 11b–14, 17–20, 28–39, 41, 43–45
John 20:30–31
John 21:1–14

It is necessary to underline scattered lines in the story of the raising of Lazarus and elsewhere; the remaining lines were added by the author of John to supplement and interpret the miracle. It is by no means certain exactly which lines are from the source and which are from John. Those listed above are a good guess, but not a conclusive list. Because in style and substance John 21:1–14 fits the signs source pattern it may have originally been part of it, indeed it may have been the third numbered sign to have taken place in Galilee.

Now you have the raw material for examination and analysis of a very early Christian document. Read it.

In reading these accounts you are not reading John but a pre-Gospel document John used. This can be exciting; you are reading material about Jesus written before any evangelist wrote.

The miracles source in John reveals its central point of view. It does this in several passages:

John 2:11. "This deed at Cana in Galilee is the first of the signs by which Jesus revealed his glory and led his disciples to believe in him."

John 4:53. "The father noted that this was the exact time when Jesus had said to him, 'Your son will live,' and he and all his household became believers."

John 6:14. "When the people saw the sign Jesus had performed, the word went round, 'Surely this must be the prophet that was to come into the world.'"

John 11:45. "Now many of the Jews who had come to visit Mary and had seen what Jesus did, put their faith in him."

John 20:30–31. "There were indeed many other signs that Jesus performed in the presence of his disciples, which are not recorded in this book. Those here written have been recorded in order that you may hold the faith that Jesus is the Christ."

The last example is probably the conclusion of the miracles source itself. It is not John's central point of view or the conclusion of the Gospel of John. Miracles are evidence, part of a cause-and-effect sequence: Jesus did so and so, this led people to believe in him; if you concede he did so and so, you too should believe in him.

The source tells us some people concluded he was "the prophet who was to come into the world" and also that people ought to conceive of him as the Christ or even perhaps the Son of God. The meanings and implications of the terms *prophet, Christ,* and *Son of God* existing in the twentieth century derive from the whole collection of New Testament texts and from nearly two thousand years of denominational speculation about those texts. It is wrong to presume that the meanings you associate with these terms are the same ones held by first-century Christians. Indeed, even in the New Testament different authors use different terms in different ways. What the word *Christ* meant to Paul, for example, is a different thing from what it meant to the compilers of miracles. The terms *prophet* and *Christ* were applied to Jesus, and the compilers of miracle stories used evidence of miracles to justify the use of the terms—to convince people to have faith in Jesus. But based on the textual evidence in the source we are studying, we cannot say more than that in the miracles source the prophet or the Christ was considered an outstanding worker of miracles.

Mark used both oral and written sources in writing his Gospel. It is likely, but not certain, that among those sources were written lists of miracles, sources probably quite similar in structure and point of view to the miracles source used by John. The sources used by Mark, like those in John, may be isolated and examined apart from the Gospel in which they appear. It is likely Mark used two similar written sources, because there clearly is duplication among the miracles reported. But it would be stretching our limited knowledge too far to attempt to state precisely which stories were taken from which source.

Highlight or underline the following passages and read them more than once.

Mark 4:35–39, 41
Mark 5:2–20
Mark 5:22–23, 35–36, 38–42
Mark 5:25–30, 33–34
Mark 6:34–44
Mark 6:45–51
Mark 7:25–30
Mark 7:32–35
Mark 8:1–10
Mark 8:22–25

Remember, you are not reading a Gospel; this is not Mark, but a source used by Mark. In fact, as we shall see, Mark was not altogether sympathetic to the point of view of the miracles sources he used. The gaps in the sequences you have outlined are probably editorial insertions by the author of Mark, and Mark has interpolated one story in the middle of another to indicate the passage of time.

The groups of stories you have underlined in Mark and John are likely not the only collections of miracle stories circulated in written form prior to the composition of the Gospels, but they are the only ones we can reconstruct. Other stories were handed down by oral tradition, but apparently not many others, since the Gospels of Matthew and Luke contain few stories not also in the Gospel of Mark. The many letters in the New Testament contain no detailed miracle stories at all.

The stories in Mark to some extent show a difference in point of view from the stories in John. For example, the stories in Mark frequently assume faith is necessary to produce a miracle, while the stories in John often presume faith was brought about because miracles occurred. This may just show two ways of looking at the same thing, for in Mark's Gospel the miracles done by Jesus often led to others having faith in him.

The miracle sources do not agree on the methods Jesus used to do remarkable things. Sometimes miracles just happened, as when Jesus is said to have taken a few loaves and fishes, blessed them, and broke and distributed them to thousands of people (Mark 6:41, 8:6; John 6:11). In another instance Jesus was apparently unaware that a healing by his power had taken place until it was over, for in the story of the woman suffering from hemorrhages, she touched his clothes and he, "aware that power had gone out of him, turned round in the crowd and asked, 'Who touched my clothes?'" (Mark 5:30). In other cases Jesus went though procedures of some complexity to achieve the desired result. In healing a man who was deaf and had an impediment in his speech, Jesus "took the man aside, away from the crowd, put his fingers into his ears, spat, and touched his tongue. Then, looking up to heaven, he sighed, and said to him, '*Ephphatha,*' which means 'Be opened'" (Mark 7:33–34). This miracle was not a spontaneous result of the person's faith but the result of a somewhat elaborate set of actions on Jesus' part. The same is true for a story told in John 9:6–7 about a man blind from birth. Jesus "spat on the ground and made a paste with the spittle; he spread it on the man's eyes, and said to him, 'Go and wash in the pool of Siloam.' . . . The man went away and washed, and when he returned he could see." If the miraculous cures attributed to Jesus happened spontaneously through people's faith in Jesus, it is hard to imagine that a few decades later anyone in the Christian movement would want to claim Jesus used such techniques as making a compound of mud and spit and then rubbing it on the eyes of a sightless man. It is likely that earlier traditions telling about Jesus' miracles contained reports of more detailed procedures and that later accounts tended to locate the cause of miracles in simple commands.

Topics

The remainder of our consideration of miracles sources will follow a format used in all subsequent chapters except the last chapter. The following topics will be examined: sources, Jesus' life, Jesus' death, eschatology, Torah Law, community, and sometimes controversies. After this there will be discussion of the interaction of ideas between the document under consideration and those already considered. Of course the section on interactions will continually expand as more documents have been studied. This format will allow the summary of material already presented and also allow the introduction of significant new information.

Sources

Miracle stories came into being in three different ways. These are not competing explanations; all three are probably true for different stories.

1. Jesus of Nazareth was known in his lifetime as a healer, one who cast out demons, had access to the Spirit of God to assist him, and therefore was able to counteract the effects of sin. People in the first century would have found it reasonable that, as illness was due to sin and Jesus cured illness, Jesus therefore cured the effects of sin and, indeed, could forgive sin.

   Stories of Jesus' healings and exorcisms circulated during his lifetime and thereafter. Our first source is stories told and retold by word of mouth. The stories transmitted in this way would have been somewhat altered over time, as is inevitable in oral story transmission. The impression given by the healing and exorcism stories, that Jesus went about Galilee and Judea curing those who had faith in his abilities and casting out demons from those who felt themselves possessed, is historically reliable.

2. Miracle stories existed less as historical documents than as arguments to prove the special excellence of Jesus so that people would have faith. Christians presumed that since Jesus did many awe-inspiring miracles it would be appropriate to heighten the miraculous elements in stories or even to create awe-inspiring stories to convince others Jesus deserved special respect. The nature miracles probably originated from this tendency.

3. The miracle source in John depicts people as concluding on the basis of Jesus' actions that he was a great prophet. Mark also shows people thought of Jesus as a prophet because of his miracles. Some people apparently concluded Jesus was not a new prophet but a prophet returned to life: "The fame of Jesus had spread; and people were saying, 'John the Baptist has been raised to life, and that is why these miraculous powers are at work in him.' Other said, 'It is Elijah.' Others again, 'He is a prophet like one of the old prophets'" (Mark 6:14–15).

   If people interpreted Jesus' miracles as those of a prophet, and they wished to know what kinds of miracles prophets did, they would turn to Hebrew Scriptures stories of prophets to find out. Chapter 4 of the book entitled 2 Kings is a collection of miracle stories much like the collections John and Mark contain. This collection contains accounts of miracles supposedly done by the prophet Elisha, who was the prophet Elijah's successor. At least one and perhaps more of the miracles attributed to Jesus apparently tried to show that Jesus not only could do what Elisha did but could do it on a considerably larger scale. The account in 2 Kings 4:42–44 of the miraculous feeding of one hundred men probably underlies the story of Jesus feeding thousands with a few loaves and fishes.

In summary, miracle stories originated from three sources: oral traditions of Jesus' activities as a healer and exorcist, legends created to heighten people's reverence for him, and accounts based on Hebrew Bible prophetic models.

Because the miracle sources are short and simple documents, few conclusions can be drawn from them. Those we can draw will later provide some basis of comparison with other New Testament materials.

Jesus

For the miracle sources *the life of Jesus* was obviously of principal importance. What he did counted most; what he said or taught counted little. The conclusion reached by the source in John and probably also by the sources in Mark is that the many miracles Jesus did during his life give convincing evidence he was a great prophet and/or the Christ. We should be cautious about drawing complex conclusions about what those terms meant to them.

John's miracle source probably concluded, "Those signs [miracles] here written have been recorded in order that you may hold the faith that Jesus is the Christ, the Son of God, and that through this faith you may possess life by his name" (20:31). Biblical translations can be misleading here, for the New English Bible and some other translations use the phrase *eternal life* in the passage, but the term *eternal* does not appear in the Greek. In the context of the miracle sources the idea of having life by Jesus' name would mean a person might be healed, given longer life, or even be raised from the dead like Lazarus through Jesus' power (or through the power of his followers acting in his name). The resurrection of Lazarus does not bring him eternal life, nor does the resurrection of the son of the widow in Nain (Luke 7:11–17) guarantee he will never die again. There is nothing in the miracle sources to prove they know of the concept "eternal" life.

Jesus' death does not seem to have much interested those who put together the miracle collections. Some scholars have argued that the story of Jesus' resurrection was contained in John's miracles source, but this is not the opinion of the majority. Even if it had been contained there it may have been considered little more than a great miracle. The miracles sources give no hint that salvation came through the death of Jesus. This negative conclusion is significant, contrasting as it does with the ideas of such authors as Paul and Mark, and showing it may have been possible to be Christian in the early first century without having faith oriented to Jesus' death and resurrection.

Eschatology

Eschatology is a term referring to ideas about the future, especially the end of the world. The prevalent eschatology of the New Testament is the idea that this world will come to an end and will be replaced with another improved world. The miracles sources, as far as we can determine, have no concern with eschatology.

Torah Law

Two stories (or two versions of one story) in our sources have to do with a point of Torah Law. In John 5:1–15 (and also Mark 3:1–5) Jesus heals a crippled man on the Sabbath. According to Torah Law, no work was allowed on the Sabbath. Did healings count as work? Yes, they did, but exceptions were made in emergency situations, and saving a life on the Sabbath would not have been condemned. If there was any legal problem with Jesus' Sabbath healings it was that the healings were not always life-or-death emergencies; a cripple could be expected to wait a few hours, to be healed when the Sabbath would be over.

In the case described in John's Gospel, the problem is not that the man was healed but that Jesus told him to carry his bed. From an ultra-conservative perspective on Law, carrying a bed on the Sabbath constitutes work. It is possible, therefore, that Jesus was criticized by certain legal authorities. But well before the time of Jesus Judaism possessed a strong tradition that works of mercy and kindness could take precedence over strict detailed adherence to the Law. As a Sabbath healer, Jesus might have been considered a liberal interpreter of Law. But his death was not a direct result of his healing people on the Sabbath. No Pharisees or scribes or other legal authorities would have threatened his life for that reason.

Community

The miracle stories provide few clues about the community or communities that compiled and used them. We can speak knowledgeably about early Christians who believed Jesus expected them to go forth and become workers of miracles (that is, healings and exorcisms), but such information is drawn mainly from Acts and the oral source called "Q" and will be dealt with under those topics.

The one clue we do have derives from the purpose of the miracle stories—convincing their audience that Jesus is the Christ or a great prophet. Miracle sources derived from groups dedicated to the proposition that belief in Jesus should be spread. This means the communities were not secret sects or self-enclosed cult groups.

The sayings source

Everyone who has read the New Testament has noticed substantial repetition in the first three books. Having read Matthew, one finds Mark to contain much of the same material. Having read Matthew and Mark, one finds story after story in Luke to be the same as one has read before. In the Gospel of John, however, the stories change, the style of Jesus' sayings change, and for the first time since Matthew one seems to be reading a very different account.

Matthew, Mark, and Luke, when their stories are set side by side, look very similar. They are called the synoptic Gospels. The term *synoptic* comes from the Greek and means "seen together." Clearly, the three have a special relationship, but what is it? Are all three versions of a lost original Gospel? Did Matthew revise Mark and then Luke revise Matthew? Is Mark a shorter version of both Matthew and Luke? Many theories have been offered during the past century, but the one now accepted by the vast majority of New Testament experts is called the Two Document Hypothesis or Two Document Theory.

The Two Document Hypothesis is quite simple. It is as follows: Mark wrote the first Gospel. Matthew and Luke each read Mark and decided it should be revised. Among other things, Matthew and Luke wished to improve Mark's Gospel by adding substantially more of the sayings of Jesus passed down by tradition. Both Matthew and Luke independently added sayings to Mark's Gospel and, therefore, each contains sayings the other does not have. In addition, both Matthew and Luke used the same written collection of sayings, a collection Mark did not have.

You can imagine, then, Matthew at his desk in one town and Luke at a desk in another town. Both have before them two written documents, a copy of the Gospel of Mark and a copy of the same collection of sayings attributed to Jesus. Both of them used those two documents to compose their own Gospels. This is the meaning of the term Two Document Hypothesis, that two documents were used by Matthew and by Luke in the writing of their Gospels. Because Matthew and Luke often agree on the order of Q sayings, and rather frequently contain word-for-word identical Greek phrases in their Q material, we can be certain Q was a written, not oral, source and that it was in Greek rather than in Aramaic.

The other principal hypothesis is known as the Griesbach Hypothesis after the German scholar who constructed it. A minority of New Testament scholars believe it to be true, but they are firm in their confidence that ultimately it will win over many other experts. The Griesbach hypothesis is based, in part, on the observation that there are a few passages in Matthew, Luke, and Mark where the versions in Matthew and Luke are identical, but the Mark version is different. How can this be, they wonder, if both of the others used Mark as a source? The Griesbach hypothesis is that Matthew was the first gospel and Luke was a rewritten form of Matthew. Mark then made a synopsis of both Matthew and Luke in producing his gospel.

In this book, as in practically all introductory books to the New Testament, we will follow the Two Document Hypothesis. The German scholars who first theorized Matthew and Luke used the same sayings collection called that collection the "source." The word for source in German is *Quelle*. This became abbreviated to "Q," and the term *Q* is now universally used for that sayings collection. Q does not now exist in separate written form; it was probably considered superfluous after it was incorporated into Matthew and Luke.

Every passage in Matthew and Luke can be put into one of three categories: (1) unique material shared with no other New Testament document (for example, the different stories of Jesus' birth found in the two Gospels); (2) material Matthew and/or Luke borrowed from the Gospel of Mark; (3) material Matthew and Luke borrowed from their common source for sayings, Q. Remember, Mark did not use the source Q. The common material in Matthew and Luke, the passages they both have and Mark does not have, is Q.

The existence of Q has received strong confirmation with the discovery in 1945 of a collection of more than 114 sayings attributed to Jesus called the Gospel of Thomas. It is just what Q was thought to be, a list of sayings one after the other without much commentary and with no stories or biography attached. Thomas shows no interest in Jesus' death and, unlike Q, presents the Kingdom of God as existing in the present both within people and spread throughout the world. Thomas seems to have as a principal theme the idea that although the Kingdom of God has been present since the seven beginning days of Genesis, people needed Jesus to encourage them to discover that important fact. This Gospel of Thomas is not Q, but it is much the same sort of thing Q was and probably was written down about the same time. The study of the Gospel of Thomas is sure to have increasing impact on the study of the New Testament texts in the coming years. There is an increasing consensus among scholars that Thomas' many sayings that are similar to sayings found in the New Testament are not taken from New Testament gospels but were written down from other sources or from oral tradition; there are, of course, scholars who

---

Thomas

The Gospel of Thomas is attributed to Didymus Judas Thomas, who was revered in the Syrian church as an apostle (Matt 10:3, Mark 3:18, Luke 6:15, Acts 1:13; cf. John 11:16, 20:24, 21:2) and as the twin brother of Jesus (so claimed by the Acts of Thomas, a third-century C.E. work). The attribution to Thomas may indicate where this gospel was written, but it tells us nothing about the author.

disagree and believe Thomas' sayings were derived from the New Testament. The Thomas nevertheless may be a very valuable source of evidence about the teachings of Jesus himself and about the development of Christianity in the mid first century. But as this book is about the New Testament, and the Gospel of Thomas is not part of that collection of texts, it appears only as an appendix in this book.

Form criticism

New Testament scholars use a variety of techniques to analyze biblical texts. Rather than discuss them all at the same time, this book will introduce several of them at relevant points. The first is called form criticism.

Form criticism, or form analysis, is a technique for analyzing specific New Testament pericopes. A *pericope* (pronounced purr-íck-uh-pee) is a single unit of tradition, a saying or story that can be taken from its Gospel context and analyzed independently. Since most of the sayings and stories in the Gospels were transmitted by word of mouth (oral tradition) before being written down, the analysis of individual pericopes can, scholars hope, lead to some understanding of the teachings of Christians prior to the writing of Gospels. A primary skill of the form analyst is the ability to distinguish the original form of a saying or story from its form in the Gospels.

Generally form criticism is applied to sayings and stories found in Mark, Matthew, Luke, and the newly discovered Gospel of Thomas. The sayings of Jesus in the Gospel of John are rarely derived from oral tradition, and so form analysis is not as often applied to them.

Form analysts organize sayings and stories into categories. The following are some of the most important of those categories.

Proverbs are short pithy sayings. Their meaning is immediately obvious. Some may have been spoken first by Jesus, but many proverbs attributed to him were probably in circulation prior to his lifetime. "Do not be anxious about tomorrow; tomorrow will look after itself" (Matt 6:34) is a proverb.

Parables, a characteristic form of Jesus' teaching, are short stories making a point. Jesus' parables, however, seem to have been deliberately designed to be somewhat ambiguous, and their point is rarely obvious. Many form analysts believe those parables found in the New Testament that make a clear and unambiguous point are probably not from Jesus. Here is an example of one of Jesus' parables: "A sower went out to sow. And it happened that as he sowed, some seed fell along the footpath; and the birds came and ate it up. Some seed fell on rocky ground, where it had little soil, and it sprouted quickly because it had no depth of earth; but when the sun rose the young corn was scorched, and as it had no root it withered away. Some seed fell among thistles; and the thistles shot up and choked the corn, and it yielded no crop. And some of the seed fell into good soil, where it came up and grew, and bore fruit; and the yield was thirtyfold, sixtyfold, even a hundredfold" (Mark 4:3–9).

Explanations of parables in the New Testament are composed by the Gospel writers or other members of the early church. Jesus seems to have left his audiences to seek their own understanding of his parables and not to have explained them. Following the parable quoted immediately above, Mark gives a lengthy explanation beginning, "The sower sows the word. Those along the footpath are people in whom the word is sown, but no sooner have they heard it than Satan comes and carries off the word which has been sown in them . . ." (Mark 4:14–15).

Apocalyptic sayings are predictions and descriptions of events to take place at the time of the end of this world. The word apocalyptic refers to revelations of the supernatural world, especially regarding the end of time and usually including final catastrophes and the raising of the dead. Mark's chapter 13 contains many such sayings. One example is: "But in those days, after that distress, the sun will be darkened, the moon will not give her light; the stars will come falling from the sky, the celestial powers will be shaken" (Mark 13:24).

Community rules derive from a time later than Jesus when the structured church was coming into being. An example of a community rule is, "If someone sues you, come to terms with him promptly while you are both on your way to court; otherwise he may hand you over to the judge, and the judge to the constable, and you will be put in jail" (Matt 5:25).

Miracle stories, similarly, are divided into categories. Some of the most prominent are *healings, exorcisms,* and *nature miracles.*

After having categorized New Testament pericopes, form analysts proceed to theorize about the purpose of the category during the time when oral tradition was the main form of Christian preaching. Each category, they believe, played a particular role in preaching Christian doctrine or in teaching moral principles or in organizing Christian communities. The purpose of each category is called its *Sitz im Leben,* German for "situation in life." Scholars sometimes refer to the *Sitz im Leben* of a particular pericope as its reason for existence; pericope X continued to exist because it served purpose Y. Form analysts believe that sayings without specific usefulness to the later community would have been forgotten.

Form criticism seldom leads to definitive conclusions. Rarely do two scholars come up with exactly the same categories or agree which sayings fit which categories. The attempt to determine a pericope's *Sitz im Leben* cannot help but be speculative. Still, historical scholarship can rarely be definitive, and so, although form analysis is less well respected today than it was a few decades ago, people should be aware of it and know what a form critic does.

Reading Q

The Q "document" can be recovered, read, and discussed. *You should now underline or highlight those passages in Luke and, if you wish, also Matthew, which were taken by their authors from Q, the sayings they have in common that are not found in Mark.* The sayings are not identical in the two Gospels, for both Matthew and Luke felt free to revise them in accordance with what they thought Jesus would have said. It would be better to read them with as little revision as possible, however, and on the whole the versions of Q sayings in Luke are often closer to the original than the versions in Matthew are and it seems that while Matthew reorganized Q sayings to fit the scheme of his gospel, Luke generally maintained their order in Q.

There are, therefore, two related, but rarely absolutely identical, versions of each passage. If you choose to study only one, use the passages in Luke. In some passages elements of narrative and interpretive comments have been added by the envangelists. Those labeled "probable" appear only in Luke, but fit the pattern of Q sayings and it is likely Matthew chose not to use them.

Luke 3:7–9	Matt 3:7–10
Luke 3:16–17	Matt 3:11–12
Luke 4:1–13	Matt 4:1–4, 9–12, 5–7, 13
Luke 6:12, 17	Matt 5:1–2
Luke 6:20–23	Matt 5:3, 6, 4, 11–12
Luke 6:24–26	probable
Luke 6:27–36	Matt 5:44, 39–42; 7:12; 5:46–47, 45, 48
Luke 6:37–38	Matt 7:1–2
Luke 6:39–40	Matt 15:14; 10:24–25
Luke 6:41–42	Matt 7:3–5
Luke 6:43–44	Matt 7:16–20; 12:33–35
Luke 6:46–49	Matt 7:21, 24–27
Luke 7:1–10	Matt 7:28; 8:5–10, 13
Luke 7:18–20, 22–23	Matt 11:2–6
Luke 7:24–28	Matt 11:7–11
Luke 7:31–35	Matt 11:16–19
Luke 9:55–62	Matt 8:19–22
Luke 10:2–12	Matt 9:37–38; 10:7–16
Luke 10:13–15	Matt 11:21–24
Luke 10:16	Matt 10:40
Luke 10:21–22	Matt 11:25–27
Luke 10:23–24	Matt 13:16–17
Luke 11:2–4	Matt 6:9–13

Luke 11:9–13	Matt 7:7–11
Luke 11:14–23	Matt 12:22–30
Luke 11:24–26	Matt 12:43–45
Luke 11:29–32	Matt 12:38–42
Luke 11:33	Matt 5:15
Luke 11:34–36	Matt 6:22–23
Luke 11:39–40	Matt 23:25–26
Luke 11:42	Matt 23:23
Luke 11:43	Matt 23:6–7
Luke 11:44	Matt 23:27–28
Luke 11:46	Matt 23:4
Luke 11:47–48	Matt 23:29–32
Luke 11:49–51	Matt 23:34–36
Luke 11:52	Matt 23:13
Luke 12:2–3	Matt 10:26–27
Luke 12:4–7	Matt 10:28–31
Luke 12:8–9	Matt 10:32–33
Luke 12:10	Matt 12:32
Luke 12:11–12	Matt 10:19
Luke 12:13–14	probable
Luke 12:22–31	Matt 6:25–33
Luke 12:33–34	Matt 6:19–21
Luke 12:39–40	Matt 24:43–44
Luke 12:42–46	Matt 24:45–51
Luke 12:49, 51–53	Matt 10:34–36
Luke 12:54–56	Matt 16:2–3
Luke 12:57–59	Matt 5:25–26
Luke 13:18–21	Matt 13:31–33
Luke 13:24–27	Matt 7:13–14, 22–23
Luke 13:28–30	Matt 8:11–12; 20:16
Luke 13:34–35	Matt 23:37–39
Luke 14:11	Matt 23:12
Luke 14:16–24	Matt 22:1–10
Luke 14:26–27, 17:33	Matt 10:37–39
Luke 14:34–35	Matt 5:13
Luke 15:4–7	Matt 18:12–13
Luke 16:13	Matt 6:24
Luke 16:16	Matt 11:12–13
Luke 16:17	Matt 5:18
Luke 16:18	Matt 5:32
Luke 17:1–2	Matt 18:6–7
Luke 17:3–4	Matt 18:15, 21–22

Luke 17:6	Matt 17:20
Luke 17:22–24, 26–30, 34–35, 37	Matt 24:26–28, 37, 39–41
Luke 19:12–26	Matt 25:14–30
Luke 22:28–30	Matt 19:28

Now, having reconstructed Q by isolating it in Luke (and, if you wish, Matthew), go back and read it carefully. Nobody can underline or highlight and read carefully at the same time. Remember, you are not reading Luke's Gospel when reading the Q material in Luke. Luke must have agreed generally with the Q material or he would not have used it, but Luke's ideas are not identical to those in Q and must be considered separately. In reading the Q material you are reading a separate and different document than Luke (or Matthew).

The origin of Q

Because Matthew and Luke so frequently use identical Greek constructions when borrowing from Q, we know the Q material was written in Greek. The best guess for the date of Q is somewhere between C.E. 50 and 70. The ideas and way of life reflected in Q are primitive, meaning they do not reflect the more sophisticated concepts of Christ and of Christian community structure that developed as the early church developed. Certainly Q was in existence before the writing of Matthew and Luke. But much more than this we really cannot say. As to the author of Q, no name is attached to it. Probably if it had not disappeared some name would have been attached to it in the second century and it might have been called the Gospel of Andrew or the Gospel of Simon. This happened with the similar sayings collection called the Gospel of Thomas, which was not written by the apostle Thomas.

Some early Christians put the Q collection together by choosing, from the sayings known to them, those they thought to be of particular interest and importance. The sayings they selected reflect not only aspects of Jesus' teachings but also aspects of their own teaching and their way of life. People do not try to preserve traditions with which they are in disagreement or which cast doubt upon their own way of life. In speaking of the Q material, then, we should think not of one person but of a group of people, the "Q people," or the "Q community." Scholars often refer to the "Q community," but as the term *community* evokes the idea of a settled group, a village or a neighborhood, the term *Q people* is preferable. The Q people left a record of their activities in the sayings they created or preserved. As with all material in the New Testament, we should be careful not to attribute all sayings in Q to Jesus himself. Some, possibly most, sayings in Q derive from sayings of Jesus, but others do not. Further, the selection made by the Q people of sayings attributed to Jesus may give a distorted notion of his main themes. They made the selection, Jesus did not.

In many places the sayings in Q describe a way of life, and we will examine that way of life in the next few pages. Scholars differ, however, on whether the way of life described in Q was lived by the Q people or only valued by them. In other words, were the people, who compiled the Q sayings itinerant Christian prophets or were they individuals living in a more settled community who respected and assisted itinerant Christian prophets? In either case a particular way of life, strange by our standards, was valued and implicitly lived. We shall assume in this book that the Q sayings were compiled by people who lived in accordance with them even though that is not altogether certain.

Q way of life, Q ideas

While scholarship on the New Testament has made great advances during the past hundred years, the main technique of scholars remains the same. We read the material over and over again and try to make sense of it in its own context and to take it seriously as it stands. In other words, we must presume Q and the other New Testament materials mean what they say. Sayings and ideas that do not sound right to us cannot be wished away, rewritten, or ignored. This is particularly important in analyzing Q, for, fortunately or unfortunately, the Q version of Jesus' sayings often reveals perspectives on human life and Christian expectations alien to us today.

Q can best be understood by first looking at the way of life of the Q people, including their reactions to their society. Then we can examine their ideas about Jesus and their vision of the future in the context of their behavior rather than in the abstract.

The Q people regarded themselves as the last in a long line of Jewish prophets, who (in their opinion) had been sent from God to the Jewish people but had been rejected, persecuted, and killed by the people to whom they had been sent. In Luke 11:49-51, it is said in reference to both the prophets of the Hebrew Scriptures and Q prophets, "'I will send them prophets and messengers; and some of these they will persecute and kill'; so that this generation will have to answer for the blood of all the prophets shed since the foundation of the world." The Q people were itinerant, people who moved from town to town and depended on the charity of those who accepted them as prophets. They were poor, hungry, and afraid. Their way of life is depicted in Q in a long passage where Jesus is said to be giving instructions to his disciples. The Q people, of course, identified themselves with the disciples. *Re-read Luke 10:2–12.* . . . A similar account of this set of instructions can be found in Mark 6:7–13. It appears twice in Luke, once borrowed from Mark (Luke 9:2–6) and once from Q. In these passages early Christian prophets are depicted as extremely poor people, whether by choice or by necessity. They possessed neither walking stick nor pack, neither bread nor money, neither purses nor shoes; they did not even have a change of clothes. They had no place to sleep, and their principal image of themselves was as tenant farmers (laborers harvesting an absentee landlord's crop).

Use your imagination. Picture the people who followed this way of life. They were dirty. They were hungry. They did not adhere to customary rules of politeness: "exchange no greetings on the road." They were entirely dependent on the kindness of strangers, even though the strangers they encountered were themselves poor Galilean villagers.

The Q people would come to a small village and hope to be welcomed. Their duty was to announce, "The kingdom of God has come close to you," but there was no guarantee anyone would agree. They might bestow their blessing (their "peace") on a house, but that might make no different and they still might be rejected. Then their blessing, their peace, would be removed from the house and returned to them.

They sought the repentance of the people. Repentance did not mean feeling sorry for misdeeds but a radical change of life in light of the prospect that "the kingdom of God has come close." Their evidence for the truth of their message was their ability to do miracles, meaning to heal the sick and to cast out demons. That was not necessarily good enough. Luke 10:13 indicates that in the villages of Chorazin, Bethsaida, and Capernaum such miracles had been done, but no one cared, no one repented, and therefore presumably no one gave the Q people food or a place to lay their heads and rest. Notice, incidentally, Q does not say that the non-Jewish areas of Tyre and Sidon did accept them, only that if they had gone there Tyre and Sidon would have been more impressed than some Galilean villages were.

There is nothing odd about the strong concern with persecution we find in Q. It derives from the response of ordinary people to destitute extra-ordinary people, which usually is to get the destitute extraordinary people to leave as quickly as possible.

Q sayings, spirit sayings

Among the most famous of all Q passages are the Beatitudes. They are found in Luke 6:20–23 and announce that poor, hungry, unhappy people will inherit the Kingdom of God. But the Q people were not primarily concerned with just any poor person but with those poor people who were prophets of Jesus and of God. It is not that anything you do for any poor or humble person you do for Jesus, but that when you listen to Q prophets or assist them you assist Jesus.

An important concept for the understanding of Q sayings, and indeed of many of the sayings of Jesus recorded in the New Testament, is found in

Luke 10:16: "Whoever listens to you listens to me; whoever rejects you rejects me. And whoever rejects me rejects the One who sent me." Similarly, in Matthew 10:40: "To receive you is to receive me, and to receive me is to receive the One who sent me." It is also one of the very few Q sayings found in John: "He who receives any messenger of mine receives me; receiving me, he receives the one who sent me" (13:20). Although Q has several distinctive points of view, in this matter at least it is in accord with most of the rest of the New Testament. Even an author who repudiates this point of view by weakening it (Mark 9:37) shows he is aware of it. These sayings solve two problems for us. They solve the problem of why the Q people regarded themselves as having such importance that their rejection would lead to the destruction of entire towns (Luke 10:15), and the problem of how it could be that many of the sayings attributed to Jesus in the New Testament were not said by Jesus.

The Q people did not believe they were to carry on the mission of Jesus only by repeating sayings they had memorized. Rather, they were able to do as he did because the Spirit he had they now had. The Spirit is the crucial link. There is a Spirit of God able to possess people. Jesus, at his baptism, received this Spirit, and so one may regard the sayings of Jesus as the sayings of God through this Spirit. This idea stems from the Jewish theory of prophecy, that through God's Spirit prophets communicated God's words. New Testament gospels agree that a divine Spirit came to Jesus' followers after his crucifixion. This entitled his followers to speak words from the Spirit or to have their statements attributed to the Spirit. Therefore, to listen to them was to listen to God's Spirit. To disbelieve them was to disbelieve God's Spirit, and to reject them was to reject God's Spirit. From this perspective, just as Jesus spoke and one thereby heard God's Spirit, so if a Q person spoke one would thereby hear God's Spirit, and this would be the same thing as hearing Jesus. For this reason the Q people reasoned that they, like Jesus, were prophets of God. If one wrote down what a Q person said one wrote down what the Spirit of God said. That saying then could be attributed to the Spirit of God (see Luke 10:21) or to Jesus.

Many people are astonished to discover that some sayings attributed to Jesus in the New Testament were not said by Jesus but came into existence well after his crucifixion. But when one considers that his early followers believed they too had the Spirit Jesus had, then what is surprising is not that some of their sayings were attributed to him but that so many of his original personal sayings survived word-of-mouth transmission and translation from Aramaic to Greek and are available to us at all.

Q mission

The Q people believed themselves to be of great, even cosmic importance, conveying God's message to people, proving their message true by healing the sick. But often they were rejected by those to whom they came. Rejection did not just hurt their pride; it threatened them with starvation, for they were poor people with serious concern for basic survival. *Re-read the Q passages Luke 12:22–31*. . . . Certainly Q people hoped God would take care of them, but what they needed most was food to keep them alive and clothes to cover their bodies. Of course they set their minds on food and drink and did worry. Who would not in their circumstances?

Their vision of the Kingdom of God was of a place where there was plenty to eat and plenty to drink: "You shall eat and drink at my table in my kingdom" (Luke 22:30). As to the people who so often rejected them, "There will be wailing and grinding of teeth then, when you see Abraham, Isaac, and Jacob, and all the prophets, in the kingdom of God, and yourselves thrown out. From east and west people will come, from north and south, for the feast in the kingdom of God" (Luke 13:28–30).

Most Q people were probably from the ranks of tenant farmers, shepherds, fishermen, and other impoverished groups. They left their homes, went on the road to various villages, and announced the imminent arrival of the Kingdom of God. But what of the people they left at home when they went on the road? To understand Q it is necessary to imagine the condition of families when a spouse or parent suddenly took off, never to return. This would have been an emotional tearing apart of the nuclear family structure, leaving scars on all concerned. Yet this tearing apart, repudiation of basic family obligations, was demanded and expected.

From their perspective families were social units working against the possibility of going forth and preaching the coming of the Kingdom of God. Families, therefore, were to be put aside along with other normal elements of human social life, business, planting of crops, building houses, and so forth (Luke 17:26–30). Some sayings in Q are called "hard sayings" because they reject the values many Christians have believed to be of major importance. But the radical perspective of Q as a whole is consistent. Consider these:

Luke 14:26. "If anyone comes to me and does not hate his father and mother, wife and children, brothers and sisters, even his own life, he cannot be a disciple of mine."

Luke 12:52. "Do you suppose I came to establish peace on earth? No indeed, I have come to bring division. For from now on, five members of a family will be divided, three against two and two against three; father against son and son against father, mother against daughter and daughter against mother, mother against son's wife and son's wife against her mother-in-law."

Luke 9:59. Jesus said to a man, "'Follow me', but the man replied, 'Let me go and bury my father first.' Jesus said, 'Leave the dead to bury their dead; you must go and announce the kingdom of God.'"

Although some exaggeration is present in these sayings, the Q people presumably did what these sayings expect them to do. They did leave their families; they did cause division within their families; they did repudiate even the ordinary duties to their families, including sometimes the burial of their fathers. What of the rest of social life? It was condemned. As every Jewish person of the time knew, only Noah's people were righteous enough to be saved from the flood; only Lot was righteous enough to be saved when God sent fire and sulphur to destroy the town of Sodom. Every one else died. They deserved to die because, according to Q (Luke 17:26–30), they ate, drank, married, bought, sold, planted, and built. Following a normal social life does not enable one to go and announce the coming of the Kingdom of God, and so such normal life is implicitly condemned. The Q people did not value what we now value and, indeed, did not value what most people then valued. They valued only one thing: the Kingdom of God.

Since the Kingdom of God is their main interest, we might expect them to describe it in some detail, but Q sayings do not do this. It is only mentioned in a few places and described little. From what we know we can say this: The Kingdom of God is a condition coming to earth in a very short time. The desires of the Q people (especially for food and drink) will be satisfied. Those who have believed the pronouncements of its coming and repented will be welcomed into it; those who have not will be destroyed.

This radical perspective cannot be compared to later Christian notions of an ethereal heaven above for those who die and who are acceptable in the eyes of God. The Q notion of the Kingdom of God is of something coming here soon. People do not die and eventually go there; it will come here, quickly, in a matter of months or, at most, a few years. When it comes the condition of human life will be entirely changed, and only a few people will be permitted to survive and enter it. When it comes it will be like the flood of Noah or the fire and brimstone that destroyed the towns Sodom and Gomorrah. The kingdom is a promise for those who repent, but a threat for the rest of the world.

The Q sayings do not give many directions for behavior in advance of the coming kingdom. Repentance is necessary. To repudiate normal social and family life and go forth to warn others is necessary. But some of the Q sayings taken to be moral principles are probably more in the line of practical advice. For people who have no staff, no money, no means of defense, it only makes sense that "when a man hits you on the cheek, offer him the other cheek too; when a man takes your coat, let him have your shirt as well. Give to everyone who asks you; when a man takes what is yours, do not demand it back" (luke 6:29–31). This advice is similar to that given novice bank tellers: if people come to rob the bank, give them the money in front of you, and give them what is in the drawer as well. People visiting large cities are advised to give muggers what they want, never to be heroes, and so forth.

But the Q material does contain one great moral principle, one way of looking at human relationships special to the Q people and in accord with their perspective on the world. It may well be a perspective going back to Jesus. It is fairly simple, and it comes down to this: "Do to your fellow human beings what you wish God to do to you on the day of judgment." Luke's chapter 6 contains this advice: "You must love your enemies and do good; and lend without expecting any return; and you will have a rich reward: you will be sons of the Most High, because he himself is kind to the ungrateful and wicked. Be compassionate as your Father is compassionate. Pass no judgment, and you will not be judged; do not condemn, and you will not be condemned; acquit, and you will be acquitted; give, and gifts will be given to you" (Luke 6:35–38).

The principle here is if you expect God to forgive you, you must forgive others. If you expect God to be compassionate to you, you must be compassionate to others. This is not a set of abstract principles but practical advice. Given that the Kingdom of God will come soon, that Jesus will return as judge and few will survive to enjoy the kingdom, how can you behave so as to be able to enter it? You must act to other people the way you wish God to act to you on that great and terrible day.

Scholars have recently been intrigued by a carefully reasoned book by John Kloppenborg in which he tries to prove that Q developed over a period of years and that it is possible to identify which sayings go with which levels of development. He argues that only in the latest level, Q3, do we find biographical interest such as the story of Jesus' temptation and insistance on the importance of following Torah. Sayings about the coming day of the Son of Man and warnings about the end and threats against people who reject Jesus and his messengers were inserted into the text at the Q2 level as the Q people reacted angrily against those who refused to accept them or their message. The earliest level, Q1, contained sayings of a proverbial nature advocating that people leave the constraints of ordinary society for the freedom of the itinerant life. His theory is already influential. . . but by no means can it be said to be completely accepted fact and many scholars have found reason to be somewhat sceptical of it.

Topics

Sources

Jesus spoke in Aramaic and his disciples remembered some of what he said. They, in turn, told others in Aramaic what he said. From one person to another his sayings were repeated and, with each transmission, changes might take place. Eventually the sayings were translated from Aramaic to Greek, and today we know them only in their Greek form. One of the main sources for the Q sayings is material in the Aramaic language, originating with Jesus, passed down by word of mouth (with some inevitable changes), translated into Greek and eventually written down.

There is another source for Q sayings. Many of Jesus' followers (including the Q people) felt the Spirit Jesus had received they also had received. The Spirit that gave Jesus his knowledge of divine things also gave them such knowledge. As it was the same Spirit, to listen to them was to listen to Jesus and to the One who sent Jesus. (Luke 10:16). Accordingly, some things said by later Christian prophets were taken down and attributed to Jesus. There is nothing dishonest about this procedure, but it does greatly complicate the task of trying to determine what Jesus himself said as distinct from what his later followers said in his name.

The sources for Q, then, are two: the sayings of Jesus transmitted by word of mouth until finally written down in Greek, and the Spirit-inspired sayings of some of Jesus' later followers that were attributed to him.

Jesus

Jesus' life was of great importance to the Q people, forming, they thought, a model for how they should live their lives and providing them with the key for their hopes for the future. Although Jesus was thought to be in the line of persecuted prophets going back all the way to Abel (Luke 11:51), he was certainly much more than a prophet. Even John the Baptist, described as inferior to the least person in the Kingdom of God, was more than a prophet (Luke 7:27–28).

A key term in Q is *Son of Man* but, despite the best efforts of scholars over the past decades, the background of the term *Son of Man* is still obscure. The term frequently is used in a cosmic sense in the New Testament as a heavenly being or an angel in the form of a man. But the only place in the Hebrew Scriptures where the term is used in a cosmic sense is in Daniel 7:1–28, where an angelic being who looks like a human being, literally "like a son of man," appears in what early Christians took to be a judgment scene. This passage strongly influenced early Christian thinking, including that of the Q people.

But "son of man" has another meaning. In Aramaic the phrase *Son of Man* was ordinarily used to mean "a person like me," and sometimes it is used that way in Q sayings. For example, "Foxes have their holes, the birds their roosts; but the son of man has nowhere to lay his head" (Luke 9:58) means that, unlike the animals, people like me have nowhere to lay their heads. It is sometimes hard to determine whether this common usage was intended in sayings, or whether one should read them with the image of the cosmic Son of Man in mind.

Son of Man is the term used most often for Jesus in Q. During his life on earth Jesus proved his special role in bringing about the Kingdom of God by his actions and by his words, and some thought the kingdom was beginning to be present in his ministry. But the Q people focused most of their attention on the near future, not on the present. In the near future would come the "Day of the Son of Man." Suddenly the Son of Man would come to earth in judgment (Luke 12:40; 17:26–30), and at that time only those who responded positively to Jesus and his messengers would be approved by the Son of Man. From the Q perspective, both Jesus and the Q people were entitled to say, "Anyone who acknowledges me before men, the Son of Man will acknowledge before the angels of God; but he who disowns me before men will be disowned before the angels of God."

While Q uses the term *Son of Man* to refer to Jesus, it is not always clear that Jesus and the Son of Man are one and the same. Some Q sayings can be read to imply Jesus and the Son of Man are the same, others that Jesus is speaking of the Son of Man as someone else. Son of Man can mean God's agent at the end of this world as it does in Luke 17:23–24, 26–30. But is this Jesus? Neither here nor elsewhere is it absolutely clear. Nevertheless, while it does not seem likely that Jesus openly and directly declared himself to be a cosmic Son of Man to come the Q people probably believed he did and included sayings to that effect in their collection.

Jesus' death was of no apparent interest to the Q people, for his death and his resurrection are not mentioned. Considering that Jesus' death and resurrection were of substantial importance to other branches of the early church it is surprising the Q material does not mention them. The term *cross* is used once: "No one who does not carry his cross and come with me can be a disciple of mine" (Luke 14:27), but this saying probably derived from a common saying meaning "shoulder a terrible burden" and does not refer to Jesus' own crucifixion. The Gospel of Thomas, which like Q does not show any interest in Jesus' death and resurrection, also contains that saying, and there too it is the only time the word *cross* is used.

Eschatology

For Q people the end of this world was a matter of utmost urgency. It was expected immediately, certainly within their lifetimes. This world, they thought, will end after a time of destruction. On the Day of the Son of Man, all the world will be judged, and those who had not already repented will be destroyed. The remaining few will enter the Kingdom of God. Logically following from Q's stress on repentance is the fact that those who thought themselves most righteous will be least likely to repent; those who felt themselves poor, sinners, outcasts will be most likely to change their ways. Q favors the poor and condemns such leaders as those Pharisees who were so convinced of their own righteousness they saw no need of repentance.

It is possible to understand the Q sayings to imply that on the Day of the Son of Man, Jesus, who came first in disguise, will return in glory and be known by all to be God's agent. But then it will be too late. Those who had been hungry, poor, weeping, persecuted for the sake of the Son of Man (Q people and those who accepted them), will soon begin to feast and drink in the Kingdom of God. All others will die.

Torah law

The Q people preserved the saying, "It is easier for heaven and earth to come to an end than for one dot or stroke of the Law to lose its force" (Luke 16:27), so we can conclude they thought the Law should be obeyed. Following the Law, however, was not all that was necessary to be saved from destruction on the Day of the Son of Man. One must also forgive others and be compassionate to others if one helped to find God willing to forgive and be compassionate.

In light of this, the passage in Luke 16:16, "Until John, it was the Law and the prophets: since then, there is the good news of the kingdom of God, and everyone forces his way in" cannot be taken to mean the Law is over and done with any more than that prophets ceased to exist. Rather, the good news of the kingdom was added to the previous messages of the Law and the prophets. People were encouraged to follow the Law in detail while keeping in mind the necessity of living in accordance with more abstract moral principles. The Law required that 10 percent of agricultural produce should be supplied to the priests. People often applied this to major crops only, but some more strict legalists found it also to apply to small garden herbs. The Q attitude is not to criticize detailed concern for Law but to insist it must be accompanied by concern for the general principles of justice and love of God. This is clear in Luke 11:42: "Alas for you Pharisees! You pay tithes of mint and rue and every garden herb, but have no care for justice and the love of God. It is these you should have practised, *without neglecting the others.*"

Community

The startlingly radical style of life of the Q people has been surveyed in the preceding pages. But, to summarize it, let us look at the Lord's prayer, which is a Q passage (Luke 11:2-4). The idea that God's name should be hallowed is traditional Jewish piety urging that God be respected, glorified, and obeyed. "Thy kingdom come" reflects the Q desire that the Day of the Son of Man arrive so they might enter the kingdom. "Give us each day our daily bread" is not a vague generality but a serious request by people who probably went many days with no bread or food at all. "And forgive us our sins, for we too forgive all who have done us wrong" reflects their key moral principle: as people forgive other people so they anticipate God will forgive them. Finally, the often-misunderstood last clause (it does not refer to temptation to sin), "And do not bring us to the test," means they hoped to avoid the times of testing, the period of tribulation when the fires and destruction they anticipated would be let loose upon the world. Even those who felt confident God would forgive them and that they would be acknowledged by the Son of Man before the angels of God were frightened of the prospect of such terrible times and asked God to let them avoid it.

Controversy

There is no sign in Q of any controversies within the Christian community. Jesus' disciples, insofar as they are mentioned at all, are mentioned favorably. Q perhaps reflects the kind of preaching you would have heard from Peter, James, John, and the other historical friends and associates of Jesus.

On the other hand, passages between Luke 11:39 and 11:53 show the Q people were engaged in controversy with Pharisaic Judaism. The Pharisees were accused of concerning themselves only with detailed legal observance and not with principles of love and justice, and the Pharisees were thought to be guilty of the persecution of God's prophets. Neither accusation is true of all Pharisees, but it is not hard to imagine that people who thought themselves to be prophets would have great resentment against religious leaders (including Pharisees) who did not accept them, did not repent on command, and who probably insisted (as Christian and Jewish religious leaders might today) that Q itinerants be driven away or locked up. Nothing in Q would have given the Pharisees any grounds under Torah Law to insist Q people be killed. However, as the announcement that a new kingdom would come and replace the existing kingdom was a serious crime under Roman law, the message of the Q people could easily have been thought by Roman authorities to be an illegal prediction or plot to replace the empire of Rome by an empire under Jewish leadership. Some Q people might have been executed by Roman authorities. Their founder was.

Interactions between Q and miracle stories

The miracle stories and the Q sayings collection do not contradict one another, but they are certainly different. The one focuses on action, the other on words. Miracle tales sought to convince people Jesus was the Christ or a great prophet, while the Q sayings were less concerned with people's ability to identify Jesus correctly and more concerned with people's willingness to commit themselves to a new repentant and compassionate form of life. The miracle sources show Jesus to be willing, even determined, to reveal himself as Christ; the Q sayings show him more ambiguously.

Bibliography

Achtemeier, Paul. "Toward the Isolation of Pre-Markan Miracle Catenae," *Journal of Biblical Literature* 89 (1970): 295–91.

Boring, Eugene. *The Continuing Voice of Jesus*. Louisville: Westminster/John Knox Press, 1991.

Crossan, John Dominic. *The Historical Jesus: The Life of a Mediterranean Jewish Peasant*. San Francisco: HarperSan Francisco, 1991.

Davies, Stevan. *The Gospel of Thomas and Christian Wisdom*. New York: Seabury Press, 1983.

Edwards, Richard A. *A Theology of Q*. Philadelphia: Fortress Press, 1976.

Fortna, R. T. *The Gospel of Signs*. Cambridge: Cambridge University Press, 1970.

Havener, Ivan. *Q: The Sayings of Jesus*. Wilmington: Glazier, 1986.

Kee, Howard C. *Miracle in the Early Christian World*. New Haven: Yale University Press, 1983.

Keller, Ernst. *Miracles in Dispute*. London: SCM Press, 1984.

Kloppenborg, John S. *The Formation of Q: Trajectories in Ancient Wisdom Collections*. Minneapolis: Fortree Press, 1987.

Kloppenborg John S., et al. *The Q Thomas Reader*. Sonoma, CA: Polebridge Press, 1990.

Mack, Burton L. *The Lost Gospel: The Book of Q and Christian Origins*. San Francisco: Harper & Row, 1991.

Patterson, Stephen J. *The Gospel of Thomas and Jesus*. Sonoma, CA: Polebridge Press, 1993.

Smith, Morton. *Jesus the Magician*. New York: Harper & Row, 1978.

Theissen, Gerd. *The Miracle Stories of the Early Christian Tradition*. Philadelphia: Fortress Press, 1983.

———. *Sociology of Early Palestinian Christianity*. Philadelphia: Fortress Press, 1978.

Four

Paul

The Growth of the New Testament

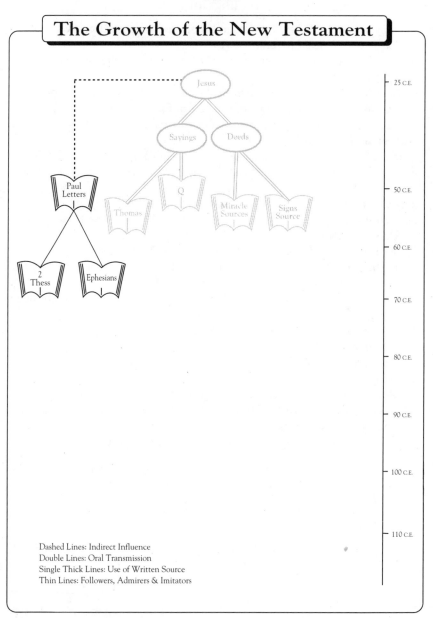

25 C.E.

50 C.E.

60 C.E.

70 C.E.

80 C.E.

90 C.E.

100 C.E.

110 C.E.

Dashed Lines: Indirect Influence
Double Lines: Oral Transmission
Single Thick Lines: Use of Written Source
Thin Lines: Followers, Admirers & Imitators

Of the twenty-seven books in the New Testament, fourteen are customarily attributed to Paul of Tarsus. All but one of these fourteen are letters; the exception is Hebrews, which is more like an essay or a sermon. Some of the letters attributed to Paul were written by Paul; others were written by followers of his who wished to carry forward his tradition and ideas by writing letters in his name.

Questions of Authorship

Scholars can often distinguish Paul's authorship from that of those who wrote in his name by analyzing the style and content of the writing. There is general agreement that Paul's letters to Christians in Rome, in Corinth, in Galatia, in Philippi, and in Thessalonika are authentically his. The short personal letter entitled Philemon is also undoubtedly Paul's. These form a solid body of information on Paul's style of writing and pattern of ideas. Other letters can then be compared with those and judgments made as to whether they deviate so far they could not come from him or whether they are sufficiently close to his style they should be attributed to him.

Scholars have counted each word and variety of grammatical construction in Paul's letters to Rome, Corinth, Galatia, Philippi, and Thessalonika. From this they have determined the frequency of Paul's use of terms and phrases. A letter attributed to Paul using words and grammatical constructions with the same frequency as they are used in other letters known to be his is probably written by Paul. If that letter also contains ideas known to be his, then it is certainly written by Paul. But a letter attributed to Paul containing many words that never otherwise occur in Paul's letters, does not have the same frequency of word use, has atypical grammatical constructions, and includes ideas inconsistent with those known to be Paul's was probably written in Paul's name by somebody else.

Virtually no analytical scholars believe 1 Timothy, 2 Timothy, Titus, or Hebrews were written by Paul. Hebrews reflects his style and concepts not at all, and the other three letters, collectively called the Pastorals, come from a later period of the church. This is evident from the developed patterns of leadership and organization in the churches to which they are written. Their author does know something about Paul's ideas but does not interpret them in the same way Paul himself does. Further, his style of writing is not Paul's.

Paul probably did not write the letter to the Ephesians, although that letter was written by a follower of his who was greatly influenced by him. The style of Ephesians is significantly different from that of the letters certainly written by Paul, and the ideas of Ephesians, although Pauline, are not sufficiently similar to Paul's to have come from him. Many scholars now believe that Ephesians was written as a cover letter or introduction to the rest of Paul's letters.

Two letters are in dispute. Did Paul write Colossians and 2 Thessalonians or did he not? Since Paul was brilliant and inventive, one cannot be too rigid in categorizing ideas as his or not-his. He may have changed his mind or come up with startling ideas that do not appear in the letters he wrote. But neither of those letters seems fully consistent with Paul's thought and they contain stylistic elements absent from his other letters. Further, 2 Thessalonians seems, in part, to be a rewritten version of 1 Thessalonians. Accordingly, many analytical scholars tend to leave Colossians and 2 Thessalonians aside in writing about Paul and regard them as having been written by associates of his who developed his thought in their own ways; but the question of their authenticity is far from being settled and a good many eminently respectable scholars regard one or both as having been written by Paul himself.

Instead of being a cause for disappointment, the discovery that some of the letters customarily attributed to Paul were written by others should be a source of pleasure. It means the range of ideas and opinions in the New Testament is much greater than it would have been if Paul had written all fourteen letters. For example, the Pastorals give insight into the state of Christianity in the early part of the second century, and Hebrews reveals Christianity as interpreted through Hellenistic Judaism. Colossians develops beyond Paul toward an even more exalted conception of Jesus in whom "everything in heaven and on earth was created, not only things visible but also the invisible orders of thrones, sovereignties, authorities, and powers: the whole universe has been created through him and for him" (Col. 1:16).

The dates given for Paul's letters are approximate (as are the dates of all New Testament documents), but here the range of uncertainty is a matter of a year or two rather than of a decade or two.

1 Thessalonians:	ca. C.E. 51
1 Corinthians:	ca. C.E. 54
2 Corinthians:	ca. C.E. 55
Galatians:	ca. C.E. 56
Philippians:	ca. C.E. 56
Philemon:	ca. C.E. 56
Romans:	ca. C.E. 59
Colossians?:	ca. C.E. 61

When you read Paul's letters carefully you may notice that his line of thought occasionally stops abruptly and shifts to another subject or that he suddenly seems to pick up a line of thinking he left many chapters earlier. Some letters seem to end twice. A convincing theory regarding these sudden shifts is that certain short letters of Paul's were combined at some later date to create longer letters. The letters within letters are not necessarily in the order in which they were received. Scholars have sought to reorder them, guided by clues from their content.

Here is a list of letters within letters, following the analysis in Norman Perrin's *The New Testament:*

Philippians:	1.	A letter thanking the Philippians (4:10–20)
	2.	Another of the same (1:1–3:1)
	3.	Fragment of a polemical letter (3:2–4:9, 21–23)
2 Corinthians:	1.	Paul defends himself (2:14–6:13, 7:2–4)
	2.	The "Tearful Letter" (10:1–13:14)
	3.	Goodwill returns (1:1–2:13, 7:5–16)
	4.	Letter recommending Titus (8:1–24)
	5.	Letter about the collection (9:1–15)
	6.	A fragment some think was not written by Paul but by someone critical of his teachings (6:14–7:1)
Romans:		Chapter 16 possibly was added to the original although it was written by Paul.

Evidence for a reconstruction of Paul's biography is found in his letters (especially Galatians and Seconld Corinthians) and in Luke's book the Acts of the Apostles, but neither his letters nor Acts is absolutely reliable as a source for Paul's biography. In his letters Paul is more interested in instructing his Christian readers than in giving accurate autobiographical details, while Luke's knowledge of Paul is based more on oral tradition and stories than on certain knowledge. But, on the other hand, Luke's sources are not greatly distorted and can often be trusted in a general way. Paul's speeches in Acts are, however, Luke's idea of what Paul would have said and cannot reliably be used to analyze Paul's thought.

Paul's Life

Paul was born to Jewish parents in Tarsus, a city of substantial size and influence located in Asia Minor (present-day Turkey). Luke informs us that he held Roman citizenship, presumably inherited from his father, which gave him considerable social prestige and legal privilege. He was well educated, both in the Greek tradition (as shown by his excellent writing and his knowledge of Greek philosophical themes) and in the Jewish tradition (as shown by his skill in argumentation based on Jewish Scripture). He may even have studied with one of the greatest Jewish teachers of the first century, Rabbi Gamaliel (Acts 22:3), although this is debatable. He was a professional maker of tents, a trade allowing him to make a living in any reasonably sized town. So he had social status from his citizenship, ethnic background, and occupation.

We do not, of course, know for sure what he looked like, but he took no pride in his appearance or physical presence (2 Cor. 10:1, 10). The Acts of Paul, a set of legendary second-century stories about Paul with almost no historical validity, does contain a description of Paul that is not the sort of thing writers of legends invent for their heroes. It may conceivably be accurate: "A man small of stature, with a bald head and crooked legs, in a good state of body with eyebrows meeting and nose somewhat hooked, full of friendliness."

In his youth Paul regarded himself as a righteous, Law-fulfilling Jew. Upon learning of Christians in the first years after the crucifixion he persecuted them. Having heard of a community of Christians in Damascus, Syria, Paul set off to continue his persecution there. He was probably in his early twenties at the time.

The greatest event in Paul's life took place during that journey somewhere on the road from Jerusalem to Damascus; Paul believed that God revealed Jesus Christ to him. Paul evidently was immediately convinced that Jesus Christ was Son of God, that he had died for the sins of all people, that salvation came only through faith in Christ, and that he, having thus seen the risen Christ, had been appointed apostle to the Gentile world.

At this point he began to travel into Gentile regions seeking to establish communities of people who would live in accordance with his vision of God's expectations. He was amazingly successful, establishing groups loyal to him (loyal to his gospel, he would say) in such areas as Macedonia, Corinth, Ephesus, Thessalonika, Galatia. Acts reports Paul arrived in Rome under arrest. Later traditions declare he was executed in Rome; this is thought to have taken place around the year C.E. 62.

It would serve no useful purpose to go into detail here about his life and travels. Many books contain such details, as best as scholars can figure them out. What is important for our purpose is to understand his overall perspective. Having looked into this we will pay special attention to two of his letters: Galatians and Romans, and survey the other letters he wrote. Paul's Letter to the Galatians will be considered in greatest detail for several reasons: in Galatians the "apostle to the Gentiles" speaks especially to Gentile Christians; he spells out central themes of his thought rather clearly; in Galatians more than in any other letter Paul discusses his own life; and, finally, it is a short and manageable letter. Having examined Galatians we will turn our attention to Paul's masterpiece, his Letter to the Romans and then examine his other letters. In an introductory book such as this our goal is to discuss the basic principles of Paul's thought, not fully to analyze each of his letters.

Each of Paul's letters contains different emphases, and each is written to address a somewhat different set of problems, but on central points concerning Jesus Christ, salvation, faith, and morals they present the same general system of ideas. But Paul's letters are *letters*, not theological treatises or carefully composed sermons. They were not designed to present a general system of ideas but to respond to conditions in communities and to respond to particular problems. They assume that readers are already familiar with Paul's thinking; in every instance except the letter to Romans Paul is writing to people who have had long and sustained contact with him personally and so he writes to remind readers of what he thinks they should already know. Even Romans, which is written to a community Paul has not yet visited, assumes that members of the community know of Paul's gospel, although he believes many of them are likely to have misunderstood it. For nearly two thousand years Christians have sought to make clear systematic sense out of Paul's letters, but never with complete success.

Readers should always bear in mind that Paul's letters address particular contingent situations in the communities he addresses. While there is a coherent center to Paul's theological thought, he does not spell out his central ideas for their own sake. Rather, Paul draws on his central ideas in addressing specific issues and situations. One ought not take any single letter of Paul's as *the* core of his thought. Rather, in each letter Paul references his ideas somewhat differently in response to differing circumstances.

Basic Pauline Ideas

Paul was a religious genius whose ways of thinking and expressing himself were different from those of ordinary people. His ideas work within a particular view of reality that is his own and that he felt he had received from God. Within his particular frame of reference much of his thinking makes logical sense. Outside his frame of reference he cannot make sense. To understand him, therefore, we must try to enter his frame of reference sympathetically.

Paul speaks of two separate ways of being human and preaches a gospel declaring people should shift from the one way to the other way. This shift is not just a change of habits or attitude, it is a shift to a whole different category of being. Here are some of the characteristics of the two alternatives:

Guilty	Justified
Cursed	Blessed
Alienated from God	Approved by God
Less than potential	Ideal
Seek approval from God	Find approval from God
by trying to follow Torah Law	by having Faith
Believe in the necessity of	
following the Law of Moses	Follow the Law of Christ
Tempted by	Assisted by
the power of the flesh	the power of the Spirit
Oriented toward the material	Oriented toward the spiritual
Destined to die	Destined to rise
Some are descendants	All are descendants
of Abraham (physically)	of Abraham (spiritually)

This list might be lengthened considerably. There is no logical limit to such a list because it stems from the premise that for each significant aspect of human life and each aspect of religious theory there is an aspect reflecting faith in Christ and an aspect not reflecting such faith.

Paul sees a new age dawning and the possibility of a new humanity. Those who, through baptism, are included "in Christ" participate in the new humanity and, in the eschatological future, will be included in the full glory of God. The dawn of this new age occurs, in Paul's view, through the death and resurrection of Jesus Christ.

Paul does not define faith in any of his letters. Christians have sought to do this for him over a period of two thousand years, but they have created not a solution but many denominations. Faith definitely involves trust in God, belief in Christ, acceptance of Christ's death as a death for all humanity, and acceptance of the idea that through faith people may be justified, or made righteous, in the eyes of God. Paul is less interested in an abstract definition of faith than in the effects of faith. Those effects include communal love, moral living and confidence in one's salvation.

Paul uses the effects of faith to reason back to a practical definition of faith. In other words, those who show the effects of faith are shown to be correct in thinking they have understood faith correctly. In the absence of the effects, faith is questionable. Faith enables Christians to receive the Spirit of God. The Spirit of God enables people to resist the temptation to sin and so to follow the way of Christ at least moderately well. Paul does not think Christians are all entirely moral, nor does he think they should act immorally. But Christians, guided by the Spirit, should be able to behave more morally than non-Christians, even if they cannot achieve perfection. The Spirit enables Christians to perform observable acts, including healing, miraculous powers, prophecy, and speech "in tongues" (1 Cor. 12:7–11). Because they have the Spirit, Christians, in theory at least, should be able to act as Jesus acted, both in the sense of obedience to God and in the sense of exercising supernatural power.

Temptations from the flesh always exist. Temptations from the material world, old habits, false gospels—all can still threaten faith. So Paul, honestly, admits the good he wants to do, he often cannot do. While the Spirit is willing, the flesh is weak. Paul does *not* believe in a hell or in eternal punishment. Death is annihilation, which is punishment enough.

The most visible effects of faith come from the Spirit as it enables the working of miracles and other signs and as it guides Christians in proper behavior. When they all have the same Spirit, which is the Spirit of the person Jesus Christ, they are all in that sense one person. In Paul's mind it logically follows from the fact of all Christians being one person in Christ that they are united with Christ and are sons and heirs of God; they are a new creation, and constitute the body of Christ (Paul uses all these ways of expressing it). Paul speaks most dramatically of identification with Christ when he writes, "I have been crucified with Christ: the life I now live is not my life, but the life which Christ lives in me" (Gal. 2:20). But he does not regard himself uniquely to be a person in whom Christ lives; he assumes this applies to all who have received the Spirit of Christ.

In the community, the body of Christ, there are to be no social divisions; there are indeed no separate people, and so "in Christ there is no such thing as Jew and Greek, slave and freeman, male and female; for you are all one person in Christ Jesus" (Gal. 3:28). Elsewhere he writes, "For Christ is like a single body with its many limbs and organs, which, many as they are, together make up one body. For indeed we were all brought into one body by baptism, in the one Spirit, whether we are Jews or Greeks, whether slaves or free men, and the one Holy Spirit was poured out for all of us to drink" (1 Cor. 12:12–13). How should people who are all the same person behave? They should love one another.

A body which is "one person in Christ Jesus" cannot allow social distinctions based on former religion or sex or wealth (Gal. 3:28) or powers given by the Spirit (1 Cor. 12:4) or roles within the church (1 Cor. 12:29) ever to be a source of division. To Paul Christian unity is absolutely essential. The Torah Law of Moses, therefore, if useful, should lead to unity. But in the real world of Jews and Gentiles, the Law of Moses led to disunity and diversion. The Law is detailed regarding permitted and forbidden foods; Pharisees interpreted the Law to make it even more restrictive with complex rules of purity and impurity. So, the social effects of following the Torah Law might include the refusal by Jews to dine with non-Jews. Gentiles did not keep, or even know anything about, the Law's purity and impurity restrictions and had no reason not to dine on such forbidden foods as ham and shrimp. For a Christian group whose main ritual occasions were frequent celebrations of the Lord's Supper—at that time a real and not a symbolic meal—this meant that adherence to Torah Law would either lead to a split within the body of Christ or to the necessity that all Christians follow the Torah Law. Neither alternative was acceptable to Paul, the first because disunity contradicted his thesis that all Christians are one in Christ, the second because it contradicted his thesis that only faith, not Law, brings salvation.

Paul believed the effort to achieve God's approval through following Law was the opposite of faith. Faith allows one to receive a gift that we term grace, from the Latin word for gift. Following Law shows you have not accepted this gift through faith. To make a commonplace analogy: if you need a thousand dollars, and a friend or relative informs you they have deposited a thousand dollars in your bank account, should you continue as before to work overtime to earn the thousand dollars it indicates you really do not think the money is in the bank waiting for you. That is one way to look at the question of Law; seeking salvation through Law indicates you have not taken seriously the idea you have already attained salvation through faith. Paul, further, does not believe salvation can be attained by obedience to Law because he regards the attempt to be saved through Law as boasting, as demanding God give a reward for proper behavior. In Paul's opinion people cannot earn salvation. It is a gift accepted through faith.

Not seeking salvation through Law, however, is not the same as disregarding all Law. Paul cautions Christians against using faith as an excuse for sinning. He is emphatic that Christians must not think they have God's permission to live immorally. He also contends that following Torah Law may be necessary to keep from offending those who are not Christians or do not understand that the Law cannot bring salvation. His position is not "never follow the Torah Law" but "never seek salvation through the Torah Law."

The crucial factor for Paul is motivation. If your motivation for following the Torah Law is to win God's approval, your failure is inevitable and you have opted not to have faith. If, on the other hand, your motivation is to keep from offending people, to live morally, to win others to the gospel, you have done nothing wrong at all.

Reading 1 Thessalonians

Read Paul's first letter to the Thessalonians.

This is the oldest piece of Christian writing we have. It dates from about C.E. 51. As Paul often does in his letters, he takes time to defend himself against various accusations: here he declares that he has no base motives, does not seek to deceive, does not flatter, seeks no praise and that he worked for his living rather than accepted money from the community (2:4–9). He speaks very bitterly of "the Jews, who killed the Lord Jesus and the prophets and drove us out" but this must not be taken to be his true assessment of Judaism or the Jewish people. In his letter to the Romans Paul writes at length very favorably about Jews and Judaism.

Perhaps the principal motivation for this letter was a perceived need to explain to the Thessalonian Christians that the physical death of believers ought not be taken to be a contradiction of Paul's gospel. Rather, he writes, Christians who have died will be brought to life again . . . they "sleep" until that occurs. Paul believes that the end of this world and the second coming of the Lord will occur in a very short time, certainly during his own lifetime. He speaks of "we who are left alive until the Lord comes," at which time there will be heard the word of command, the sound of the archangel's voice, God's trumpet call. Then the Lord will descend, the Christian dead will rise and "we who are left alive" will be caught up in the clouds to meet the Lord in the air. This passage (4:13–18) is the one to which evangelical Christians appeal when they speak of "the rapture."

Paul evidently refers to a traditional saying of Jesus in 5:1–2 when he refers to the day of the Lord coming like a thief in the night. A similar formulation is found in Q (Matt 24:43–44 // Luke 12:39–40).

Reading Galatians

Read Paul's letter to the Galatians at least twice (it is quite short). Underline every reference to Law and to circumcision. The term *circumcision* means, to Paul, accepting the necessity of following the Law to win God's approval. Paul is not so much concerned with circumcision itself but with circumcision as a symbolic act demonstrating one's determination to follow the Law. In this symbolic sense persons of either sex might accept circumcision. For Gentile men, of course, the acceptance was more than symbolic and, in days before anesthetic or antisceptic, was a very serious decision.

Jesus' disciple Peter is the person called "Cephas" in Galatians. His original name was Simon. Jesus gave him the Aramaic name Cephas, but he is now universally known as Peter. *Peter* is a Greek translation of *Cephas;* both words mean "the rock." It may sound funny, but the correct English translation of the nickname Cephas (Peter) is "Rocky."

Law

Having read Galatians carefully you will have noticed the letter is highly argumentative. The Gentile Christian community in Galatia is evidently in the process of deciding to follow Torah Law. The people, therefore, intend to accept circumcision. Paul is adamant; they should not do this. The passages you have underlined assert repeatedly that Law and faith are contradictory. You may do the one or the other, but not both. To feel a need to keep the Law is to demonstrate a lack of faith. Paul's strongest statement to that effect is: "Mark my words: I, Paul, say to you that if you receive circumcision Christ will do you no good at all" (5:2) (indicating, incidentally, that the Galatians have not yet taken this step). Justification, or righteousness in the eyes of God, comes through faith in Christ Jesus, not through following Law.

This opposition between faith and Law is spelled out clearly in Galatians. Paul writes (2:21), "If righteousness comes by Law, then Christ died for nothing." Paul believes that since Jesus' death people have the potential to shift from one category to another, from fallen people to perfected people. Should there be no need to shift, if righteousness is already available, what would have been the point of Jesus' death? Nothing significant would have changed; the Law would lead to righteousness just as much before as after. It is as essential to Paul's theory that Law does not bring righteousness and justification as it is that faith does bring righteousness and justification. Why did the Son of God have to die on a cross? That's Paul's question. If you answer that Christ's death brings one more optional way to salvation, Paul will not accept it. For Christ's death to have been *necessary* it must provide the *only* way to salvation.

Paul argues against Law as a way to salvation in various ways. Some are allegorical. Paul writes, "Tell me now, you who are so anxious to be under Law, will you not listen to what the Law says?" (4:21). Here he uses the term in two ways, Law as seeking justification by obedience to rules, and Law as the stories in the Torah. In this instance he uses the story of Abraham found in Genesis chapters 12 through 25. The allegory in 4:21–31, for example, is based on the story that Abraham had two sons, one by his slave girl Hagar and the other by his elderly wife Sarah, whose pregnancy was said to have come about in fulfillment of God's promise. Paul claims that the offspring of Sarah represents those who have faith and are free from Law, while the offspring of Hagar represents those who seek righteousness through the Law given to Moses on Mount Sinai. Paul clearly accepts the authority of Torah as divinely revealed allegorical stories even though he argues against Torah as a required set of ordinances. Because he understands those stories as allegories he feels free to interpret them in light of his own gospel, a gospel he believed to have been revealed to him by God. Christians should understand that although Jewish rabbis also read Torah allegorically, and instances of this are found even in the Dead Sea Scrolls, Paul's Christian allegorical readings would have been incomprehensible to knowledgeable Jewish people, for he argues, in effect, that Torah (story) contradicts Torah

(Law). To non-Jews, to the gentiles to whom Paul came as apostle, his allegorical readings evidently did make good sense.

All Jewish people traced their ancestry back to Abraham and Sarah. Genesis contains the story of God's establishment of a covenant with Abraham and, through him, with Abraham's offspring (or "issue"). The covenant included the promise (Genesis 12:2–3): "I will make you into a great nation, I will bless you and make your name so great that it shall be used in blessings: Those that bless you I will bless, those that curse you, I will execrate. All the families on earth will pray to be blessed as you are blessed." This promise was made to Abraham and his offspring. The Jewish people identified themselves as Abraham's offspring and regarded themselves as a people whose duty to the covenant included the obligation to keep the Law of Moses.

Paul believes the promise made to Abraham and his offspring is valid. In what would have come as a staggering surprise to any Jewish audience, Paul goes on to declare that the offspring of Abraham is Christ and, in accordance with his theory that Christians are one person through the Spirit of Christ, the offspring of Abraham is therefore any person who has faith in Christ and so does not seek righteousness through Law. According to him, Abraham's *true* offspring were the Christians of Paul's Gentile churches, for they had faith in Christ. Jews would have thought this theory turned Scripture absolutely upside down. Paul's rationale is that Abraham received the promises and covenant because "Abraham put his *faith* in the Lord and the Lord counted that faith to him as righteousness" (Genesis 15:6). The offspring of faithful Abraham are only those people who have faith. Paul assumes what the Genesis passage means by faith is exactly what he means by faith.

Today's readers rarely realize how radical Paul's ideas are. He claims that the promises made to Abraham and the covenant on which the Jewish people had based their national and religious identity for centuries were made all along only to such non-Jews (Gentiles) and Jews as were willing to renounce the obligation of obedience to the Law by accepting that they had become righteous through their faith In Paul's opinion the "new covenant" is the final version of the old, making explicit what the old covenant implied.

Paul encourages Gentile Galatians in the Christian community to think of themselves in a Jewish fashion, as heirs to the promise to Abraham and as members of the covenant (a new covenant in Jesus' blood, to be precise) (1 Cor. 11:25). They could consider themselves the ones to whom the Torah really refers and to whom it belongs, those who correctly worship the One God who was revealed to Abraham and Moses and who spoke through the prophets.

What of the Jews? In his Letter to the Romans Paul writes to a Jewish

Christian audience and is careful to be highly complimentary to Jews and the Jewish religion. Yet his conclusion there, as in Galatians, is that true Jews, true Israel, are those who have faith in Christ. Such people were, primarily, Gentiles. Jews were welcome to join Paul's communities of faith and he profoundly respects the fact that the Torah was revealed to them, indeed he regards that revelation as a mark of God's special favor. But, in the final analysis, to be Jewish without faith in Christ and to seek to become righteous in God's eyes by obedience to Torah would no more lead to salvation than to worship the gods of pagan religions.

Paul offers Gentiles a way of being "Jewish" that did not entail the rigors of Judaism, that did not involve the painful and dangerous operation of adult circumcision, and that did not require any change in habits of eating. Then, as today, dining was the central event of social life. Imagine being unable to dine with business colleagues, friends at their homes, or relatives who married members of other religious groups, and you will see the social consequences of the Mosaic food laws when taken seriously. Such laws create strong group cohesion, but at the cost of separation from those outside that group. Judaism was an attractive option to many Gentiles for reasons given in this book's chapter 2. To become "Jewish" through faith rather than through obedience to Law was an attractive option. Gentiles who followed Paul's gospel might believe themselves to have the benefits of Judaism without the social difficulties usually encountered by converts to Judaism who sought to follow Torah Law.

Gentiles evidently did wish to enter the covenant and receive the promises of Abraham through faith in Christ. Their desire to do so led to the rapid spread of the Christian religion. Jewish people, on the other hand, considered themselves already to be in the covenant, to be heirs to the promises of God, and to be the people of God. The men already were circumcised and surely most Jews then, like most Jews today, believed they had lived throughout their lives in reasonable accordance with the Law. Most Jews were confident that should they have broken the law and honestly asked God's forgiveness, they would be forgiven. Paul offered Gentiles the opportunity to enter Judaism without the Law; there is no reason to think any substantial number of Jewish people would be interested in accepting that offer for themselves.

Jewish people believed God would forgive failures to keep his Law if people were sorry, repentant, and determined to do better. For them it was not that complicated a matter; God's forgiveness was repeatedly announced in the Scriptures. It would be nonsense for the prophets to have demanded repentance if repentance did no good. Judaism affirms that God forgives sin and God will approve as righteous those who seek to obey his Law and who repent when they fail.

Here we find difficulty in Paul's line of reasoning, because, if Paul's theory is to work, repentance must be impossible. He argues, "Those who rely on obedience to the Law are under a curse; for Scripture says, 'A curse is on all who do not persevere in doing everything that is written in the Book of the Law.' It is evident that no one is ever justified before God in terms of Law" (Gal. 3:10, quoting Deuteronomy 27:26). This argument, in fact Paul's whole perspective, depends on there being no forgiveness for those who break God's Law. If God forgives those who repent, then the "curse" would apply only to those who will not repent, and Paul is absolutely convinced his theory, his revelation, applies to all humanity. Those who repent have no advantage over those who do not repent.

If God forgives, then those who break the Law can repent and be forgiven. If people can repent and be forgiven, then people can obtain righteousness through Law, provided they sincerely try to keep it and repent when they fail. This is the belief of Jews today and it was the belief of Jews in Paul's day. If that is true, however, then from Paul's perspective, "Christ died for nothing." Does salvation come *only* through faith in Christ or *also* through faith in Christ? For Paul, only the former alternative was true.

Throughout Galatians Paul appeals to the Hebrew epic story of Abraham, Hagar, Sarah and their children. Those who are in Christ are, according to Paul, the intended heirs of Abraham and a new humanity, one that was promised by God at the beginning of Hebrew mythic history. Accordingly it may be better to think of Galatians as an argument that Gentiles are included in the people of God rather than to think of Galatians too much as a discussion of sin and forgiveness.

The situation in Galatia

The letter to the Galatians immediately sets forth the general problem Paul seeks to solve: "I am astonished to find you turning so quickly away from him who called you by grace, and following a different gospel" (1:6). Here "gospel" does not mean a book but a message. Evidently, other Christians have brought a gospel message to the church in Galatia. Their gospel includes the requirement that Christians, whether born Gentile or Jewish, must keep Torah Law. If men are not circumcised, they must be circumcised. The food Laws must be kept. The Christians who preached this message are apparently near to success in convincing a church founded and instructed by Paul that Paul's teachings are unreliable. Evidently some or all of the Galatian Christians have begun trying to keep the Law of Moses (4:21) and are moving away from the Pauline point of view that salvation comes through faith and grace. Paul seems furious:

"You stupid Galatians! You must have been bewitched—you before whose eyes Jesus Christ was openly displayed upon his cross! Answer me one question: did you receive the Spirit by keeping the Law or by believing the [my] gospel message? Can it be that you are so stupid? You started with the spiritual; do you now look to the material to make you perfect? I ask then: when God gives you the Spirit and works miracles among you, why is this? Is it because you keep the Law, or is it because you have faith in the [my] gospel message?" (3:1–5).

The Law, material, is opposed to Faith, spiritual. Paul believes some of those in Galatia who have become Christians have now been convinced to return to behaviours and beliefs characteristic of their life before their conversion. This would make Paul's whole work with them a failure. No wonder he is upset. They accepted his gospel; they had evidence provided by the Spirit and miracles worked through the Spirit affirming his gospel. Now they are adopting a perspective contradicting his gospel.

What might lead the Galatians, who probably never heard of Jesus Christ before the arrival of Paul, suddenly to turn away from Paul's teachings to those of other Christians? That the Galatian Christians should obey strangers, rather than Paul who brought them the gospel, is evidence the strangers had strong arguments to support their claim that their gospel was superior to Paul's. An effort to understand Paul's letters requires an effort to understand the perspectives of the audience of those letters (a perspective with which Paul is usually *not* sympathetic). In reading Galatians one should try to comprehend how it might have been that Paul's Christians would have been tempted to turn away from Paul. Some powerful motivations must have been at work.

Clues to the identity of Paul's opponents come from Paul's self-defense. Paul defends himself in two ways. One is to argue from Scripture and from the principles of his theory of salvation from faith that seeking salvation by following the Law cancels the good results of faith. The other is to defend himself personally. He does this in the first section of Galatians, 1:1–2:16.

Apparently the claim had been made that Paul was appointed to the status of apostle by one or more human beings, for at the beginning of his letter he takes pains to defend himself from such a charge. Presumably there were Christian authorities who claimed the right to appoint apostles. Either these authorities denied ever having appointed Paul, or they thought their appointment of him gave them the right to control him. Paul responds with the assertion that he is not an apostle by human appointment or commission but by commission from Jesus Christ and from God (1:1).

When Paul outlines his life story (1:12–2:14), he does not simply tell a story; he seeks to prove his knowledge of Jesus Christ does not come from human instruction at all but from direct revelation. After his initial persecution of Christians, Paul believes God revealed His Son to him in order that he might proclaim him to the Gentiles. Immediately thereafter Paul went to Arabia and then returned to Damascus in Syria. It was after three years that Paul went to Jerusalem to meet Peter (Cephas). He stayed there only two weeks and saw only Peter and James. This section is worded to demonstrate that although Paul did meet Peter and James, he did not go to them for instruction, and that his acquaintance with them was very limited.

"Fourteen years later," he again went to Jerusalem. There he met privately with James, Peter, and John, who agreed Paul should bring the gospel to the Gentiles while they should bring the gospel to the Jews. Paul also agreed to collect money to send to them.

He is adamant in insisting that he went to Jerusalem only twice in seventeen years and that while he was there little happened other than that James, Peter, and John agreed he should bring the gospel to the Gentiles. Without their permission, he had already been doing this for many years. Paul insists his account is true. He claims, "What I write is plain truth; before God I am not lying" (1:20). These are powerful words.

Paul's argument in outlining his career is twofold: first, he was not appointed by any human being; second he did not learn his gospel from any human being. His appointment and his gospel were both given him directly when God revealed the Son to him. Not Peter nor James nor John nor their associates commissioned him or taught him; on that point he is adamant. It is interesting to note that this means that Paul's knowledge of "the historical Jesus" (whom James and Peter and John knew personally) was limited, even close to non-existent. His argument here in Galatians is that he had little such knowledge and wanted little and siezed no opportunities to get more. Knowledge of Christ Son of God that God revealed to him was, in his mind, more than sufficient.

Paul would be telling us all this only if it were essential to his defense against his opponents in Galatia. Those opponents must have claimed Paul was appointed an apostle by humans and learned his gospel from humans; otherwise it would be pointless for Paul to seek to prove such claims false. Since their gospel was contradictory to his regarding the Law, Paul's opponents presumably claimed that whatever he had learned from humans he had learned badly, and that whoever had appointed him an apostle wished to cancel the appointment or wished to assert authority over him so that he would no longer teach freedom from Law.

We do not know who came to Galatia. Many scholars use such terms as Judaizers or Jewish-Christians, with the implication they constitute a branch of the early church independent both of Paul and of the authorities in Jerusalem. This is possible but not likely. At this very early date in the history of the Christian movement it is hard to imagine there could have arisen Christian groups who both kept the Law and urged Gentile Christians to keep the Law, and who were also distinct from or in opposition to the leaders of the church in Jerusalem.

A more convincing explanation is that those who came to Galatia were sent by James or by the church in Jerusalem, which was led by James up to the time of his death. We know James believed Christians must follow Torah Law. As Paul presents it, if Christians representing James arrived in Galatia to reform Paul's Christian community, they were breaking the agreement Paul made with James, Peter, and John that he, Paul, would go to Gentiles while they, e.g. Peter, would go to Jews.

Were the Christians in Galatia "Christians" (in the sense of a separate religious category) or were they "Jews"? From Paul's perspective, the answer is that faithful Christians are the descendants of Abraham, the people of God, and therefore they are "Jews." Another way of putting this is that Paul declared that the covenant between God and his people is now open to Gentiles who have faith in Jesus Christ; thus, Christians are those who through faith have joined in the covenant between God and the Jewish people.

Suppose then the Galatians, feeling and believing themselves to have become Jewish through their faith, encountered Christians of Jewish ancestry—Christians who had seen Jesus or, at least, had met his brother James and his disciples and friends such as Peter and John—who said, "Nonsense! You must have faith in Jesus Christ *and* you must obey the Law of God, repenting any sins you may commit, receiving forgiveness in Jesus' name." The Galatian Christians might have countered, "But Paul said the Law and faith were opposed," and might have heard in response, "But what does Paul know? He never met Jesus. Everything he learned he learned from those who did know Jesus, especially our friends who are leaders of the church in Jerusalem. They allowed him to be an apostle. He has no grounds to contradict them."

The Galatians seem to have met such people and nearly to have been convinced that salvation requires obedience to God's Law. Paul hears about this and angrily, defensively, responds with his letter.

As before, in Antioch (2:11–14), Paul in Galatia seems to be in conflict with Jesus' brother James and Jesus' most important disciple, Peter (Cephas). Paul cannot claim anything like their knowledge of the life, teaching, and personality of Jesus. Rather, he claims knowledge of Jesus the risen Christ and Lord, knowledge given him directly by God. It was not James or Peter who appointed him apostle but God. God's Son taught him, not James or Peter. The Galatians should listen to him, and through him God, rather than listen to representatives of James or Peter.

Toward the end of his letter to the Galatians Paul addresses another problem, one occurring frequently in his letters. If Christians are free from the necessity to follow the Law, are they therefore free to do anything they want no matter how wild and irresponsible? Of course not. In the concluding chapters of his letter Paul is careful to emphasize that Christians must act in a moral and loving fashion despite their freedom from Law.

Reading Romans

Paul's letter entitled Romans is his masterpiece, his most sustained and systematic effort to communicate his thoughts on Christ, salvation, sin, and Law. *Read the Letter to the Romans. Underline references to faith, justification and righteousness.*

Although traditionally Romans was thought to have been sent specifically to the church in Rome, some scholars believe it to have been a general letter designed to be sent to several churches rather than just to one. It is something of a summary of Paul's basic position on many issues and would serve well to remind members of his churches of his teachings. It certainly could have served to defend Paul's ideas to Roman Christians. Paul at the time of writing Romans had never visited Rome, although he planned to travel there in the near future.

The letter to the Romans in many places contains more lengthy and complexly written versions of the same arguments as are in the letter to the Galatians. At the same time, however, it is so densely argued that it is less accessible to ordinary readers than Galatians is. In Galatians Paul addressed an audience of Gentiles. In Romans his audience included both Jewish and Gentile Christians, and the Jewish Christians may have been in the majority. Romans contains several arguments that the Jewish tradition and the Jewish people are favored by God. But Paul does not downgrade Gentiles.

The Gentiles and the Law

Toward the beginning of Romans (1:18–2:17) Paul argues against the idea that because God is the God of the Jews, and because the Jews were given God's Law, the Gentiles are irrelevant to God's plan. That idea arises from reasoning that if the problem of salvation concerns people's obedience to God's Law, and if God, who is just, would act unjustly should he punish people for disobedience to a Law they never knew, then God would neither reward nor punish Gentiles. Paul argues that the Gentiles indeed have the Law, or at least knowledge of God and God's commands equivalent to the Law. They obtain this knowledge from reasoning about the natural world or perhaps, as we might put it, from their consciences. Paul writes, "For all that may be known of God by men lies plain before their eyes; indeed God himself has disclosed it to them. His invisible attributes, that is to say his everlasting power and deity, have been visible, ever since the world began, to the eye of reason, in the things he has made. There is therefore no possible defence for their conduct; knowing God, they have refused to honour him as God, or to render him thanks" (Rom. 1:19–21). Through careful thought about the world, Gentiles can come to know the nature and requirements of God. In Paul's opinion Gentiles are just as subject to God's judgment as Jews and just as capable of achieving righteousness as Jews are.

This line of reasoning would naturally raise the question of whether Jews have any special relationship to God at all, or whether they are simply one more ethnic group out of many. Paul wishes to argue that Jews do have a special place in God's plan and also to maintain the position that "God has no favorites" (2:11–12). Jews have the advantage over Gentiles, in theory at least, because they have received God's Law directly and therefore, unlike the Gentiles, do not have to puzzle it out for themselves by reflection on the world. Paul thus concedes the Jews have a special relationship to God. Yet he denies that special means superior. "Are we Jews any better off? No, not at all! For we have already drawn up the accusation that Jews and Greeks alike are all under the power of sin" (2:9). God is the God of Jews and Gentiles equally.

Paul seems to argue two points simultaneously, and while they may seem contradictory, they are really not. He argues that the Jews were given the Law on Mount Sinai and so have the advantage over Gentiles should they have been able to keep the Law. As they did not keep it (in Paul's opinion) their advantage is canceled and they are in the same situation as the Gentiles. Still, they were first to receive special consideration by God (Torah Law), and so the Jews come first and Gentiles last. In chapter 11 of Romans Paul uses the image of a domestic variety of olive tree that has been consecrated to God; this is Judaism. But some branches are pruned off and some branches of a wild variety of olive tree (Gentiles) are grafted onto the domestic tree. These wild branches now share the nutrients provided by the roots and the sap of the consecrated tree, and all parts constitute the same tree. Because of their lack of faith the old branches were pruned off; because of their faith the new branches are grafted on. But the root of the tree remains Judaism.

In chapter 11 of Romans especially Paul argues that the delivery of the gospel to Gentiles does not mean the Jews are condemned. If anything, salvation came to them first, for Jesus was born Jewish. The Jews will be saved, Paul believes. The salvation of the Gentiles is intended, in part, to provide motivation for Jews to be saved. Paul finds Jews somewhat less receptive to the gospel than Gentiles but believes that condition to be temporary: "This partial blindness has come upon Israel only until the Gentiles have been admitted in full strength; when that has happened, the whole of Israel will be saved" (11:26). It is unlikely that Jewish audiences then (or now) have found this prospect comforting, or even acceptable.

Righteousness through faith

For Paul "righteousness" is a key principle; if God finds a person righteous, or justified, so that person is approved by God and so, Paul believes, that person will never spiritually die. But Paul believes humanity is sinful, unwilling to admit God is sovereign over all life, and incapable of living in accordance with God's will. Thus God cannot approve of humanity in the absence of complete transformation. As Paul understands it, that transformation only comes through faith.

One term Paul frequently uses to express the approval of God is *justification,* which usually means "to make righteous." In Paul's opinion people seek through Law to make themselves righteous, but in this they cannot succeed. Only God can justify people. Should people, through faith in Christ Jesus, admit they are sinful and concede God has the right to punish sin, that person is open for justification. When the person has faith in Jesus Christ, understands that Jesus died for the sins of all humanity and receives the Spirit of Christ, that person is justified, or righteous, before God. This process of justification through faith can be called "salvation," or "redemption," or even "expiation," a word most often used in reference to cleansing through sacrifice. Jesus Christ was a sacrifice for expiation, Paul believes, and through faith in his death for sin, the expiation of the sins of faithful individuals becomes effective.

Although individuals may receive justification through their faith, this does not guarantee they will subsequently live moral lives or, regardless of their behavior, rise to life with Christ after death. Strengthened with the Spirit, Christians should be better able to avoid sin than other people, but sin (conceived as a power counteracting the will of God) continues to urge people to go against God.

In chapter 7 of Romans Paul uses the first person ("I"), but this is not just self-description. The "I" of this chapter refers to all those with faith in Christ. Paul writes, "I do not even acknowledge my own actions as mine, for what I do is not what I want to do, but what I detest. But if what I do is against my will, it means that I agree with the law and hold it to be admirable. But as things are, it is no longer I who perform the action, but sin that lodges in me" (7:15–18). This is, of course, a pessimistic view of the human situation. It is countered by a statement found a little later in Romans where Paul, speaking of Christians like himself, writes, "You are on the spiritual level if only God's Spirit dwells within you; and if a man does not possess the Spirit of Christ he is no Christian. But if Christ is dwelling within you, then although the body is a dead thing because you sinned, yet the Spirit is life itself because you have been justified" (8:9–11). This reminds one of the passage in Galatians wherein Paul claims "to prove that you are sons, God has sent into your hearts the Spirit of his Son, crying 'Abba! Father!' You are therefore no longer a slave but a son, and if a son, then also by God's own act an heir" (Gal. 4:6–7). In fact, Paul was reminded of that thought when writing Romans, for he continues on in chapter 8 to write, "All who are moved by the Spirit of God are Sons of God. [Note: A small s for *sons* rather than a capital S for *Sons* is a translator's decision caused by the effort to distinguish Jesus the Son of God from other people who are sons of God; Greek manuscripts do not make the distinction.] The Spirit you have received is not a Spirit of slavery leading you back into a life of fear, but a Spirit that makes us Sons, enabling us to cry 'Abba! Father!' In that cry the Spirit of God joins with our spirit in testifying that we are God's children; and if children, then heirs" (Rom. 8:14–15). All Christians, Paul believes, have received a Spirit making them children [Sons] of God. As such they are saved, justified, righteous, heirs to the promise God made to Abraham.

Paul seems to shift from pessimism to enthusiastic optimism in a few short lines in this section of Romans. The Spirit of God in a person will war against its opposite, the spirit of sin, but final victory does not occur during a person's lifetime. Thus, a person who has received the Spirit of God should seek to do what is right with the aid of the Spirit of God. But that person should not be overconfident; the temptations of the spirit of sin, which he sometimes calls the "flesh," will continue, and even those who seek to follow the way of God's Spirit may often not do what they seek to do but find themselves doing what they detest. Paul ultimately is optimistic and believes Christians will be saved through their faith and will, through the assistance of the Spirit, be able to behave in a reasonably loving fashion.

In chapters 12 through 15 of Romans Paul outlines the course of conduct appropriate for Christians in whom God's Spirit dwells. This is not a re-creation of the Law through the back door, although some have accused Paul of doing this. Rather, Paul gives general advice based on the principle that as all Christians are united in faith, they must behave in ways appropriate to that state of union. If Christians are all one person in Christ Jesus, they must love one another as themselves, not just in a poetic way but in a way directing their behavior.

A Letter of introduction for Phoebe

Chapter 16 of Romans is perhaps not part of the original letter; some scholars doubt it was written to Rome. Paul indicates in chapter 1 he has not visited Rome, but in chapter 16 he lists many people with whom he is personally familiar. Verses 17–20 seem to be written to a congregation over which Paul exercises authority and which he seems to have founded; Paul had no authority over the Roman church prior to his arrival there. Chapter 16 makes good sense if considered a separate self-contained letter written as a reference for a respected fellow Christian leader: Phoebe.

The letter begins, "I commend to you Phoebe, a fellow-Christian who holds office [i.e. "deacon" = servant] in the congregation at Cenchreae" (16:1), and that was probably its purpose. It is a letter of introduction and recommendation for a woman who, like several other women mentioned in the letter, is an important church worker.

Reading 1 Corinthians

Read the letter called 1 Corinthians and underline passages that identify specific problems that Paul addresses: for example, 1:11–12 specifies a problem relating to divisions among the Christian community, 8:1 defines a problem having to do with whether Christians can eat food consecrated to heathen deities. Paul's purpose in writing 1 Corinthians is to comment on specific problems he believes to exist in the Corinthian Christian community. Readers can infer the theology and Christology of Paul from the letter, but the letter was not written to be a treatise on those subjects.

1 Corinthians is part of a longer correspondance more of which is preserved in the composite letter called 2 Corinthians. Like other letters of Paul's, this one has a formal style. It begins with greetings and continues with a thanksgiving statement (1:1–9). Then comes the body of the letter, a section which in his letters frequently concludes with "parenesis" or an exhortation to behave properly (16:13–18) [Galatians 5:1–6:10 is a more extended example of this.] Finally this, like other of Paul's letters concludes with mention of specific individuals.

The first portion of the letter, 1:10–6:20 is critical of Christians who believe that they have a special wisdom that elevates them above other Christians. Paul writes, with irony, that his gospel is a message of foolishness and weakness, not of wisdom and self aggrandizement. This theme he ties in with the crucial theme of the crucifixion of Jesus and he argues that the message of the cross, which seems like foolishness, is in fact the manifestation of the wisdom of God.

1 Corinthians is particularly signficant for the insight it gives into early Christian ritual life. Here we find the first recorded discussion of the ritual of the communion meal (10:14–17, 11:17–34, etc.). We hear about the practice of public prayer and prophecy in the church meetings (14:-1–19, etc.), a

practice evidently carried out by men and women alike (11:13). But in another passage, one that causes considerable dismay to many readers, Paul declares that women should not speak aloud in church (14:34–35). Scholarship is divided on the issue of whether Paul wrote this passage or whether it was written later (at about the same time as the Pastorals) and inserted into 1 Corinthians. Those who think it is a later insert argue that it contradicts the passages in Paul's letters that indicate that women did speak in churches, it contradicts the principle that "in Christ there is neither male nor female," that the flow of the letter is more smooth if the passage is removed (i.e. 14:26–33, 36–40 makes clear sense without that passage) and that Paul is not prone to argue that Christian services must be "as the law directs."

Those who accepted Paul's gospel and received the grace of God received also the Spirit of Christ. The Spirit of Christ was not conceived to be an abstract state of being but a powerful and practical new mode of being, giving an individual special power. That special power included increased ability to resist temptations and to do special things. Paul lists various possibilities in 1 Corinthians 12:7–11: "In each of us the Spirit is manifested in one particular way, for some useful purpose. One man, through the Spirit . . . can put the deepest knowledge into words. Another, by the same Spirit, is granted faith; another, by the one Spirit, gifts of healing, and another miraculous powers; another has the gift of prophecy, and another ability to distinguish true spirits from false; yet another has the gift of ecstatic utterance of different kinds, and another the ability to interpret it. But all these gifts are the work of one and the same Spirit, distributing them separately to each individual at will." The gifts of the Spirit were seen by Paul to validate his work and his gospel (Gal. 3:1–5) and to provide evidence for its truth.

His churches, composed of people filled with Spirit, tended sometimes toward chaos. In 1 Corinthians, from chapter 11 to the end, Paul tries to bring order to community meetings where the display of spiritual gifts had been leading to disorder. One of his main points is that speaking in tongues (technically: glossolalia) has no useful effect upon a communal audience unless that speech can be translated into comprehensible language (for them, Greek). While this is sometimes taken to be an effort by Paul to downplay the importance of speech in tongues, he shows great respect for that capacity when used properly. In fact he claims that he speaks in tongues more than anyone in the community (14:18). But Paul does argue that spiritual gifts of any sort are subordinate to the capacity for love. His classic passage on love is found in chapter 13: "I may speak in tongues of men or of angels, but if I am without love, I am a sounding gong or a clanging cymbal. I may have the gift of prophecy, and know every hidden truth; I may have faith strong enough to move mountains; but if I have no love, I am nothing. . . ." (1 Cor. 13:1–3). These words were written to emphasize his principle that nothing should come ahead of Christian unity through love—not Law, not even the exercise of the gifts of God's Spirit.

Reading 2 Corinthians

It is possible that 2 Corinthians is a composite of letters rather than one sustained piece of communication. *Read the letter called 2 Corinthians, but try doing so in this order*

1. The "Tearful Letter" (10:1–13:14)
2. Paul defends himself (2:14–6:13, 7:2–4)
3. Goodwill returns (1:1–2:13, 7:5–16)
4. Letter recommending Titus (8:1–24)
5. Letter about the collection (9:1–15)
6. A fragment some think was not written by Paul but by someone critical of his teachings (6:14–7:1) . . . can you see why?

Evidently other Christian itinerant apostles have come to Corinth and delivered what Paul believes is a message of another Jesus, another spirit, another gospel (11:4). They have had some success among the Corinthian Christians and Paul is outraged. He responds with bitter irony claiming that while he does not wish to boast, as he believes those other apostles boast, he nevertheless could boast if he chose to. And, for a period, he chooses to. In the process he provides very interesting biographical material, particularly in the section 11:21–12:10. Speaking of himself in the third person, he tells of an experience fourteen years past when he entered the third level of the heavens and heard secret supernatural words.

As he did in the beginning of 1 Corinthians Paul contrasts power and weakness choosing, ironically, to brag about his weakness as he bragged, in 1 Corinthians, about his supposed foolishness (and see 2 Cor. 11:16–21). Paul would have his audience believe that his weakness is, in reality, the power of God. "Hence," he says, "I am well content, for Christ's sake, with weakness, contempt, persecution, hardship, and frustration; for when I am weak, then I am strong" (12:10).

Paul's opponents come across in his letters extremely badly. We know of them only what he tells us, and he is not interested whatsoever in giving their points of view a fair assessment. But it is a good mental exercise to try and surmise what their point of view might have been and what they might have said critically of Paul. His opponents were (presumably) sincere Christians active in a very early stage of the Christian church and they may well have had significant and valuable points of view of their own.

Reading Philippians

Read Paul's letter to the Philippians. See if the letter doesn't make more sense if you consider it originally to have been three letters:

1. A letter thanking the Philippians (1:1–3:1)
2. A fragment of a polemical letter (3:2–4:9, 21–23)
3. Another letter thanking the Philippians (4:10–20)

Philippians contains a passage of principal importance for the development of Christian thought about Jesus Christ: 2:6–11. This is sometimes called "the Christ Hymn" because of its poetic structure. Most scholars today believe that it was quoted by Paul, not composed by him, because it contains words and emphases rare or unknown elsewhere in Paul's writing. On the other hand, it is likely that Paul made some changes in the Christ Hymn, probably adding the phrase "death on a cross" and possibly adding the phrase "in heaven, on earth, and in the depths." This hymn was probably in use in Christian liturgies in Philippi and perhaps elsewhere. The fact that the Hymn is not written by Paul should not be taken to mean that it is "pre-Pauline."

Paul's angry argument in chapter 3 is similar to his angry arguments in his letter to the Galatians. Here, especially in 3:9, one can see the kind of uncompromising statements that, in part, gave rise to the Protestant reformers' insistence that salvation comes by faith alone. Verses 3:12–14 echo a theme found elsewhere in Paul's letters: the perfection of salvation has not happened yet. Paul believes that Christians are transformed now, by the spirit, into people whose ultimate salvation is guaranteed but has not occurred. This is sometimes called Paul's "eschatological reservation," meaning that perfection must not be claimed now as perhaps some Corinthian Christians claimed it (as evidenced in 1 Cor. 4:8 where Paul writes sarcastically) but should be anticipated at the time of the return of the Lord (see 1 Thess. 4:15–18 in light of Phil. 3:20–21).

Reading Philemon

Read Paul's letter to Philemon This letter is written to accompany the slave Onesimus who is being returned to his master Philemon. Onesimus is probably the same person referred to in Colossians 4:7–9 as a native of Colossae and if so Philemon lives in Colossae. Paul's intention is to urge Philemon to look favorably on Onesiumus despite the fact that he could legally punish him severely.

Paul here seems to accept the institution of slavery. Elsewhere in his letters he urges slaves and servants to be obedient to their masters and urges

Christians in general to accept the orders of the civil government. Paul's revolutionary ideas were confined to the sphere of religion. He does not seem to have had any intention to urge people to seek the restructuring of secular society.

Reading Colossians

Read the Letter to the Colossians. The question of Paul's authorship of this letter is disputed but there are as many scholars who affirm it is Paul's as deny that it is. The letter contains the most elevated concept of the nature of Christ to be found in any Pauline letter. Paul declares him to be "the image of the invisible God, his is primacy over all created things. In him everything in heaven and on earth was created, not only things visible but also the invisible orders of thrones, sovereignties, authorities, and powers: the whole universe has been created through him and for him. And he exists before everything, and all things are held together in him," (1:15–17) and "in Christ the complete being of the Godhead dwells embodied, and in him you have been brought to completion" (2:9–10). These exalted views, which probably are related to the identification of Jesus Christ with God's Wisdom (cf. Proverbs 8:22–31 and 1 Cor. 1:24) are said not to correspond well with other statements of Paul's about Christ. The Christ Hymn, which Paul cites approvingly in Philippians, derives from a rather different image of Christ as one who voluntarily emptied himself of divinity. But, on the other hand, Paul's ideas may have evolved over time and have been expressed differently in different circumstances. Indeed, it would not be unlikely that as his ideas evolved he came to hold a more elevated vision of Christ's nature. If so, then, the letter to Colossians would be authentic and have been written close to the end of Paul's life, around the year C.E. 61.

Reading 2 Thessalonians

Read the Second Letter to Thessalonians. Somewhat fewer scholars believe 2 Thessalonians was written by Paul than believe that Colossians was written by Paul. The principal difficulty in ascribing it to Paul is that in 1 Thessalonians the time of the end, the return of the Lord, is anticipated very soon. But in 2 Thessalonians 1:6–2:12 that time is evidently rather far off and will not arrive until a sequence of events have already taken place. Various rather mysterious beings are referred to in the letter who are otherwise unknown from Paul's writing: a man who is the embodiment of wickedness, a restrainer. The idea that God puts people into states of delusion (2:11) does not sound like Paul and Paul generally speaks of the return of the Lord happily as something Christians should look forward to.

Here, however, the author seems rather to dread the occasion, or at least to dread the events that lead up to it.

Reading Ephesians

Read the letter to the Ephesians. Few scholars think Ephesians was written by Paul. The language of the letter is rather different from that of letters certainly written by Paul and certain ideas seem out of accord with Paul's discussion of them elsewhere. For example, while 2:8–10 in this letter is rather similar to ideas expressed in Romans, the crucial idea of justification is missing. The image found in Romans of the grafting of the Gentile branch onto the trunk of the Jewish tree is quite a different thing than the image of the two becoming one found in 2:11–16. Paul usually does not declare that Christians have already attained perfection. He reserves that for the time when the Lord comes. In this letter, however, we read that already "in union with Christ Jesus [God] raised us up and enthroned us with him in the heavenly realms" (2:6). But if not Paul's letter, it is certainly a Pauline letter written by a disciple of Paul's who is very familiar with Paul's characteristic ideas and concerns. The author repeatedly stresses the Pauline idea of unity and love within the community of Christians (e.g. 4:2–6), stresses the necessity of grace rather than Law obedience, and reflects Paul's idea of the church as bride of Christ and body of Christ (5:29–33). The letter's discussion of the relationship of husbands and wives (5:21–33) is "patriarchal" by the standards of today, but in terms of the standards of Paul's time speaks in defense of the rights and role of women in marriage.

Topics

Sources

Paul declares that the main and essential source for his ideas and teachings is the revelation he received from God and Christ. All other sources of information—human teachings, as he would put it—are secondary. "Without consulting any human being" (Gal. 1:16), Paul began his ministry. He did not feel the need to learn from anyone but God and Christ. This is not to say he did not learn from any other Christians. He must have, but he placed little value on that knowledge and does not use the "teachings of Jesus" as sources for the principal ideas of his gospel.

On certain occasions Paul seems to refer to traditions he received from human beings. For example, when he gives an account of the Lord's Supper, he writes, "The tradition which I handed on to you came to me from the Lord himself" (1 Cor. 11:23). Scholars usually find the term *tradition* to govern that sentence and to imply Paul's knowledge of the Lord's Supper comes from other people to whom it was a crucial event recalled from Jesus' life. Another point of view, however, is that "the Lord himself" spoke of the matter to Paul in a revelation. Paul's denial, in Galatians, of the influence of human information on his thought would support this idea. The sentence as it stands is ambiguous. It may mean the Lord himself revealed to Paul an account subsequently passed on as a tradition, one eventually written down by Mark and then adapted by Matthew and Luke. John, Q, and Thomas do not record this tradition.

We may be certain Paul knew something of Jesus' life and of his sayings. Therefore, oral tradition must have had some influence in shaping his point of view. Indeed, Paul does not insist that he refused ever to know anything about the "historical" Jesus. But from Paul's own perspective, historical traditions were not nearly as important in the formation of his thought and beliefs as private revelation from the Lord.

Jesus

Paul's interest in the events of *Jesus' life* is limited. He never discusses in any detail Jesus' birth, miracles, or teachings. Once in a while Paul quotes words spoken by Jesus, but usually to support his own teachings and even then not in a way that indicates that he relies on Jesus' words for his own ideas. If we knew of Jesus' life and teachings only through Paul's letters, we could say little but that he was born "under the Law" and that he was crucified.

We do not know what, if anything, Paul told strangers about Jesus' life to lead them to faith. From his letters it does not seem likely he told them tales of Jesus' miracles for he never refers to them. Paul would not have denied Jesus did any or all of the miracles attributed to him in the miracles sources. Rather, Paul would have argued they were details of little importance compared to the cosmic importance of the death of Christ for the sins of all people and the resurrection of Christ giving all people the opportunity to choose to rise from the dead with him. Similarly, Paul does not consider his gospel a version or continuation of the oral "gospel" spoken by Jesus and transmitted by tradition. He might not have denied that Jesus said what traditions said he said, but he does not anywhere indicate that he is dependent on, or even particularly interested in, explaining and carrying on the traditions of Jesus' sayings.

Jesus' death is of crucial significance to Paul. When Christ died, he died for the sins of all people and so, in Paul's opinion, the option of accepting his death rather than having to die one's own death became available to anyone. This, for Paul, was the most important event in human history since the fall of Adam. It provided the opportunity to achieve eternal life, to be justified through faith, and thus to be united with Christ and be children of God (Gal. 3:26). The idea of "the sacrifice of Christ on the cross" comes from Paul; "sacrifice" is another way of indicating that Jesus' death brings forgiveness of sins and escape from death to anyone with faith.

Eschatology

Paul's clearest statements about the coming end of this world can be found in his first letter to the Thessalonians. There he makes clear the end of this world will come quickly and that one mark of Christian life is that Christians "wait expectantly for the appearance from heaven of [God's] Son Jesus . . ." (1:10). They will wait a short time; Paul speaks of "*we* who are left alive until the Lord comes" (4:15); he was confident the Lord would return during his own lifetime but says that no one knows exactly when this event will take place.

The faithful who are embodied in flesh now will receive immortality and spiritual bodies. Paul reveals this secret in 1 Corinthians 15:51–53: "Listen! I will unfold a mystery: we shall not all die, but we shall all be changed in a flash, in the twinkling of an eye, at the last trumpet-call. For the trumpet will sound, and the dead will rise immortal, and we shall be changed. This perishable being must be clothed with the imperishable, and what is mortal must be clothed with immortality." Note that Paul expects he and most of his audience will be alive when this happens.

Paul's expectation of the end of this world and the return of the Lord Jesus Christ in a short time affects his ideas about how people should live. He believes it might be best to avoid such long-term commitments as marriage since the remaining time is so short.

When the Lord returns those who are in the Lord will be more perfectly with him, free from constraints brought about by material life. Paul's perspective on the world's end is optimistic for himself and his followers, but others will suffer and die: "While they are talking of peace and security, all at once calamity is upon them, sudden as the pangs that come upon a woman with child; and there will be no escape" (1 Thess. 5:3).

There is no Judgment Day for Paul; nor does he anywhere mention hell or eternal punishment. The common concept of Judgment Day contradicts Paul's essential ideas. To be judged whether you have or have not lived in obedience to God's intentions falls into the category of Law rather than faith. Those who have faith will be with Christ, those who do not will die and exist no more. The judicial idea of judgment, with people on trial before God or Christ, has no place in Paul's system of ideas.

Torah

Much of this chapter has dealt with the Law as Paul conceived of it. His ideas come down to this: (1) Although the Law may provide useful instruction in morality, anyone who seeks to be justified in the eyes of God by following it is doomed to failure. All will break it and so all will be cursed.

(2) Faith in Christ brings about justification in the eyes of God. Anyone already justified by faith must not seek justification through following Law. (3) Anyone may follow the Law if it is convenient; no one should live immorally or feel under any obligation deliberately to break the Law. The second point caused Paul considerable trouble. His followers occasionally believed freedom from Law meant freedom to do anything at all and his opponents accused him of teaching immorality. Repeatedly he denies any such intention. His letters insist that Christians are not free to behave immorally and that such behavior will lose them the rewards their faith would otherwise bring them.

Paul thinks the Law could have unacceptable social consequences. Since Christian unity is essential, for otherwise Christ's body would be divided into rival groups, any time Laws tended to lead to division (and they would tend to divide Gentiles from Jews), the Law should be put aside for the sake of unity. It is on this point that Paul disagreed with Peter and Barnabas in Antioch (Gal. 2:11-14).

Paul's message to Gentiles includes the important point that Gentiles can become members of God's community ("Jews") through faith without following the Law of the Jews. It should not be surprising he ran into opposition from Jewish Christians who insisted the contrary, that to be members of God's community one must necessarily follow God's Law. This may have been the most significant conflict within the Christian movement during the first century. By the second century Paul's perspective prevailed.

Community

Paul was probably the founder of the Christian communities to which he wrote, with the exception of the community in Rome. His letters show he felt responsible for those communities, and, even when absent, he felt he had the right to exert influence and control. To what extent the members of the communities thought of Paul as their leader, in his absence, is unclear, but certainly their respect for him gave him strong influence.

Controversy

Paul wrote his letters because of controversies and, therefore, controversies fill them. Because we have only Paul's side of the argument, and Paul has no interest in detailing, much less explaining, the positions taken by his opponents, it is usually unclear exactly what the controversies were about or with whom Paul found himself in disagreement. It is significant, however, that Paul's opponents are practically always other Christians. Sometimes, as in 1 Corinthians and Romans, Paul apparently was engaged in more than one argument at once. In Galatians, Paul argues against Jewish Christians who seek to convince his Gentile Christians they should follow the Law.

Paul's defense indicates that his opponents represented, or claimed to represent, the Jerusalem church, whose principal figures were James, Peter, and John. As we have but the one letter to go by we do not know who won, but in the long run Paul's perspective on the Law came to be that of the whole Christian church.

Interactions

The Miracles sources

The miracles sources argue faith that Jesus is Christ should be based on his miraculous power. This is not Paul's position. Faith for him is faith in Christ leading to transformation, not simply faith that Jesus was in fact Christ. Paul believed that through the Spirit Christians receive they can perform miracles, and those miracles serve as evidence that faith is effective. As all Christians can do miracles of some sort or another, to argue Jesus did miracles would be, from Paul's perspective, simply to argue that Jesus had the Spirit. Jesus, to Paul, was much more than just somebody with the Spirit.

The Q source

None of the sayings in the Q source criticizes Jesus' disciples. They encourage repentance and demand the Law be followed. It is tempting, therefore, to link the Q source to Jesus' disciples. Perhaps the Q source contains the sort of gospel taught by James, Peter, and John. As we shall see in the chapters on their Gospels, it is reasonable to infer that Matthew and Luke traced the Q source to disciples such as James, Peter, and John.

Does this mean, then, that Paul's opponents in Galatia, who evidently were linked to the Jerusalem church led by Jesus' disciples, were Q people? No, not really; because we know little of what Paul's Christian opponents in Galatia taught, we cannot claim they were Q people, although it is hard to imagine they would have thought the emphasis on Law, eschatology, and the Son of Man's return for judgment, as found in the Q sayings, were mistaken ideas.

Still, as we know something of both the ideas of Q and the ideas of Paul, we can conclude that serious differences exist. For Q, following Law was essential; the questions raised in Q reflect differences of opinion about which parts of the Law taken precedence over others. Repentance leading to forgiveness and ultimately to God's approval is a central theme of Q, while for Paul only grace through faith leads to God's approval. The fact that Q does not find Jesus' crucifixion to be a crucial factor for salvation means that Q Christianity and Pauline Christianity were not the same thing.

But Paul and Q agree on one major point. Both believe that Jesus will return soon and at that time faithful Christians will be saved.

Bibliography

Beker, Christian. *The Triumph of God: The Essence of Paul's Thought.* Minneapolis: Fortress Press, 1990.

Betz, Hans Dieter. *Galatians*. Philadelphia: Fortress Press, 1979.

Black, Matthew, *Romans* (New Century Bible Commentary). Grand Rapids: Wm. B. Eerdmans Pub. Co., 1989.

Davies, W. D. *Paul and Rabbinic Judaism: Some Elements in Pauline Theology.* 4th ed. Philadelphia: Fortress Press, 1980.

Hengel, Martin. *Between Jesus and Paul.* Philadelphia: Fortress Press, 1983.

———. *The Pre-Christian Paul.* Philadelphia: Trinity Press International, 1991.

Hock, Ronald F. *The Social Context of Paul's Ministry.* Philadelphia: Fortress Press, 1980.

Jewett, Robert. *A Chronology of Paul's Life.* Philadelphia: Fortress Press, 1979.

Longenecker, Richard N. *Galatians* (Word Biblical Commentary 41). Dallas: Word Books, 1990.

Neyrey, Jerome H. *Paul in Other Words.* Louisville: Westminster/ John Knox Press, 1990.

Perrin, Norman, and Dennis Duling. *The New Testament: An Introduction.* New York: Harcourt Brace Jovanovich, 1982.

Sanders, E. P. *Paul, the Law, and the Jewish People.* Philadelphia: Fortress Press, 1983.

Sandmel, Samuel. *The Genius of Paul: A Study in History.* Philadelphia: Fortress Press, 1979.

Soarcos, Marion L. *The Apostle Paul: An Introduction to his Writings and Teachings.* Mahwah, N.J.: Paulist Press, 1987.

Tambasco, Anthony J. *In the Days of Paul.* Mahwah: Paulist Press, 1991.

Theissen, Gerd. *The Social Setting of Pauline Christianity.* Philadelphia: Fortress Press, 1982.

Five

The Gospel of Mark

The Growth of the New Testament

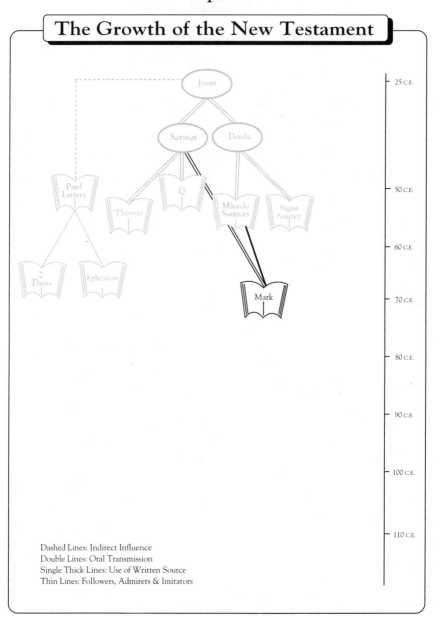

Jesus — 25 C.E.

Sayings   Deeds

Paul Letters — 50 C.E.

Thomas   Q   Miracle Sources   Signs Source

— 60 C.E.

2 Thess   Ephesians

Mark — 70 C.E.

— 80 C.E.

— 90 C.E.

— 100 C.E.

— 110 C.E.

Dashed Lines: Indirect Influence
Double Lines: Oral Transmission
Single Thick Lines: Use of Written Source
Thin Lines: Followers, Admirers & Imitators

Read Mark from verse 1:1 to verse 16:8 and underline all references to Jesus' disciples, to Jesus' family, and to Jesus' demands for silence or secrecy. Be sure to use a different colored pen or highlighter whenever you are under- lining different kinds of material. If, for example, you have used yellow to highlight Mark's miracle stories, use pink or blue to highlight other mate- rial. In the pages following we will be examining Mark's ideas about Jesus' followers and family as well as possible reasons for Jesus' commands for silence, and therefore it will be useful to isolate passages concerned with those subjects. Reread Mark. As with other New Testament material, one reading is never enough. Gospels are not difficult reading, but readers raised in Christian cultures approach them with many preconceptions. Repeated reading lets a Gospel's own messages come through; with a single reading one will frequently find only what is expected.

Author, date, and place of origin

The Gospel of Mark is usually dated around the year C.E. 70. Like the dates for all the Gospels, this date is approximate and may be off by a decade or so. The reason for the date C.E. 70 is that chapter 13 suggests Mark knew about the Jewish insurrection against Rome and the resulting destruction of the temple in Jerusalem in C.E. 70. We have no other evidence about Mark's date.

An early tradition says that Mark's Gospel originated in Rome. Mark does not know Palestinian geography well and assumes his readers know little of Palestinian Judaism (7:1–8). There is, however, no solid evidence that Mark is Roman in origin, and the few Latin terms used in the Gospel are terms that would have been commonly used throughout the empire. However, Rome is as good a guess as any for the Gospel's place of origin.

The beginning of the gospel

The Gospel of Mark starts at an interesting point. Having introduced John the Baptist, immediately Mark gives a short account of the baptism of Jesus. Quickly he tells of the arrest of John, and of Jesus coming into Galilee proclaiming the gospel of God: "The time has come; the kingdom of God is upon you; repent, and believe the Gospel" (1:15). Jesus immediately selects Andrew and Simon to follow him and they quickly do so. The repeated use of *immediately* and *quickly* in the sentences above gives you an example of one trait of Mark's writing. Unlike the other evangelists, he introduces many of his paragraphs with *immediately,* as though to give his Gospel a sense of rushing and urgency, a tendency supplemented by later passages urging people to "keep awake!" (13:35, 37). Mark's use of Greek is not at all sophisticated, and his writing style is clumsy. Like Matthew and Luke, who both revised Mark, modern translators generally work to improve Mark's style.

Notice this Gospel does not begin with an account of Jesus' cosmic origin (as John's poem about the "Word" does) or of his birth (as Matthew's does) or of his birth and childhood (as Luke's does). For Mark, Jesus' importance began at the time of his baptism, at the moment when the Spirit, as a dove, descended and a voice spoke from heaven saying, "Thou art my Son, my Beloved; on thee my favour rests" (1:11). The fact that Mark begins the Gospel with Jesus' baptism entitles us to believe he knew nothing of the story of Jesus' virgin birth. Therefore, from the outset, Mark's perspective contrasts somewhat with that of the other evangelists. It contrasts least with John's, for, although that Gospel places Jesus in a cosmic setting with an introductory poem, John's story of Jesus' life begins with the baptism just as Mark's does. Even Luke, who has the most extensive account of the birth of Jesus of any Gospel writer, begins a summary of Jesus' life story in the book of Acts with Jesus' baptism. "Starting from Galilee after the baptism proclaimed by John . . . God anointed him with the Holy Spirit and with power. He went about doing good and healing all who were oppressed by the devil, for God was with him" (Acts 10:37–39).

As we begin to study each of the Gospels, we will briefly examine the roles of two individuals, one prominent at the beginning, the other at the end of Jesus' life ministry: John the Baptist and Pontius Pilate. Each of the four evangelists was faced with similar problems regarding those individuals, and each of the four chose somewhat different ways to solve those problems. Comparing the Gospels in this regard will show something of how evangelists went about solving the problems they faced.

John the Baptist

It is historically likely that John the Baptist believed he had a mission from God to baptize people "in token of repentance, for the forgiveness of sins"

Mark

The Gospel of Mark is attributed to John Mark, a companion of Paul (Acts 12:12, 25, 13:5, 15:36–41, Phlm 24, Col 4:10, 2 Tim 4:11), a cousin of Barnabas (col 4:10), and perhaps an associate of Peter (1 Pet 5:13). The suggestion was first made by Papias (ca. 130 C.E.), as reported by Eusebius (d. 310), both fathers of the ancient church. In this, as in other matters, Papias is unreliable, because he is interested in the guarantees of an eye-witness rather than in the oral process that produced Mark.

(Mark 1:4), that John baptized Jesus, and that, on that occasion, Jesus believed he received God's Holy Spirit. At this point Jesus began the mission leading ultimately to his crucifixion. Two difficulties arise for the evangelists: First, was Jesus sinful, then repentant, then willing to submit to baptism? Second, does the fact that John baptized Jesus imply John is superior to Jesus, as the followers of John surely would have claimed? No evangelist believed Jesus sinful, nor did any believe John superior. But the logic of the basic story is as follows: John baptized the repentant people who came to him and so he was superior to them; Jesus came and so was repentant; John baptized Jesus and so he was superior to him. All of the evangelists rejected this logic.

Mark introduces John at the very beginning of his Gospel. He outlines John's mission in the passage quoted above (Mark 1:4) and categorically states Jesus "was baptized in the Jordan by John" (Mark 1:9). To demonstrate John's inferiority to Jesus, Mark reports John said, "After me comes one who is mightier than I. I am not fit to unfasten his shoes. I have baptized you with water; he will baptize you with the Holy Spirit" (1:8). It is likely John said these words, but it is debatable whether he meant them to refer to Jesus or to God, who John expected would come in the immediate future to usher in his kingdom. Mark presumably believes John's statement demonstrated John's inferiority to Jesus. Mark does not explicitly contradict the assumption one could draw from 1:4 that Jesus, like others who came for baptism, came in response to John's call for repentance.

Pontius Pilate

The problems the evangelists faced in regard to Pontius Pilate are more urgent and more difficult than the problems they faced in regard to John the Baptist. Pontius Pilate was a procurator appointed by Rome, and was the chief Roman official in Palestine during Jesus' life. As far as we can determine historically, Pilate brought Jesus to trial (perhaps after a preliminary examination of his case by the Jewish court, the Sanhedrin) and found him guilty of treason and ordered his execution. Precisely what Jesus did that Pilate thought treasonous is uncertain, but it is likely that Jesus' announcement of the coming of the Kingdom of the Jewish God (and thus, implicitly, the end of Roman control of Palestine) would have been sufficient for a charge of treason.

The evangelists, and Christians generally, did not seek the overthrow of the Roman Empire and did not intend to be traitors. Jews would not offer formal sacrifices to images of the emperor, for they regarded the ceremony as idol worship. They were legally excused from doing this. Christians similarly refused to offer sacrifices, but Roman law contained no similar provisions for Gentile Christians. Thus Christians, by refusing to offer sacrifices to the emperor's image, created the impression that they were traitors, an impression seemingly confirmed by the fact that Christians worshiped a legally convicted traitor as the Son of God. Thus Christians throughout the empire were in danger of persecution for their seemingly anti-Roman beliefs.

The fact of Jesus' execution was universally known and could not be denied. But Christians did not believe him to have been a traitor to the empire. Evangelists, therefore, were faced with the difficult task of demonstrating that a person legally convicted and executed of treason was not a traitor. Toward the end of their Gospels, the four evangelists wrote differing accounts of Jesus' trial before Pilate and Pilate's decision to execute Jesus. They shared the desire to demonstrate Pilate did not believe Jesus to be a traitor and even that Pilate had found him innocent. The responsibility for Jesus' execution is said not to be Pilate's at all but rather to be the responsibility of the only non-Roman people present: the leaders of the Jewish people, or the Jewish people as a whole.

In Mark's account, the "chief priests and the whole council [Sanhedrin] tried to find some evidence against Jesus to warrant a death-sentence, but failed to find any" (14:55). However, after Jesus admits he is the Messiah, the Son of the Blessed One, "their judgment was unanimous: that he was guilty and should be put to death" (14:61–64) on the grounds of blasphemy against the Jewish God. This is no crime in Roman law. Jesus is brought to Pilate and questioned by him, but Jesus does not respond to the charges "they" (not Pilate) are bringing against him. Mark informs us Pilate asked the people, "'Do you wish me to release for you the king of the Jews?' For he knew it was out of malice that they had brought Jesus before him" (15:9–10). Pilate asks, "What harm has he done?" but receives no answer (15:14). Finally, Pilate "in order to satisfy the mob" (15:15), orders the execution.

Mark's account presents an image of Pilate as so weak and vacillating that he executes a man, against whom he knows he has no evidence, simply to satisfy a mob. Some find this, and similar Gospel accounts, anti-Semitic, for they place blame on the Jewish people for Jesus' execution. But it is likely the evangelists were motivated more by the need to shift responsibility away from the Roman procurator than to shift it toward the Jewish people. Unfortunately, apart from Romans, the only other people present were Jewish.

In historical fact Pilate was brutally repressive and cared little about the desires and wishes of the Jewish people and their leadership. Far from granting them favors and following their wishes, he despised them. Rather than giving in to the urging of a Jewish mob, he more likely would have brought in soldiers to attack the mob. Pilate was so hated by the people over whom he had authority that eventually his superiors removed him from office.

The ending of the Gospel

The conclusion of the Gospel of Mark raises several interesting questions. The first and perhaps most interesting is, what is its ending? The answer is that the Gospel of Mark has *five* different endings. One is usually printed in Bibles as chapter 16, verses 9 through 20. It begins, "When he had risen from the dead early on Sunday morning he appeared first to Mary of Magdala. . . ." A second, very short ending, is also usually printed in Bibles, but without verse numbers, and it begins, "And they delivered all these instructions briefly to Peter and his companions. . . ." The third is the ending of the Gospel of Matthew, for, remember, Matthew is an extensively re-written version of Mark. The fourth ending, that of the Gospel of Luke, includes the entire book of Acts. The fifth, though, is the authentic ending. It is Mark 16:8: "They said nothing to anybody, for they were afraid."

How do we know Mark 16:8 is the real ending? There are two excellent reasons. The first is derived from source criticism. Since Matthew and Luke used Mark as a source, and since Matthew and Luke differ completely in their accounts of Jesus' resurrection appearances, it is impossible that both used Mark as a source for their accounts. Further, it is unlikely only one did; the accounts in Matthew's and Luke's Gospels are written entirely in their own styles and not at all in the style of Mark. Apparently neither had a version of resurrection appearances written by Mark to copy or to adapt.

Text criticism

Text criticism, or text analysis, is the study of various manuscripts of the New Testament to determine which words, phrases, and passages are original and which are the results of changes in the original. In the ancient world the only way copies of books could be made was to have copies written out by hand. There were no printing presses, no photocopiers, no laser printers, no movable type, no mechanical printing of any kind. All copies were handwritten on scrolls of papyrus, or possibly booklets of papyrus, by scribes who often took down what they wrote from verbal dictation.

Handwritten copies of manuscripts are never absolutely the same as their originals, especially if (as was often the case in the ancient world) they are based on verbal dictation instead of sight reading. All kinds of mistakes occur: letters may be omitted, words left out, sentences copied twice or not at all, and so on. Copyists may choose to make changes, to correct or delete phrases with which they disagree, to add explanations for difficult passages, to improve grammar, or to add stories or sayings where they seem appropriate. This means every single manuscript of the New Testament is different in many small ways, and in some greater ways, from every other manuscript.

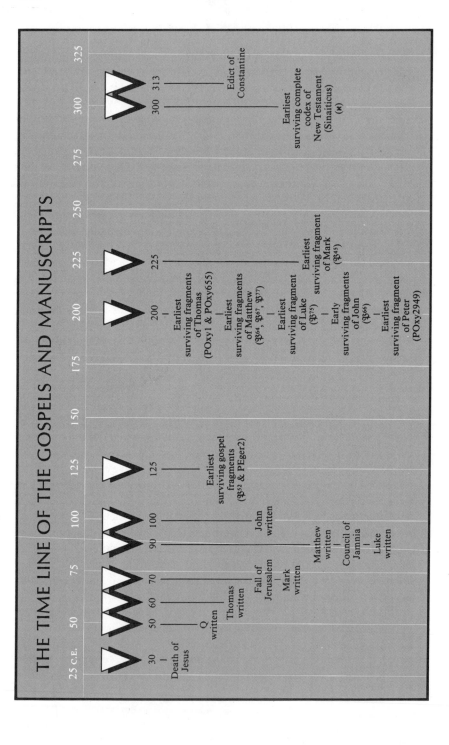

THE TIME LINE OF THE GOSPELS AND MANUSCRIPTS

25 C.E.   50   75   100   125   150   175   200   225   250   275   300   325

30 — Death of Jesus

50 — Q written

Thomas written

70 — Fall of Jerusalem / Mark written

90 — Matthew written / Council of Jamnia / Luke written

100 — John written

125 — Earliest surviving gospel fragments ($\mathfrak{P}^{52}$ & PEger2)

200 — Earliest surviving fragments of Thomas (POxy1 & POxy655)

Earliest surviving fragments of Matthew ($\mathfrak{P}^{64}$, $\mathfrak{P}^{67}$, $\mathfrak{P}^{77}$)

Earliest surviving fragment of Luke ($\mathfrak{P}^{75}$)

Early surviving fragments of John ($\mathfrak{P}^{66}$)

Earliest surviving fragment of Peter (POxy2949)

225 — Earliest surviving fragment of Mark ($\mathfrak{P}^{45}$)

300 — Earliest surviving complete codex of New Testament (Sinaiticus) ($\aleph$)

313 — Edict of Constantine

More than 1,500 different manuscripts exist which contain New Testament texts, some complete, some fragmentary. Most of these derive from the centuries after C.E. 400, although we have some fragments of copies of New Testament texts written on papyrus and dated from the middle of the third century (ca. C.E. 250). Not even fragments remain from the first century. More complete texts exist from the fourth century. The later the date of copies, the more likely it is that errors have occurred in transmission.

Clear connections exist between many different copies, because errors are perpetuated. A mistake made in a second-century copy may consistently occur in later copies of that copy, and in copies of the later copies. Text analysts seek to sort out the history of copies and to trace them back to earlier and earlier versions by grouping related copies into categories and developing family histories of the copies. The hundreds of later versions derive from four basic families of copies. These are the Alexandrian text (probably the most accurate), the Byzantine text (less accurate and the basis for the King James Version), the Western text, and the Caesarean text. None of these four texts now exists in a pure form; all must be re-created by careful comparison of their many surviving various forms.

Any particular modern version of the New Testament is a single collection of choices made from the many options the ancient manuscripts make available. Text analysts use both external and internal evidence to make their choices. External evidence is, primarily, the result of the past century's scholarly efforts to decide preferable readings from the many extant manuscripts. It is often easy to determine preferable readings. Nonsense words, obvious later theologizing, doubled phrases, and so forth can be corrected without difficulty. But some questions simply cannot be precisely answered, and different text analysts will make different decisions about what to accept and what to reject.

Internal evidence comes from comparison between what a particular variant reading (a phrase or passage different from most versions) says and the general perspective and literary style of a particular author. It is reasonable to prefer passages that match an author's general opinions and usual style of writing and to reject those that do not. Also reasonable is the principle that a more difficult variant reading ("difficult" either because it is grammatically clumsy or because it does not fit the theologies of later centuries) is likely to be more accurate than an easy reading. This principle derives from the common-sense observation that copyists tend to make the reading of their copy polished and precise, not awkward and careless.

The earliest and best manuscripts of the Gospel of Mark end with verse 16:8; only later and inferior manuscripts have verses 16:9–20 or the other shorter ending. From a text analytical perspective this is not a difficult problem. Mark's ending at 16:8 is a more difficult reading (for Christians came to expect an account of resurrection appearances), and it is supported by superior manuscripts.

From a theological perspective the other endings of Mark may be canonical, but they are not therefore considered to have been written by Mark. Such problems as this have led fundamentalist Christians to declare the Bible is inerrant *in the original autograph.* They mean by this that the original authors were inerrant, but errors may have crept in through scribal inattention or deliberate efforts by scribes to improve the original. Many translations contain, as footnotes throughout the Bible, comments like "other manuscripts have . . ." or "some witnesses give . . ." followed by variants on the verse in the text. This is simply honest admission that while a text analytical choice has been made, the reader should be aware that other possibilities exist and that they could be original.

The original end of the Gospel of Mark is unique. There alone the resurrection of Jesus is not followed by an appearance to any of his followers. The easiest way to explain this is that Mark believed Jesus would shortly reappear on earth in Galilee, this time "coming in the clouds with great power and glory" (13:26), but this event had not yet happened. Judging by the end of chapter 13 (verses 33–37), Mark assumed Jesus' reappearance would take place soon, certainly within a few years, and "the present generation will live to see it all" (13:30). But other passages in chapter 13 (verses 7–8 and 24–27, for example) indicate that Mark did not think it would take place immediately. Indeed, it is from Mark that we are told that "About that day or that hour no one knows, not even the angels in heaven, not even the Son; only the Father" (13:32). What Mark seems to regard as one event, Jesus' appearances upon his return, other sources regard as two, Jesus' resurrection appearances followed at a later time by his "second coming."

The organization of the Gospel

1. An introductory section wherein Jesus travels through the countryside speaking in parables and performing many miracles (1:1–8:21).
2. A central section wherein Jesus plainly reveals the true mission of the Son of Man (8:22–10:52).
3. A section reporting several areas of controversy between Jesus and Jewish authorities in Jerusalem (11:1–12:44).
4. An extended discourse (13:1–37).
5. A passion narrative (14:1–16:8).

Throughout the first half of the Gospel Jesus repeatedly commands people not to tell about him, not to announce his miracles, not to spread the word about his healings. People and demons alike must keep silent. Demons are not weird, red-colored creatures with tails; *demons* refers to people who believe themselves to be possessed by an evil spirit. When Jesus speaks to a demon or a demon speaks to Jesus, two people are in conversation. Demon here is shorthand for "a person supposedly possessed by a demon." Mark, it may be presumed, did not doubt such people were possessed.

Jesus' requests for silence in Mark's Gospel have come to be known as the Messianic Secret, although exactly what was to be kept secret, and why, are still subject to dispute among scholars. One theory is that only after Jesus' crucifixion did his disciples begin to believe him to be the Messiah. Mark, realizing it was not clear in the traditions that Jesus claimed to be Messiah, and yet believing Jesus was the Messiah, decided Jesus must have wished it kept secret until after his resurrection. This theory emphasizes Mark 9:9, when after the transfiguration Jesus "enjoined them not to tell anyone what they had seen until the Son of Man had risen from the dead."

Repeated requests for silence in Mark seem especially curious because they so obviously were ignored. Mark reports people spoke about Jesus' exorcisms and healings whether he wanted them to or not. No other source suggests Jesus wanted this miraculous aspect of his ministry to be kept silent, and the miracles sources show that proclamation of Jesus' miracles was a main interest of at least some early Christians. Why, then, might Mark have depicted Jesus as seeking to maintain secrecy regarding exorcisms and miracles? We shall return to this question shortly.

Those who misunderstood Jesus

Reread with an open mind the passages you have underlined regarding the disciples; you will almost certainly be in for a surprise. The disciples are depicted as failing to understand Jesus at all. Twelve are selected (early and apparently at random) and given every opportunity to understand. They are present at his miracles, listen to him speak, and receive special information not available to others (4:10–12; 7:17–18; 9:2; 9:30–32; 14:33). James, Peter, and John are especially singled out for attention. Significantly, Paul somewhat sarcastically calls these the three pillars of the church in Jerusalem (Gal. 2:9). These three disciples witness such scenes as the transfiguration and Jesus' prayers in the Garden of Gethsemane, but to no avail. They continue to misunderstand Jesus and his message.

Many who read Mark assume this situation is temporary, that while the disciples may have had trouble understanding what they witnessed and heard, eventually they managed to overcome doubt and skepticism and came to follow Jesus correctly. Maybe so, but this is not Mark's idea. At the end of Mark, one disciple has betrayed him and the other eleven have run off, one of whom publicly denies knowing him. The women who discover the empty tomb do not tell the disciples about it or about what they heard from the young person (not the *angel*) at the tomb. End of Gospel.

Jesus' family does not come off much better. In chapter 3 Mark reports, "He entered a house; and once more such a crowd collected round them that they had no chance to eat. When his family heard of this, they set out to take charge of him; for people were saying that he was out of his mind" (3:20–21). There is some doubt about the meaning of *he was out of his mind,* but the prevailing idea in the first century would have been that one out of his mind was one possessed by a demonic or unclean spirit. There follow in Mark several passages regarding demon possession, including the startling passage stating that anyone who declares Jesus possessed of an unclean spirit, rather than the Holy Spirit, has slandered the Holy Spirit and cannot be forgiven. Then Jesus' mother and brothers arrive and send a message in to him. They receive the response, "'Who is my mother? Who are my brothers?' And looking round at those who were sitting in the circle about him he said, 'Here are my mother and my brothers. Whoever does the will of God is my brother, my sister, my mother'" (3:31–35). A charitable interpretation of this is that Jesus includes his family in the category of those who do the will of God, but the passage is more easily seen to contrast the former family (outside) with the new family (inside). Mark's chapter 3 implies that his family believed those who said, "He is out of his mind."

In chapter 6, Jesus returns home, teaches in the synagogue, and the crowd is amazed. "'Is not this the carpenter, the son of Mary, the brother of James and Joseph and Judas and Simon? And are not his sisters here with us?' So they fell foul of him. . . . [Jesus] could work no miracle there, except that he put his hands on a few sick people and healed them; and he was taken aback by their want of faith." This passage surprises many Christians who have been taught Jesus had no brothers or sisters. The words translated "brothers" and "sisters" can occasionally mean cousins, or step-brother and step-sister. However, the reports of Paul, Luke, Mark, Matthew, and John indicate the Christians of the first century had no problem with the tradition that Jesus did have brothers. (Only Mark and Matthew [13:56] specifically mention sisters.)

Jesus' brother James became the leader of the church in Jerusalem after the crucifixion. Paul mentions "James, the Lord's brother" in Galatians 1:19 and later gives evidence for the disciples' high position when he refers to "those reputed pillars of our society James, Peter and John" (Gal. 2:9). James is prominent in Acts. The Letter of James in the New Testament is thought by some scholars to have been attributed to Jesus' brother James, and the letter of Judas (commonly called Jude to avoid confusion) is attributed to Judas the brother of James and, presumably, brother of Jesus.

According to Mark, Jesus returned to his hometown, Nazareth, and while there amazed the people who heard him speak in the local synagogue. "They fell foul of him. Jesus said to them, 'A prophet will always be held in honour except in his home town, *and among his kinsmen and family.*' He could work no miracle there, except that he put his hands on a few sick people and healed them; and he was taken aback by their lack of faith" (Mark 6:4–6). In analyzing this passage we have information beyond that given by Mark. We have two first-century reactions to the passage produced by the authors of Luke and Matthew. Further, a first-century version of this saying exists in the Gospel of Thomas. Let us consider this information.

Matthew takes the version of the saying in Mark and presents it as, "A prophet will always be held in honour, except in his home town, and in his own family" (Matt. 13:57). This slightly tones down Mark's doubly stressed "kinsmen and family." Luke goes further, retaining only, "No prophet is recognized in his own country" (Luke 4:24). We can presume, then, that Matthew and Luke, the two earliest biblical analysts we know of, both thought the saying in Mark was too critical of the family of Jesus; Luke deleted all the implied criticism.

Should we assume that Jesus implied by the saying that his family did not hold him in honor, or did Mark introduce that idea? If we check our other source of information, Thomas, we find saying 31, "A prophet is not acceptable in his own village; a physician does not heal those who know him." This has the appearance of being a proverb generally applicable to prophets and healers in peasant societies and not a biographical statement. Apparently Mark added the clauses critical of family and relatives, and Luke, recognizing this, deleted them.

But perhaps Mark did more than this. Perhaps he had in front of him a saying in the Thomas version, "A prophet is not acceptable in his own village; a physician does not heal those who know him," and wondered what caused Jesus to say this. Most of the sayings of Jesus now in the New Testament originally were passed down by oral tradition and then in written lists without any narrative to place them in biographical context. Mark, in his effort to create a coherent narrative out of scattered sayings and miracle stories, may have assumed Jesus could have said such a thing only when he returned to his village, was not accepted there, and could heal few people there. Moreover, Mark had no particular interest in the inhabitants of Nazareth but was interested in Jesus' family, who he did not think were supportive of Jesus.

What Mark may have done is to take the original saying, add clauses critical of "family and kinsmen," create for the saying a logical biographical context, and write the account we now read in 6:1–6, where it is narrated that Jesus could heal few of those who knew him because they had no faith in him. Matthew and Luke, in turn, came across Mark's passage and revised those elements they found inappropriate, Matthew revising a little in 13:54–58 and Luke much more in 4:16–24.

The disciples of Jesus and the family of Jesus have one crucial thing in common. After the crucifixion they became the leaders of the new church and, based in Jerusalem, sought to spread the gospel as they understood it throughout first the Jewish and then the Gentile world. Mark's unflattering portrayal of both disciples and family certainly does not come from reports traceable back to John, Peter or James, since we may be confident they thought they understood Jesus well enough. Their failure is an opinion of Mark's.

At the climax of Mark's first section, 1:1 to 8:21, Jesus reacts with anger to his disciples' inability to understand him: "'Have you no inkling yet? Do you still not understand? Are your minds closed? You have eyes: can you not see? You have ears: can you not hear? Have you forgotten? When I broke the five loaves among five thousand, how many basketfuls of scraps did you pick up?' 'Twelve,' they said, 'And how many when I broke the seven loaves among four thousand?' They answered, 'Seven.' He said, 'Do you still not understand?'" Here, midway in the Gospel, the disciples evidently understand nothing. But they have been with Jesus from the Gospel's beginning, have heard his teaching, seen his miracle working powers, and received special instruction. What purpose might Mark have had in portraying them as so obtuse? One major clue to the solution of the problems of the Messianic Secret and of Mark's desire to show the disciples in a bad light may be found by close analysis of Mark 8:27–34:

"Jesus and his disciples set out for the villages of Caesarea Philippi. On the way he asked his disciples, 'Who do men say I am?' They answered, 'Some say John the Baptist, others Elijah, others one of the prophets.' 'And you,' he asked, 'who do you say I am?' Peter replied: 'You are the Christ.' Then he gave them strict orders not to tell anyone about him; and he began to teach them that the Son of Man had to undergo great sufferings, and to be rejected by the elders, chief priests, and doctors of the law; to be put to death, and to rise again three days afterwards. He spoke about it plainly. At this Peter took him by the arm and began to rebuke him. But Jesus turned round, and, looking at his disciples, rebuked Peter. 'Away with you, Satan,' he said; 'you think as men think, not as God thinks.'"

This passage is almost universally regarded as a turning point in Mark's Gospel. In the chapters preceding it Jesus speaks publicly only in parables, which Mark regards as opaque riddles (4:10–13), and performs miraculous works. After this passage Jesus instead teaches his disciples privately, journeys to Jerusalem, is executed, and rises from the dead. Public parable preaching and miracle working rarely occur in the later chapters. This passage contains both Mark's assessment of Jesus' central purpose and a major clue to the reason for the disciples' difficulties.

Jesus asks, "Who do men say I am?" His question sets up all that follows. In Mark's opinion there are two perspectives on Jesus: human and divine. The human perspective is misguided. It is that Jesus is a prophet, probably a prophet who formerly lived and died and now has come back to life. People do not seem clear on which prophet he is: John the Baptist? Elijah? Another altogether? Their answers repeat the opinion of Herod and those about him that Jesus was John come back, or Elijah, or at least that he was like the old prophets (6:14–16). These opinions are based on the idea that "miraculous powers are at work in him" (6:14). The opinion that Jesus is a prophet is denied by Mark. People generally, and Herod specifically, are wrong.

Peter declares Jesus is Christ. This, in some sense, is the right answer. But do not be misled. Mark, like any good teacher, is clever enough to know the right word may be a correct or incorrect answer depending on what the word is thought to mean. What did Peter mean by Christ? The Son of Man who was to suffer and die and rise again? A miracle-working prophet? A political messiah destined to overthrow Roman rule?

Mark does not believe Jesus primarily to be either a miracle worker or a political revolutionary. From the gospel of John we learn that the term *prophet* sometimes implied both ideas. At the conclusion of John's account of the miraculous feeding of the five thousand, "When the people saw the sign [miracle] Jesus had performed, the word went round, 'Surely this must be the prophet that was to come into the world'" (John 6:14). The passage continues with a sentence probably added by the author of John's Gospel indicating the term *prophet* may sometimes have implied a political claim: "Jesus, aware that [those who called him the prophet] meant to come and seize him to proclaim him king, withdrew again to the hills by himself." In Mark's Gospel, Jesus does not claim earthly kingship. Mark takes the political term *Son of David* (implying Jesus is a descendant of the royal house and therefore technically eligible for the kingship) and in one instance puts it in the mouth of a man who is blind (Mark 10:37–48) and in another instance quotes Jesus as denying the Messiah is the Son of David at all, basing the denial on an interpretation of Psalm 110:1 (Mark 12:35–37). So for Mark, the term *Christ* means neither a prophet nor an earthly king.

What does Mark think Peter means by *Christ?* Peter hears from Jesus that the Son of Man has come to suffer, die, and rise again. Peter's initial reaction to this is to "rebuke" Jesus. The word *rebuke* is the same term used by Mark to describe Jesus' response to demons (1:25; 9:25). In response, Jesus immediately "rebukes" Peter, calls him Satan, sends him away, and states that Peter thinks as humans think, not as God thinks. We know both what people think (that Jesus is a prophet come back to life or a prophet like the old prophets) and what God thinks (that Jesus is the suffering Son of Man). Whatever Peter meant by his statement "you are the Christ" is *not* what Jesus and God mean, according to Mark.

Mark distinguishes between using correct terms and understanding terms correctly. To proclaim Jesus the "Son of God" and the "Christ" is correct, from Mark's perspective,only if the meaning of the terms is properly understood. Peter names Jesus "Christ" and shows he misunderstands the term. In response, Jesus treats Peter like a demon: rebukes him, names him Satan, and demands he depart. The demons (possessed people) Jesus has previously encountered stated who he was, "Son of God," but "he insisted that they should not make him known" (3:12). Demons get the terms right, but their knowledge is necessarily inadequate, based solely on their experience of Jesus' power to cast them out, to exorcise and heal. Mark believes Jesus is more than a miracle worker, and so in his Gospel the demons are instructed not to proclaim their inadequate knowledge. This then is one of the elements behind the "messianic secret."

The disciples, too, throughout the first seven chapters of Mark, have witnessed Jesus' public speaking in parables and performing miraculous works. Peter, it appears, like people generally and Herod particularly, understands Jesus to be a prophet and probably a miracle-working prophet. The miracle story most likely to have been derived from an Old Testament prophetic model (2 Kings 4:42–44), the miraculous feedings, is used twice in leading up to Peter's confession. But again, Mark is not satisfied with this view of Jesus. He does not want people to think of Jesus as a prophet, but he recognizes that some of Jesus' activities led people mistakenly to think of him that way.

Mark's central section

In a tightly organized segment of his Gospel Mark gives three versions of what he believes the correct interpretation of Jesus to be. *Read Mark 8:22 through 10:52 carefully, noting the following:*

1. The section begins with a story of a blind man who is given sight, 8:22–26, and ends with a story of a blind man who is given sight, 10:46–52. These stories form a frame around the section. Mark is using the idea of gaining sight to symbolize the idea of gaining understanding.
2. Three separate sections begin with the mention of a journey (8:27, 9:30, 10:32). These soon are followed by the key passages about the suffering Son of Man (8:31, 9:31; 10:33).
3. These three sections are followed by passages critical of disciples (8:33; 9:32–34; 10:35–40). This criticism leads to passages insisting that Christians, especially Christian leaders, should be self-sacrificing, show humil-

ity, and serve others. The disciples, according to Mark, were too eager to put themselves forward and to inhibit those not in their particular group (9:38–41).

Mark's central section is very carefully constructed, so carefully that an appreciation of its construction is the best evidence that Mark (and the other evangelists) did not primarily intend accurately to write down factual sequences of historical events. Rather, they designed narratives to dramatize their own views of what Jesus was about. The central section repeatedly highlights Mark's main point: that people should, first and foremost, think of Jesus in terms of his suffering, death and resurrection. The blindness of the disciples evidently leads them to misunderstand this. Because they misunderstand they are shown repeatedly to strive for power among themselves as insiders (9:34), or for themselves against outsiders (9:38–41), or for themselves as individuals (10:27–40). Jesus insists that such quests for personal power are completely inappropriate: "anyone who wishes to be a follower of mine must leave self behind" (8:34), "whoever does not accept the kingdom of God like a child will never enter it," (9:15), "whoever wants to be great must be your servant, and whoever wants to be first must be the willing slave of all" (10:43–44). He presents himself as an example of proper leadership "for even the Son of Man did not come to be served but to serve, and to surrender his life as a ransom for many" (10:45).

The gospel's first section 1:1–8:21 *seems* to show Jesus' principal role to be a divinely empowered man. This would encourage his followers, should they wish to be like him, to seek to exercise power. But the second section 8:22–10:52 is designed, quite deliberately, to contradict this impression. Mark is an extraordinarily clever author. He doesn't write simply to say "this is the right view, that is the wrong view," he writes to explain through narrative how it came to be that people came to hold the wrong view (the gospel's first section) and then, through narrative, how it should be that people should come to hold the right view (the remainder of the gospel).

Mark thinks Jesus is misunderstood even by some of those who use correct terms about him, possessed people and even Peter. It is likely that Mark thinks the misunderstandings come from focusing on Jesus' miracle-working powers instead of his suffering and death. Mark's is sometimes called a corrective Christology (a *Christology* is a theory of the nature and significance of Christ), for he seems to introduce false impressions of Jesus, as a miracle worker or a resurrected prophet, and then to cancel these impressions by repeatedly stating what the correct impression should have been. Mark's own Christology is quite explicit in his Gospel. Jesus is made to repeat the same point four separate times in 8:31, 9:12, 9:31, and 10:33–34, the last of which reads, "the Son of Man will be given up to the chief priests and the doctors of the law; they will condemn him to death and hand him over to the foreign power. He will be mocked and spat upon, flogged and killed; and three days afterwards, he will rise again."

Having shown Jesus repeatedly to insist that he must be understood in light of his suffering, death and resurrection, Mark concludes his gospel with a long sustained narrative that portrays those very events (14:1–16:8). Mark is quite good at transferring abstract points into narrated stories. For example, he shows Jesus concluding chapter 13's apocalyptic discourse with the admonition to "stay awake!" (13:37) because the Son of Man will return at any moment. Shortly thereafter Mark relates the story of Gethsemane (14:32–42) which portrays Peter, James and John as being instructed to stay awake but, three times, failing to do so. Mark here, as elsewhere, uses the disciples as examples of people who do just the wrong thing.

In one interesting passage, Mark cancels what was earlier a strong claim to authority found in both Q and John. This claim is, "Whoever receives a messenger of mine receives me, whoever receives me receives the One who sent me." Those who created the Q sayings list would have identified themselves as disciples and messengers of Jesus and would have used this saying to justify themselves as persons of significance. So, presumably, did Jesus' disciples. Mark alters the saying to "Whoever receives *one of these children* in my name receives me; and whoever receives me, receives not me but the One who sent me" (9:37). This is not the same thing at all. Mark has made a claim to special messenger of God status into a general statement applicable even to children.

It is likely that Mark was aware of the preaching of Jesus' disciples (and of such leading family members as James) and thought it misguided. He did not believe them entitled to leading positions in the church and felt they were entirely too prone to seek power. They (or their successors who lived during Mark's time) claimed position and authority because they (or their predecessors) had been with Jesus during his lifetime.

If Mark wished to counteract the claims to authority of such people he faced a serious dilemma. He could not deny Jesus' disciples accompanied Jesus and were taught by him and did witness his miracles. But Mark can deny these privileges did them any good. Mark purposefully presents Jesus' teachings in his Gospel in such a way that the reader of the Gospel understands Jesus (as suffering Son of Man) better than the disciples did. At the same time, the reader can see how it was the disciples came to be mistaken (through excessive interest in Jesus' miracles). Mark probably knows (as Paul did, 1 Corinthians 15:3–9) that witnesses to the resurrection had special claim to status in the church (*apostle* is the term used by Paul) and, to counteract any such claims, ends his Gospel denying the disciples were even aware of the resurrection, much less that they witnessed it.

As odd as it may seem, Mark notes that Jesus deliberately spoke in enigmatic parables to keep people from understanding him. He says to the disciples, "To you the secret of the kingdom of God has been given; but to those who are outside everything comes by way of parables, so that [as Scripture says] they may look and look, but see nothing; they may hear and hear, but understand nothing; otherwise they might turn to God and be forgiven" (4:11–12). The fact the disciples are given the secret does not necessarily mean they understood it. Mark misquotes the Scripture reference, Isaiah 6:9–10. The original blames the people for refusing to understand, while in Mark's version the people are deliberately kept from understanding. This is curious, especially since Mark introduces Jesus' message as the time has come; the kingdom of God is upon you; repent and believe the Gospel" (1:15), and so Jesus is said to have encouraged people to repent, turn to God, and be forgiven. Perhaps Mark, in showing Jesus to request repentance and then seemingly to make repentance impossible, is simply inconsistent. But, on the other hand, Mark's Gospel is motivated not only by his desire to explain the true nature of Jesus' mission as he understands it, but also to reveal that during his life people in general, and the disciples in particular, did not understand that mission correctly. Mark may have regarded Jesus' parables as riddles almost impossible to understand and have concluded both that Jesus must have deliberately made them difficult and that this accounts in part for people's misunderstanding of Jesus. Mark's judgment is harsher on the disciples. To them "the secret of the kingdom of God has been given" (4:11), and, unlike the common people, they were expected to understand Jesus' parables. In any event, understanding Jesus primarily as a teacher would be a mistake, in Mark's view. One should understand him in reference to his suffering death, and resurrection.

Four important themes come together in the central segment of Mark: the Messianic Secret, Mark's critical appraisal of the disciples, the requirement that Christians behave with humility, and the concept of the suffering Son of Man. It is probably because Mark conceives of the people as having been misled by Jesus' miracles that he portrays Jesus as eager to have demons and people healed of illness keep silent. Jesus is seeking to avoid misconceptions about his mission. Jesus' efforts fail. People do not keep silent. The disciples, with knowledge unavailable to all, are mistaken. Mark shows Jesus revealing "plainly" (8:32) that he is to suffer and die and rise in contrast to his previous custom of speaking in "parables" (4:2). In Mark's perspective, parables are riddles.

Those who understand Jesus

Some do understand Jesus correctly, although possibly as few as one. The person who most clearly understands Jesus correctly in the Gospel of Mark is an unnamed woman (14:3–9) who, while he is alive, anoints his body for burial. This shows she anticipates his death and his resurrection for, when raised, his body cannot receive the customary anointing. The disciples, typically for Mark, do not understand what she is doing; "They turned upon her with fury." In the greatest praise bestowed on anyone in the Gospel of Mark, Jesus says, "I tell you this: wherever in the world the Gospel is proclaimed, what she has done will be told as her memorial."

The Roman centurion (*centurion* is a rank roughly equivalent to an army captain today) mentioned in 15:39 directed, and therefore was immediately responsible for, the crucifixion of Jesus; an officer is responsible for the orders he gives his men. Mark probably intended his readers to believe that this man correctly understood Jesus. This centurion, when he saw how Jesus died, declared, "Truly this man was a son of God." From Mark's perspective a declaration that Jesus is a Son of God because of his death (not, for instance, because of his miracles) is correct. It is unclear whether Mark's intention in the phrase *a Son of God* was to make the centurion's declaration ambiguous; he may simply have regarded *Son of God* and *a Son of God* as synonymous. Joseph of Arimathaea is another whom Mark may have believed understood Jesus correctly (15:43). Joseph is praised as "a man who looked forward to the kingdom of God." He received Jesus' corpse from Pilate. "A respected member of the council," he presumably had joined in the unanimous council vote declaring that Jesus should be put to death (14:64).

The woman who anoints Jesus, Joseph who eagerly awaits the Kingdom of God, and the centurion who proclaims Jesus a Son of God together have voted to condemn him, directed his execution, anointed his body for burial, and buried him. But from Mark's perspective these people do the opposite of rebuking Jesus for declaring the Son of Man must suffer and die; they willingly participate in those events.

Mark's apocalypse

Special attention must be paid to Mark's chapter 13. There Jesus gives a lengthy speech in response to a question put privately by Peter, James, John, and Andrew. "'Tell us,' they said, 'when will this [destruction of the temple] happen? What will be the sign when the fulfillment of all this is at hand?'" This speech can be categorized as *apocalyptic,* as it foretells in some detail the ominous events scheduled by God to take place before the end of this world and its replacement or renewal by the Kingdom of God. The speech alternates between the cosmic scale and the local scale, between events to occur in the world at large and events to occur in the lives of local Christians, presumably those living in Mark's community. The local events are thought by scholars to reflect real social conditions and therefore to be a valuable source of evidence about Mark's community and the events resulting in the writing of this Gospel.

"Local" events, referring probably to Mark's own community, are found in chapter 13, verses 5–6, 9–13, 21–23. They reflect a time of persecution both on the level of the state and on the level of the family. People (probably Christians) come, claiming Jesus' name, with "signs and wonders" (probably healing miracles and exorcisms) who may mislead "God's chosen." Threats arise from within and outside the Christian movement. Significantly here, as in the first section of Mark's gospel, signs and wonders tend to mislead.

Cosmic apocalyptic material is found in the following verses: 7–8, 14–20, 24–27, 32. They state the end of this world is to come and will be introduced by terrible disasters. This may provide one answer to the obvious question raised by Mark's perspective: *why* did the Son of Man have to suffer and die? The answer could be that Jesus' tragic death was a part of a whole sequence of tragic events taking place before the end, and it, like the suffering taking place in Mark's community and the suffering and death of John the Baptist, was planned by God.

Mark's little apocalypse, as it is sometimes called in scholarship, seems designed to reinterpret the idea of the imitation of Christ. To be like Christ seemed, evidently, to some Christians to require them to be prophets, to do signs and wonders, even to come in Jesus' name claiming "I am he!" But Mark believes, and emphasizes, that the imitation of Christ is done by those who are submissive, who are persecuted, who, like the Son of Man, may be required to suffer, to die and ultimately to rise again.

Only two phrases, obscure but highly important, are present in Mark's gospel as clues to his interpretation of the significance of Jesus' death. The first is, "The Son of Man did not come to be served but to serve, and to give his life as a ransom for many" (10:45). This is the final sentence of Mark's crucial central section and plays, in literary terms, the role of a climax. It is supplemented by a statement at the Last Supper when Jesus announces, "This is my blood, the blood of the covenant, shed for many" (14:24). These two clues support speculation that for Mark Jesus' death began a new covenant with people (the old covenant being God's establishing a special relationship with the Jewish people who kept the Law of the Torah), and that people were ransomed by Jesus' death. But we are told little of what the new covenant involves in terms of the relationship between people and God except people should be servants of one another. We are told nothing of what "many" are ransomed from, and nothing of why Jesus' death for ransom was necessary. These two clues, insufficient as they stand, do not allow us to state with certainty what Mark believed the purpose of the death of Jesus was. A theologian will recognize in those sentences echoes of the Christology of Paul and use Paul to help explain Mark's meaning. This is perhaps a valid procedure, as Mark seems in several respects to agree with Paul's view of Jesus. But, even though use of Paul's ideas to interpret Mark may be valid, it is good to remember that as it stands, in and of itself, Mark gives only two difficult clues to his idea of the purpose of Jesus' death. Mark assumes his audience understands the purpose of Jesus' death. Thus he does not tell them that purpose.

Mark does tell us that, at a climactic point of his trial before Jewish authorities, Jesus replied to the High Priest's question "Are you the Christ, the Son of the Blessed One?" with the response "I am. And you will see the Son of Man seated on the right hand of God and coming with the clouds of heaven" (14:61–62). This bold statement confirms the prediction found in Mark's apocalypse (13:26). One might wonder, however, whether it was made by Jesus or by the Spirit speaking in Jesus (those who attack him demanding he prophesy evidently think it was the Spirit) for in 13:11 we hear Jesus say "when you are arrested and taken away, do not worry beforehand about what you are to say, but when the time comes say whatever is given you to say; for it will not be you that speak but the Holy Spirit."

For many years scholars casually reasoned that as Mark was the first Gospel, at least a decade earlier than the other three, it must therefore be the most historically reliable. This is not necessarily true. Mark's particular perspectives, especially his antagonism to Jesus' disciples, make suspect his accounts of Jesus' interactions with his closest associates. Further, Mark's careful structuring of his Gospel, from early stories of miracle working to his carefully structured central section focusing on the suffering Son of Man, to his lengthy account of Jesus' betrayal, trial, and execution, reflects more his own organization of Jesus' life than any research into the actual events in Jesus' life. Mark must be judged as an evangelist, not a biographer; evangelists set forth the meaning of Jesus life as they see it within a narrative framework, while biographers seek as nearly as possible to render a factual account of a life. The two are not the same, and the common assumption that the evangelists were biographers has led to much misunderstanding of the nature of the New Testament.

Topics

Sources

It is impossible to be certain what Mark's sources were, but intelligent guesses can be made. As Mark's version of Jesus' trial and death is quite similar to John's it is likely both derive from a common source. Since Jesus' death was of supreme importance to some branches of the early Christian church it is likely that accounts of it were written down before anyone wrote a longer biography. Mark, therefore, probably adapted a previously written passion narrative to his Gospel.

In addition, Mark seems to have used two small written collections of miracles (which you have already underlined) in the first half of his book.

Along with these Mark may have made use of short written collections of Jesus' parables. Some scholars think Mark's chapter 4 comes from such a collection.

Otherwise, Mark seems to be working from an oral tradition he edits, revises, and interprets in his own fashion.

Jesus

In Mark's Gospel *Jesus' life* is not an uninterrupted story of success. He comes to reveal himself as the suffering Son of Man who also is Christ and Son of the Most High God, yet those closest to him fail to understand this correctly. Neither his miracles nor his teachings were of major importance, for, when Jesus gives the central purpose of his life, they are not mentioned (8:31; 9:12; 9:31; 10:33). In Mark's short book, from chapter 8 through chapter 16, Jesus speaks of his approaching death, travels to Jerusalem where it will take place, and undergoes the legal prosecution and eventual execution he had predicted. A cliché in the study of the Gospel of Mark is that it is a passion narrative with an extended introduction.

The Son of Man has power on earth (to exorcise, heal, forgive sins: all somewhat synonymous), but his great power will come later. Perhaps it would be best to think of Jesus in Mark's Gospel as the Son of Man come in disguise, and only those who see through the disguise and are not misled will be privileged to live eternally with him when he comes in the future (10:29–31).. Eternal life will, apparently, be given to those who repent (1:15, but see also 4:12), who behave in a moral fashion (7:21–23; 10:19), who sell all they have and give the proceeds to the poor (10:21), who follow Jesus despite personal sacrifices of many kinds (10:29–31), and above all who recognize the importance of Jesus' death (10:45; 14:24).

Jesus' death is a crucial part of his mission from God. It is toward death that the Gospel is directed, in both a literary sense and a Christological sense. Jesus, the Son of Man, was to suffer and die and rise. But why was Jesus' death of such importance? Only Mark 10:45 and 14:24 hint at answers, but those short, puzzling comments do not let a reader see very deeply into Mark's conception. Presumably those for whom his Gospel was written understood the purpose of Jesus' death, so Mark feels no need to discuss the matter at length. This means it would be wrong to say Mark wrote his Gospel to explain the meaning and nature of Jesus' life and death. Rather, Mark is writing for an audience who believe they know this and are puzzled why others do not.

Although Mark clearly believes Jesus Christ can be understood only from the perspective of his death and resurrection, no resurrection appearances are given; Mark apparently believes Jesus will appear only in the future, in Galilee (14:28; 16:7), when as the Son of Man he returns "in the clouds with great power and glory" and "sends out the angels and gathers his chosen from the four winds, from the farthest bounds of earth to the farthest bounds of heaven" (13:26–27). Then those who do understand and live correctly will live eternally with him.

Eschatology

Chapter 13 is a self-contained unit outlining the events taking place leading up to the catastrophic end of this world and the glorious return of the Son of Man. Mark insists, on the one hand, the end is still some time away and, on the other, it will soon come. This can be seen, for example, in verses 7 and 8, "When you hear the noise of battle near at hand and the news of battles far away, do not be alarmed. Such things are bound to happen; but *the end is still to come.* For nation will make war upon nation, kingdom upon kingdom; there will be earthquakes in many places; there will be famines. With these things *the birthpangs of the new age begin.*" The events leading up to the end are occurring in his own time, Mark believes, but this does not mean that in a matter of months all will be over. In times to come "the sun will be darkened, the moon will not give her light; the stars will come falling from the sky, the celestial powers will be shaken" (13:24–25), but those things have not yet happened.

Mark believes he and his community are living in the midst of eschatological events. When they will finally culminate God knows, but no one else, not even the angels in heaven or the Son (13:32). "The present generation will live to see it all" (13:30), but they have not seen it all yet. There is here a fluctuation back and forth between "*now* is the time of the end of this world," and "keep awake for the end of this world is *soon* to come." The events of the end time are terrible; nothing good is mentioned in chapter 13 until finally the Son of Man comes in power and glory. The events of Jesus' life were, similarly, terrible. He was misunderstood, rejected, betrayed, tried, convicted, executed. Mark's Gospel must be understood in terms of this bleak but hopeful perspective. If members of Mark's community were being persecuted, handed over to the courts, flogged in synagogues, summoned to appear before governors and kings, arrested and taken away, betrayed by family members, and generally hated (13:9–13), it probably was part of his intention in writing to show that such terrible occurrences were predicted by Jesus and essential to God's plan. What happened to the Son of Man and to John the Baptist would happen to faithful Christians, and they ought not to be in despair when this occurred.

For Mark, eschatology provides an explanation for otherwise incomprehensible events. If his Christian community is approved by God, how could it be that it was being brutally victimized? Mark's answer is, this is the way God planned it for the community as also for John the Baptist and also for Jesus. Those seeking signs and wonders (rather than faithfully enduring persecution) make the same mistake as the disciples did during Jesus' life when they failed to understand his statements about the necessity of his persecution and his death.

Torah law

Mark's attitude toward Torah Law is somewhat casual. He does not have the passionate concern with it found in Paul's writing. "Commandments" are quoted in Mark: "Do not murder; do not commit adultery; do not steal; do not give false evidence; do not defraud; honor your father and mother" (10:19), to which he adds, "Sell what you have and give to the poor" (10:21), but the laws of Moses here are apparently regarded as general moral guidelines to which others can be added. "Do not defraud" is not one of the ten commandments, and neither, of course, is the command to sell what you have. Only half of the Ten Commandments are quoted. Jesus quotes two passages from the Hebrew Scriptures as the two greatest commandments: "Hear, O Israel: the Lord our God is the only Lord; love the Lord your God with all your heart, with all your soul, with all your mind, and with all your strength" and "Love your neighbour as yourself" (12:30–31). Both are general admonitions, not specific rules for behavior. Pharisees and rabbis would have agreed that these are great and essential commandments.

When it comes to ethnic Jewish commandments such as the complex detailed requirements of food selection, preparation, and purity developing later into "kosher" practices, Mark's Gospel shows Jesus to have eliminated them all: "Thus he declared all foods clean" (7:20). What defiles people is not impure foods but "evil thoughts, acts of fornication, of theft, murder, adultery, ruthless greed, and malice; fraud, indecency, envy, slander, arrogance, and folly" (7:22–23). It is hard to imagine a teacher in any religious tradition disagreeing with this checklist of moral "defilements." The commandments in Mark derive from universal human social standards. They are neither specifically Jewish nor specifically Roman nor Greek. When it comes to ethnic Jewish commandments, Jesus declares them no longer to be in effect.

Paul is deeply concerned about the Torah Law; Mark is not. Mark uses it as a point of reference, but commandments are added and deleted by Jesus in brief statements. Mark's audience was not predominately composed of Jewish people, for Jews would have had no need to be told "the Pharisees and the Jews in general never eat without washing the hands, in obedience to an old established tradition . . ." (7:3). Probably neither Mark nor his audience regarded the Laws of Moses as more than general moral guidelines to which various ethnic Jewish customs (like the food laws) had been added. The perspective on Law found in Mark's Gospel is that of a Gentile who is sympathetic to Judaism but who has no desire to advocate detailed obedience to specifically Jewish laws and customs.

Community

On the assumption that chapter 13 reflects something of the conditions in Mark's community when he wrote his Gospel, that community was in a situation of great danger. The Jewish religious courts were sources of persecution, and some Christians known to Mark had been "flogged in synagogues" (13:9). Others were brought to trial before "governors and kings" and faced the death penalty. It is not clear why Christians might have been in so much legal danger in or about the year C.E. 70, but Mark's Gospel certainly conveys the impression they were.

Not only were external forces (synagogues, government officers) inimical to Mark's Christians, but so also were some members of their families. "Brother will betray brother to death, and the father his child; children will turn against their parents and send them to their death. All will hate you for your allegiance to me" (13:12). A dreadful situation is outlined here. Parents betray children to the courts and to their deaths; children do the same to parents. "All will hate you"—a terrible thing to think or say. But it is from this context (or at least from a situation perceived to be this terrible) that Mark writes.

The surprising themes of Mark's Gospel do not come out of Mark's personal reflections alone. They come out of a particular social situation demanding radical explanations. Mark writes for people who ask, "If we are God's chosen, why are we hated, betrayed, killed?" His Gospel gives an answer referring to Jesus, a model for Christians who fear being hated, betrayed, and killed.

Controversy

Mark's is a Gospel filled with controversies. With few exceptions Jesus is opposed, misunderstood, or forsaken. His family and his neighbors at Nazareth show no understanding in chapters 3 and 6. Throughout the Gospel the leaders of Jewish groups oppose him: Pharisees, Sadducees, Chief Priests, elders, Herodians. The Roman authorities eventually execute him. The common people, although supporting him nearly to the end, at the last are crying out, "Crucify him!" His disciples, given both secret and public evidence of his special status, understand nothing and by the time of the crucifixion they all have abandoned him. The women who were with him remain loyal longer, but the Gospel's last sentence depicts them as failing to carry out the only mission assigned to them, and their expectation of finding Jesus' corpse in the tomb shows they failed to understand. Those who understand him—the woman with anointing oils, Joseph of Arimathaea, the centurion—perceive him correctly in light of his death. And God? In Mark's Gospel Jesus' last words are "'*Eli, Eli, lema sabachthani?*' meaning 'My God, my God why have you forsaken me?'" That sentence, the longest in the New

Testament quoted in either Hebrew or Aramaic, comes from the first stanza of Psalm 22, a psalm coming eventually to an affirmative conclusion. But as it stands it is a cry of desolation, and at the end Jesus is alone.

Do the obtuse, self-important disciples of Mark's Gospel represent the people of Mark's community? Some scholars believe so, arguing Mark presents the disciples as weak and inadequate at first while knowing in the end the disciples showed both courage and understanding. So, the argument goes, did Mark regard his community—as a group who at present feel weak and inadequate and yet, like the disciples, can hope to come through well in the end. But this argument is based not on Mark but on other New Testament books where the disciples do at last understand. In analyzing Mark all we can conscientiously use for evidence is Mark. And in Mark the disciples do not come through well in the end at all.

It is more likely Mark portrays the disciples in such a negative light because Mark was personally in direct conflict with the disciples or with their successors. He thought they did not emphasize the suffering and death of the Son of Man as he thought they should but, improperly, emphasized Jesus' miraculous powers. To counteract their claims to authority (time spent with Jesus, family relationship with him, perception of him risen from the dead), Mark denies either that these things were the case or that they did the disciples any good. One motivation for Mark's Gospel could have been Mark's need to assert and validate his authority against the claims to authority of Jesus' disciples or their successors.

Interactions

Miracles sources

Mark's interaction with the sources he used for stories of Jesus' miracles is most interesting. While using them as sources, and as far as we can tell rewriting them little, he does not support their underlying idea. After all, if Mark's idea of Jesus is of a servant destined by God to suffer (10:45), and the compilers of miracle stories believe he was an extremely powerful and compelling worker of wonders, conflict would inevitably be present. Mark allows his reader to assume Jesus did the miracles attributed to him and that they did, as the sources wished, encourage faith that he was a prophet, Christ, or even Son of God. But the miracle stories are placed in his Gospel in such a way that doubt is cast on the wisdom of those who take them too seriously. Those who based faith on miracles are like the demons who claim Jesus is Son of God because of his exorcisms, or like Peter who says Jesus is Christ but who does not approve the suffering Son of Man and who is treated like a demon. Mark uses the miracles sources, apparently believes them reliable, but offers a subtle reinterpretation of them. The faith the miracles sources wish to call forth is made to seem inadequate or even

Miracle Stories

Healing Stories	**Mark**
1. Jesus Gives Orders to an Unclean Spirit	1:21-28
2. Jesus Heals Simon's Mother-in-Law	1:29-31
3. Sick and Demon-Possessed Come to Jesus	1:32-34
4. Jesus Cures a Leper	1:40-45
5. Jesus Cures a Paralytic	2:1-12
6. Jesus Heals on the Sabbath Day	3:1-6
7. The Demon of Gerasene	5:1-20
8. Jesus Cures Jairus' Daughter	5:21-24a, 35-43
9. Jesus Cures the Woman with a Menstrual Flow	5:24b-34
10. Greek Woman's Daughter	7:24-30
11. Jesus Cures a Deaf Mute	7:31-37
12. Jesus Cures a Blind Man	8:22-26
13. The Man with the Mute Spirit	9:14-29
14. Jesus Cures Blind Bartinaeus	10:46-52
Nature Wonders	**Mark**
15. Jesus Rebukes the Wind and the Sea	4:35-41
16. Loaves and Fish for Five Thousand	6:35-44
17. Jesus Walks on the Sea	6:47-52
18. Loaves and Fish for Four Thousand	8:1-9
Epiphanies	**Mark**
19. John Baptizes Jesus	1:9-11
20. Jesus, Elijah, Moses on the Mountain	9:2-8

demonic, and their perspective is presented as "what men think" and not "what God thinks."

Q source

Mark did not use the Q document as a source. But, as most sayings in the Q source circulated independently of the written document containing them, it is not surprising Mark knows and uses some of them. He does not always do so without revision, however. Sometimes he alters them in ways appropriate to his general perspective. For example, the saying "Whoever receives a messenger of mine receives me" is softened to "Whoever receives a child in my name receives me" as discussed above. In another instance the startling saying "If anyone comes to me and does not hate his father and mother, wife and children, brothers and sisters, even his own life, he cannot be a disciple of mine. No one who does not carry his cross and come with me can be a disciple of mine" (Luke 14:26–27) is softened to rad, "Anyone who wishes to be a follower of mine must leave self behind; he must take up his cross, and come with me" (8:34). Mark's perspective on Christian life, like that of Q, is founded largely on the expectation of imminent disasters accompanying the end of this world and the arrival of the Kingdom of God. But unlike Q's perspective, Mark does not have a bleak view of family and social life. Disruption of family may occur, but Mark regards such disruption as tragic (13:12) and temporary (10:30). In Q disruptions are expected, if not required (Luke 9:59–62).

Mark and Q differ on the Torah Law, the Q people apparently wishing it to be kept strictly in the traditional way: "It is easier for heaven and earth to come to an end than for one dot or stroke of the law to lose its force" (Luke 16:17). Mark does not regard the Law as crucially important. The food laws are suspended, the laws of Moses are hastily summarized and altered. Mark respects Torah law only as a set of general moral guidelines.

Paul

Did Mark receive his central ideas through Paul's influence, or do both Mark and Paul receive their ideas from earlier levels of Christian tradition? Scholars have argued that question for decades. On the one hand it looks as if Mark's focus on Jesus' death derives from Paul's similar focus on his death. But, on the other hand, Paul is eager to interpret Jesus' death in terms of his own Christology, while Mark barely interprets it at all. Death "for the ransom of many" sounds like it has Paul's ideas behind it, even though it is difficult to say what that phrase means.

Perhaps Mark's casual approach to Jewish legal matters derives from Paul's passionate attempt to free Christians from the obligation of following that Law. On the other hand, Christianity, in moving away from the Jewish world of Palestine into the Gentile world, may have been destined to reject the particular customs of Judaism with or without Paul's influence.

Mark does not use any of Paul's characteristic language, nor does Mark reflect any substantial and thoroughgoing understanding of Paul's complex theology. One might list a dozen Pauline themes missing in Mark, from the idea of justification to the concept of the church as the body of Christ. This convinces many that Mark is not a follower of Paul. Others argue that conversion of Christianity from a Jewish movement of repentance and renewed legal obedience focused on the miracles and teaching of its founder to a mainly Gentile movement free from the Law and focused on the death of its founder could have come only through the work of a single genius—Paul—and that therefore Mark reflects Paul's influence if not the details of his teaching.

Perhaps a compromise perspective is best. Paul personally established many communities, and his associates established more. Some, perhaps, kept and studied Paul's letters, while most simply remembered him and his teachings as best they could. As with the teachings of Jesus, the teachings of Paul were communicated by word of mouth and gradually were altered over the years. It may be best to imagine Mark having grown up in a community founded by Paul, or one of Paul's associates, retaining Paul's emphasis on the death of Christ and respecting Torah Law only as a general moral code. Many Gentiles throughout the ancient world respected the Torah in this way. Such an image of Mark would allow many of his ideas to come, ultimately, from Paul and would also explain why Mark shows no signs of having studied Paul's letters or the technicalities of his philosophy. Both Paul (especially evidenced in Galatians) and Mark appear to have been in conflict with Jesus' personal disciples and family, individuals who probably were convinced that Christians, like Jews, should follow Torah Law.

Bibliography

Kealy, Sean P. *Mark's Gospel: A History of Its Interpretation*. New York: Paulist Press, 1982.

Kee, Howard C. *Community of the New Age: Studies in Mark's Gospel*. Philadelphia: Westminster Press, 1980.

Kelber, Werner, ed. *The Passion in Mark*. Philadelphia: Fortress Press, 1976.

Kingsbury, Jack Dean. *Conflict in Mark*. Minneapolis: Fortress Press, 1989.

Marxen, Willi. *Mark the Evangelist*. Nashville: Abingdon, 1956.

Perrin, Norman. *The Resurrection According to Matthew, Mark, and Luke*. Philadelphia: Fortress Press, 1977.

Rhoads, David and Michie, Donald. *Mark As Story*. Philadelphia: Fortress Press, 1982.

Räisänen, Heikki, *The "Messianic Secret" in Mark's Gospel*. Edinburgh: T. & T. Clark Ltd., 1990.

Taylor, Vincent. *The Gospel According to Mark*. London: Macmillan and Co., 1959.

Waetjeu, Herman. *A Reordering of Power: A Sociopolitical Reading of Mark's Gospel*. Minneapolis: Fortress Press, 1989.

Weeden, Theodore J. *Mark, Traditions in Conflict*. Philadelphia: Fortress Press, 1979.

Wrede, W. *The Messianic Secret*. Cambridge: James Clarke, 1971.

Six

The Gospel of Matthew

The Growth of the New Testament

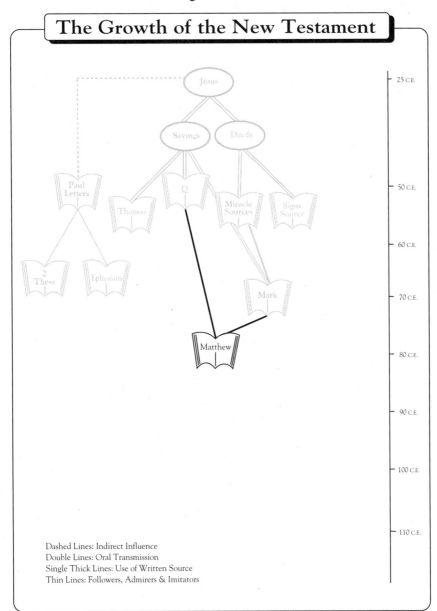

25 C.E.

50 C.E.

60 C.E.

70 C.E.

80 C.E.

90 C.E.

100 C.E.

110 C.E.

Dashed Lines: Indirect Influence
Double Lines: Oral Transmission
Single Thick Lines: Use of Written Source
Thin Lines: Followers, Admirers & Imitators

The Gospel of Matthew is probably the most popular of the four Gospels. It begins with the Christmas story; it contains the Sermon on the Mount, which many regard as the principal statement of Jesus' message; it is more concerned with church order than is any other Gospel. Matthew presents Jesus as a miracle worker who came both to fulfill prophecy and to fulfill the Law of God, as one whose disciples struggled but were eventually successful in understanding him. This is a more comfortable perspective than Mark's, and it contributes to Matthew's popularity.

Read the Gospel of Matthew and underline references to prophets and the fulfillment of prophecy. Although all the evangelists believe Jesus' life often fulfilled prophecy, this theme is most prominent in Matthew's Gospel, and we will investigate it with some care.

Author, date, and place of origin

We do not know who Matthew was. An early report claims he originally wrote his Gospel in Hebrew and he was a disciple of Jesus, possibly "Matthew the tax collector." But this is not true; Matthew's use of Mark as a source proves both that he wrote in Greek (as Mark did) and that he is not relying on his own memory for an account of the events of Jesus' life. He never claims to be an eyewitness. His references to the Hebrew Bible are taken from the Greek translation of it rather than from the original Hebrew; no author writing in Hebrew would have done that. Jesus is repeatedly said to have dined "with tax collectors and sinners," probably a true report, but to Matthew tax collectors are examples of people who should not be allowed into his church. Matthew, showing his concern for church order, writes that Jesus instructed church members to treat a member who will not reform as they would "a pagan or a tax gatherer" (18:15–17) or, in other words, to expel him or her.

Matthew

It is Papias again, as reported by Eusebius, who names Matthew (Matt 10:3) as the author of the first gospel. Matthew may have another name, Levi, which is the name given to the tax collector in Mark 2:14 and Luke 5:27, but who is called Matthew in the parallel passage, Matt 9:9. We cannot account for the differences in name. Papias' assertion that canonical Matthew was composed in Hebrew is patently false; Matthew was composed in Greek in dependence on Q and Mark, also written in Greek by unknown authors.

His sympathetic interest in Torah Law and his frequent use of the Hebrew Scriptures indicates Matthew considered himself Jewish. Whether he was born to a Jewish family or whether he was a Gentile convert to Judaism is debated by scholars. On the one hand he defends the validity of the Law more than any other evangelist does; on the other hand his knowledge of the Torah is limited ("hate your enemy," Matt 5:43, is not in the Torah).

Matthew may have written his Gospel in the Roman province of Syria. That is the guess of many scholars, although there is no firm evidence for it. His use of Mark and Q, and the evidence in his Gospel that the church of his day was becoming rather well organized, indicate a date well after the year C.E. 70. The year C.E. 85 is frequently given for Matthew and is a reasonable guess; but it may be off by a decade either way.

The beginning of the Gospel

The Gospel of Matthew prefaces Jesus' baptism with an account of his birth. This account is entirely composed by Matthew and shows his own style as an author in contrast to most of the remainder of his Gospel, where he is revising and reorganizing the Gospel of Mark. After presenting his version of Jesus' genealogy (quite different from that found in Luke 3:23–38), Matthew argues in three ways that Jesus is Messiah. He argues Jesus is Messiah because God revealed this to Joseph in dreams. In the ancient world dreams were commonly believed to be messages from a deity. He argues Jesus is Messiah because the prophets of the Hebrew Scriptures announced in advance events of his life. Finally, he argues the magi (Persian astrologers held in high esteem throughout the empire) found evidence of Jesus' special status in the stars.

John the Baptist

John the Baptist plays a role at the beginning of Jesus' ministry, as he does in Mark. More than in Mark, John is shown to know he is inferior to Jesus. We are *not* told that those who came to John did so as a token of repentance for forgiveness of sins. Rather, while Matthew notes that people who were baptized did so confessing sins (3:6), Jesus' baptism is separated from theirs. When Jesus came to be baptized, "John tried to dissuade him. 'Do you come to me?' he said; 'I need rather to be baptized by you.' Jesus replied, 'Let it be so for the present; we do well to conform in this way with all that God requires'" (3:14–15). This passage is found only in Matthew. The baptism here is said to occur because of the mysterious will of God and not even implicitly because of any need on Jesus' part for forgiveness.

Matthew portrays John as believing that he is more in need of baptism than Jesus.

The ending of the Gospel

Matthew concludes, like Mark, with an account of Jesus' trial, but, unlike Mark, Matthew also gives a brief account of a resurrection appearance. At the end of Matthew's Gospel the risen Jesus appears to his disciples (28:2–20), but in a surprisingly short passage. Much of the conclusion is concerned with dispelling a rumor, present in Matthew's day, that Jesus' body was stolen by his disciples (27:62–66). The women at the tomb meet the risen Jesus, who tells them the same thing the youth in white clothes told them in Mark's account. In Mark the women told no one what they heard and saw; in Matthew they "hurried away from the tomb in awe and great joy, and ran to tell the disciples.' When the disciples saw Jesus on a mountain in Galilee "they fell prostrate before him, though some were doubtful. . . . He said: 'Full authority in heaven and on earth has been committed to me. Go forth therefore and make all nations my disciples; baptize men everywhere in the name of the Father and the Son and the Holy Spirit, and teach them to observe all that I have commanded you. And be assured, I am with you always to the end of time'" (28:17–20). This passage is a good clue to Matthew's understanding of Jesus and Christianity, for it concludes his Gospel and it presumably states what Matthew believes to be his own mission in life. The mission Jesus conducted during his life in Israel among Jews is now to expand to "all nations." Jesus' followers are to baptize and teach observance of commandments, confident that Jesus remains with them.

Pontius Pilate

More than Mark's, Matthew's Gospel insists Pilate believed Jesus to be innocent. Only in Matthew do we find the story that Pilate's wife had Jesus' innocence revealed to her in a dream (27:19). The story of Pilate literally and symbolically washing his hands of the matter saying, "my hands are clean of this man's blood" (27:25) is, likewise, found only in Matthew. This graphic scene heightens the impression given in Mark's Gospel that Pilate believed Jesus innocent. It is not to Matthew's credit that he further inserts into Mark's account a fictional passage designed to demonstrate that the Jewish people deserve responsibility for Jesus' execution. Matthew's Gospel quotes them as saying, "His blood be on us and on our children" (27:25). This passage has been used to justify much persecution of Jewish people by Christians.

The organization of the Gospel

From Mark's organization Matthew retains (with additions) only Mark's concluding parts: the apocalyptic discourse and the passion narrative. After the story of Jesus' birth, Matthew divides Jesus' ministry into five central speeches or discourses, each concluding with the phrase "when Jesus had finished this discourse." The five discourses are separated by narratives of travel, teaching, and miraculous actions, which three times conclude with a description of Jesus' great popularity. Matthew's five sections of narrative and discourse are as follows:

1. Jesus' ministry begins: 3:1–4:25 (narrative) concluding, "He went round the whole of Galilee, teaching in the synagogues, preaching the gospel of the Kingdom, and curing whatever illness or infirmity there was among the people. His fame reached the whole of Syria; and sufferers from every kind of illness, racked with pain, possessed by devils, epileptic, or paralyzed, were all brought to him, and he cured them. Great crowds also followed him, from Galilee and the Ten Towns, from Jerusalem and Judaea, and from Transjordan."

1a. This narrative section is followed by the discourse called the Sermon on the Mount: 5:1–7:29 concluding, "When Jesus had finished this discourse the people were astounded at his teaching; unlike their own teachers he taught with a note of authority.

2. Jesus displays his power: 8:1–9:35 (narrative) ending, "So Jesus went round all the towns and villages teaching in their synagogues, announcing the good news of the Kingdom, and curing every kind of ailment and disease."

2a. Next comes a discourse directed to his disciples explaining how they are to conduct their missions: 9:36–11:1 concluding, "When Jesus had finished giving his twelve disciples their instructions, he left that place and went to teach and preach in the neighboring towns."

3. Announcement of the kingdom's coming: 11:2–13:1 (narrative) concluding, "That same day Jesus went out and sat by the lake-side, where so many people gathered round him that he had to get into a boat."

3a. Matthew's chapter of parables follows: 13:2–53 concluding, "When he had finished these parables Jesus left that place, and came to his home town."

4. The disciples see wonders: 13:54–17:27 (no conclusion).

4a. This is followed by a discourse on discipleship and community order (18:1–19:1) concluding, "When Jesus had finished this discourse he left Galilee and came into the region of Judaea across Jordan. Great crowds followed him, and he healed them there."

5. Conflicts with Jewish authorities: 19:2–24:2 (no conclusion).

5a.   The final discourse (revised from Mark chapter 13) is apocalyptic, revealing the events to take place at the end of this world: 24:3–26:1, and it concludes, "When Jesus had finished this discourse he said to his disciples, 'You know that in two days' time it will be Passover, and the Son of Man is to be handed over for crucifixion.'" This serves as the introductory passage to the remainder of Matthew's Gospel: his version of the passion narrative.

Some scholars believe that by this fivefold organizational scheme Matthew intends his readers to think of the five books of the Torah. A few go so far as to believe Matthew intends his Gospel to be a new Torah. Most scholars, however, are content simply to acknowledge there are five discourses set apart by Matthew and to draw no conclusion from that fact. Most of Matthew's gospel, like Mark's central section especially, shows through its careful organization that Matthew is not intending to write an historical biography but, rather, an evangelical narrative: a Gospel.

In the following pages we will first survey a scholarly technique called redaction criticism helpful in analyzing Matthew. Then a useful tool called Gospel parallels will be introduced and used to analyze an important passage in the gospel. After that we will analyze several of Matthew's main themes.

Redaction criticism

The Two Document Hypothesis, discussed previously, is the most important single factor in twentieth-century study of the Gospels of Matthew and Luke. To summarize that hypothesis: both Matthew and Luke used two documents, as well as their own insights and oral tradition, to write their Gospels. One was a list of sayings attributed to Jesus now called the Q document, and the other was a short narrative now called the Gospel of Mark. This hypothesis, accepted by the majority of scholars today, is a valuable insight into the history of the New Testament. In addition, it allows the reconstruction of a Q source, which can then be considered (as in chapter 4) a separate element in the New Testament, one giving information about an early and influential variety of Christianity. The Two Document Hypothesis gave rise to the scholarly approach called redaction criticism. Redaction criticism (or redaction analysis) refers to analysis of the editorial work of New Testament authors.

Redaction analysis pinpoints changes that an author made in the sources he or she was using. If we know the source an author used and can see how the author changed the source in preparing the text, we can make intelligent guesses about why the author made those changes. We then have a window into the editorial perspective of the author; we know something about the author's motivation to make certain changes. This may sound trivial, but you will see it is not.

When we do have a source, an author's editing is easily seen. For example, the little Letter of Jude found toward the end of the New Testament seems to have been a source for the New Testament letter called 2 Peter. We can learn more about 2 Peter's author by comparing what he wrote with the Letter of Jude than by reading his letter alone; we see what he found important in what he expanded, what he found unimportant or inaccurate in what he left out, what some of his thoughts were by what he changed.

Redaction analysis presupposes the New Testament writers were creative authors rather than people who wrote down traditional material. This sounds obvious, and we have been taking it for granted throughout this textbook, but earlier in the twentieth century it was argued that the evangelists primarily transmitted traditional material without adding anything themselves. Luke's introductory paragraph (Luke 1:1–4) indicates he thought the "many writers" who preceded him had not done an adequate job. Hence, he tells us, he has decided to write an accurate account. Redaction analysis assumes that is true for all the evangelists; to convey what they thought was true they felt compelled to revise their sources.

Matthew revised Mark. We have the original of Mark in the New Testament, and the two can be compared easily. To compare Matthew's version of Mark 8:27–33 with the original, you flip pages back and forth from Matthew 16:13–23 to the passage in Mark. Nothing could be simpler ... Well, yes, something could be: a tool called Gospel Parallels.

Gospel parallels

In books of Gospel parallels the three synoptic Gospels are set either in columns side by side on the page, or they are set one under the other so that the eye may follow each across the page from left to right. Some students of the New Testament prefer the one, some the other method. The three-column method is probably most widely used. Every library should have a copy of *Gospel Parallels* by Burton H. Throckmorton, Jr. It is an essential tool for serious study and is something a novice will have no trouble using.

To begin consideration of the Gospel of Matthew, the following page contains two revised versions of Mark 8:27–33 and the original.

Read through them carefully, making note of every single change you can find.

Mark 8:27–29

Jesus and his disciples set out for the villages of Caesarea Philippi.

On the road he started questioning his disciples, asking them, "What are people saying about me?"

In response they said to him, "⟨Some say, 'You are⟩ John the Baptist,' and others 'Elijah,' but others 'One of the prophets.'"

But he continued to press them, "What about you, who do you say I am?"

Peter responds to him, "You are the Christ!"

Matt 16:13–16

When Jesus came to the region of Caesarea Philippi, he started questioning his disciples, asking, "What are people saying about the Son of Man?"

They said, "Some ⟨say, 'He is⟩ John the Baptist,' but others 'Elijah,' and others 'Jeremiah or one of the prophets.'"

He says to them, "What about you, who do you say I am?"

And Simon Peter responded, "You are the Christ, the son of the living God!"

Luke 9:18–22

And on one occasion when Jesus was praying alone the disciples were with him; and he questioned them asking: "What are the crowds saying about me?"

They said in response, "⟨Some say, 'You are⟩ John the Baptist,' while others ⟨say,⟩ 'Elijah,' and still others ⟨claim,⟩ 'One of the ancient prophets has come back to life.'"

Then he said to them, "What about you, who do you say I am?"

And Peter responded, "God's Christ!"

Mark 8:30–33

And he warned them not to tell anyone about him.

He started teaching them that the Son of Man was destined to suffer a great deal, and be rejected by the elders and the ranking priests and the scholars, and be killed, and after three days rise. And he would say this openly. And Peter took him aside and began to lecture him. But he turned, noticed his disciples, and reprimanded Peter verbally: "Get out of my sight, you Satan, you, because you're not thinking in God's terms, but in human terms."

Matt 16:17–23

And in response Jesus said to him, "You are to be congratulated, Simon son of Jonah, because flesh and blood did not reveal this to you but my Father who is in heaven. Let me tell you, you are Peter, 'the Rock,' and on this very rock I will build my congregation, and the gates of Hades will not be able to overpower it. I shall give you the keys of

Heaven's domain, and whatever you bind on earth will be considered bound in heaven, and whatever you release on earth will be considered released in heaven."

Then he ordered the disciples to tell no one that he was the Christ.

From that time on Jesus started to make it clear to his disciples that he was destined to go to Jerusalem, and suffer a great deal at the hands of the elders and ranking priests and scholars, and be killed and, on the third day, be raised.

And Peter took him aside and began to lecture him, saying, "May God spare you, master; this surely can't happen to you."

But he turned and said to Peter, "Get out of my sight, you Satan, you. You are dangerous to me because you are not thinking in God's terms, but in human terms."

Luke 9:21-22

Then he warned them, and forbade them to tell this to anyone, adding, "The Son of Man is destined to suffer a great deal, be rejected by the elders and ranking priests and scholars, and be killed and, on the third day, be raised."

Many observations could be made. Here are a few:

1. Luke does not mention the location of the event. It is characteristic of Luke to organize the travels of Jesus into a reasonably straight line from Galilee to Jerusalem, and he tends to omit location references conflicting with this pattern. Matthew makes the location slightly more vague, ("territory") rather than ("villages.")
2. Matthew tries to spell out passages he regards as ambiguous. For example, he changes "What are people saying about me?" to "What are people saying about the son of man?" and he goes on to add Jeremiah to the short list of prophets. Luke 9:7-8, probably influenced by Mark 6:14-15, adds that people believe Jesus was a prophet come back to life.
3. Both Matthew and Luke expand Peter's answer. Both are convinced that Peter's answer is absolutely correct. Here they differ from Mark where, although Peter replies with the correct term, he does not show correct understanding.
4. Matthew continues with a lengthy passage of substantial significance to the later development of the Christian church. On this passage the Catholic church bases its belief in the primacy of the pope (bishop of Rome). Since Matthew wants it clearly understood that Peter's answer is correct, his revision of Mark states both that God revealed Peter's answer to him and that Jesus awarded Peter authority on the basis of it.
5. Luke omits the section of Mark critical of Peter. Matthew revises it slightly by telling us what he believes Peter said to Jesus. In Mark, Jesus'

severe reaction implies that Peter repudiated Jesus' interpretation of the Son of Man. In Matthew we hear that Peter, as any friend would, hopes aloud that Jesus would not have to suffer. Further, in Matthew Jesus does not simply rebuke Peter and call him Satan; his version adds to Jesus' words the phrase "you are dangerous to me." Matthew retains the criticism of Peter found in Mark but softens it; Peter is wrong, but out of friendship rather than out of misunderstanding. Further, Peter has been highly praised in the preceding passage, and so Jesus' comments to him are made in a very different context than they are in Mark where they follow upon Mark 8:14–21, a passage declaring the disciples' utter ignorance.

Matthew as a redaction critic

This example of the use of Gospel parallels shows the kinds of judgments one can made regarding the evangelists' redactional work. Every passage in Mark was either omitted, expanded, condensed, or left unchanged by Matthew and Luke, and they had reasons for doing each of those things. Often their motivations for their revisions can be inferred. But not only modern scholars use redaction analysis. *Matthew and Luke were redaction critics.* They believed Mark had acted as an author, editing his sources and sometimes adding perspectives that were not always correct. Both, for example, disagreed with Mark's view of the disciples as failures. Luke in his way (largely by editing out what he thought excessive criticism) and Matthew in his way (by revising critical passages to make the disciples more admirable) sought to change Mark to make it acceptable to people who respected the disciples. Their understanding of Mark is not unlike that of scholars today; they believed Mark had access to some historically reliable information which he altered to suit his own perspective. Both Matthew and Luke sought to correct that perspective by revising Mark's Gospel. *Mark had done something similar;* through his Gospel he sought to correct the perspective of Jesus' disciples or their successors by criticizing what he believed to have been their understanding of Jesus and supplementing theirs with his own perspective on the suffering Son of Man.

It is unlikely Matthew knew much more about Jesus than we do. After all, his main source for Jesus' life, Mark, was a book with which he somewhat disagreed. He also used, and occasionally revised, a collection of Jesus' sayings we do not have but can reconstruct (the Q source). Finally, he had oral traditions, received from persons in his community, that he used to supplement his other two sources. Many people think the evangelists had immense amounts of knowledge about Jesus life' and teachings they never committed to writing. But it is likely they told us most of what they knew.

Special Matthew

You have had the opportunity to underline the Q material in Matthew. *Underline the material in Matthew which is neither in Q nor in Mark.* This material is called Special Matthew. He may have taken some of the parables in chapter 13 from a short written list, but most of Special Matthew is either composed by Matthew to express what he believed Jesus taught or is derived from Oral Tradition.

Matthew 1:1–2:23	Matthew 17:24–27
Matthew 3:14–15	Matthew 18:16–20
Matthew 4:13–16	Matthew 18:23–35
Matthew 5:5, 7–10	Matthew 19:10–12
Matthew 5:19–24	Matthew 20:1–16
Matthew 5:27–28	Matthew 21:10–11
Matthew 5:31, 33–38	Matthew 21:14–16
Matthew 6:1–8	Matthew 21:28–32
Matthew 6:16–18	Matthew 21:43
Matthew 7:6	Matthew 22:11–14
Matthew 7:28–29	Matthew 23:2–3, 5
Matthew 8:17	Matthew 23:8–11
Matthew 7:28	Matthew 23:15–22
Matthew 10:5–6	Matthew 23:28, 31
Matthew 11:28–30	Matthew 24:10–12, 14
Matthew 12:17–21	Matthew 25:1–13
Matthew 12:36–37	Matthew 25:31–46
Matthew 13:14–15	Matthew 26:52–54
Matthew 13:24–30	Matthew 27:3–10
Matthew 13:35–53	Matthew 27:19
Matthew 14:28–31	Matthew 27:24–25
Matthew 15:23–24	Matthew 27:52–53
Matthew 16:11–12	Matthew 27:62–66
Matthew 17:13	Matthew 28:2–5, 9–20

Notice that by underlining the Q material and Special Matthew you have isolated everything in Matthew he took from Mark: it is the material *not* underlined. *Read the Special Matthew passages carefully and identify the ideas that occur most frequently.*

The sermon on the mount

Probably the key passage for understanding Matthew is 5:17–20. It occurs in the Sermon on the Mount (5:1–7:29), which was composed by Matthew from sayings found in his three sources.

The Sermon on the Mount begins with a list of Beatitudes or blessings (5:1–12). Two passages of praise follow (5:13–16): "You are salt to the world, . . ." "You are light for all the world. . . ."

These statements introduce the main thesis (5:17–20), which is followed by extensive discussion of the implications of that thesis (5:21–7:20), and finally by a conclusion referring back to the main thesis (7:21–29). The main thesis is as follows:

"Do not suppose that I have come to abolish the Law and the prophets; I did not come to abolish, but to complete. I tell you this: so long as heaven and earth endure, not a letter, not a stroke, will disappear from the Law until all that must happen has happened. If any man therefore sets aside even the least of the Law's demands, and teaches others to do the same, he will have the lowest place in the kingdom of Heaven; whereas anyone who keeps the Law, and teaches others to do so, will stand high in the kingdom of Heaven. I tell you, unless you show yourselves far better men than the Pharisees and the doctors of the Law, you can never enter the kingdom of Heaven."

Matthew certainly must have thought of himself as one who attempted to keep the Law and to teach others to do so, for he believes Jesus came to complete the Law and the prophets and that the Torah Law remains completely in force as long as heaven and earth endure. We will discuss Matthew's understanding of "completing the prophets" shortly. By "completing the Law" Matthew means Jesus came to give directions for behavior in accord with God's Law, so that anyone with sufficient dedication may follow the Law successfully.

Accordingly, the main thesis for Matthew's gospel is probably also the main thesis for the Sermon on the Mount: that Jesus came, in fulfillment of prophecy, in order to defend and interpret the Law of Moses. Matthew writes from in a situation of conflict both with Christians and Pharisees. Some Christians, he believes did not seek properly to follow Torah but, rather, ignored some or all of it substituting faith and supernatural powers for obedience. Pharisees generally, he believes, taught properly about Torah but failed to follow through on their teachings. Matthew had, therefore, both rivals who were Christian and rivals who were Pharisees.

Matthew's Christian rivals

Matthew's Christian rivals evidently have led people to believe Jesus came to abolish the Law and the prophets. In accordance with that teaching, they tend to relax some commandments. Oddly enough, Matthew, despite his profound disagreement with them, still believes they have a place, however low, in the Kingdom of Heaven. Who were Matthew's rivals? Paul is a name that should spring to mind. It was Paul, after all, who wrote in Galatians,

"No man is ever justified by doing what the law demands" (2:16), "Christ bought us freedom from the curse of the law" (3:13), and other similar things. Matthew may have had Paul in mind, but there is no way we can be sure he did. We do know for certain that he had Mark in mind. In Mark's Gospel we find the short but important sentence whereby Jesus cancels the Law regarding pure and impure foods: "Thus he made all foods clean" (Mark 7:19). Mark's Gospel teaches that Jesus came to abolish at least that portion of the Law. Matthew, however, would never claim Jesus "made all foods clean"; he omits the passage in his revision of Mark. Presumably Matthew, acting as a redaction analyst, regarded this as Mark's teaching, not Jesus'.

Matthew may concede that the faith in Jesus Christ of people such as Paul and Mark allows them to enter a low place in the Kingdom of Heaven, but he does not believe anyone who would cancel any or all of the Law could have understood Jesus correctly. The fulfillment or completion of the Law is the opposite of its abolition or reduction. Matthew is the Torah Law's defender, and he informs us Jesus was the Law's defender too.

Matthew's Jewish rivals

Matthew is also in conflict with the Pharisees, a rather bitter conflict, judging from the vehement language he uses in 23:1–39.

Reread 23:1–39 now.

Matthew quotes Jesus calling the Pharisees hypocrites, blind guides, snakes, viper's brood. But the first thing you read is crucial, "The doctors of the Law and the Pharisees sit in the chair of Moses; therefore *do what they tell you*; pay attention to their words" (23:2).

Matthew thought of Jesus as one who came to complete the Law and who gave, after his resurrection, the instruction to his disciples to teach all people "to observe all that I have commanded you" (28:20). Thus in 23:2 he portrays the Pharisees as similar in one respect to Jesus. Matthew urges his audience to be obedient both to the Pharisees and to Jesus. How can such commendation of the Pharisees coexist with condemnation of them?

The key term is *hypocrite,* and it is found fifteen times in Matthew but only five times in the rest of the New Testament, a fact easily learned from a concordance. The word *hypocrite* is the Greek word for actor and, by extension, anyone who pretends to be someone or something he or she is not. Matthew, on the one hand, agrees with the Law as understood by the Pharisees who "sit in the chair of Moses." On the other hand, he does not believe they keep the Law fully. That is why they are hypocrites; they teach others but do not follow their own teaching. They are more concerned with appearing pious than they are with true piety. Or so Matthew believed.

Matthew does not criticize the teaching of Jewish legal authorities, only their performance. Only through guidance from Jesus the Messiah, Matthew believes, could these leaders fulfill their own ideals. Jesus is not portrayed as opposing the Pharisees' theories, but as trying to assist them in attaining a shared goal, the fulfillment of God's Law. The Pharisees, on the other hand, are depicted as opposing Jesus during his lifetime and eventually bringing about his death. From Matthew's point of view they are more intent on maintaining their hypocrisy than on supporting God's Messiah.

How then, should people seek to fulfill God's Law? How should people live to ensure they are "far better men than the Pharisees and the doctors of the Law" (5:20)? The next two portions of the Sermon on the Mount provide some answers.

The antitheses

The first of these sections (5:21–48) is called the antitheses because in six consecutive passages Jesus quotes the Torah and then, seemingly, alters it: "You have learned that they were told . . . But what I tell you is this. . . ." The first clause quotes Torah ("told" to Moses and the Jewish people at Mount Sinai); the passages following seem to be new Law from Jesus.

Reread 5:21–6:18 now.

The meaning of the antitheses is still debated among scholars. Do they cancel Torah, add to Torah, show that Matthew felt Jesus was a new Moses, or that Matthew regarded Jesus as a divine Lawgiver? "You have learned that our forefathers were told, 'Do not commit murder; anyone who commits murder must be brought to judgment.' But what I tell you is this: Anyone who nurses anger against his brother must be brought to judgment. If he abuses his brother he must answer for it to the court; if he sneers at him he will have to answer for it in the fires of hell" (5:21–22). It is impossible never to be angry. If anger is equivalent to murder, then righteousness through obedience is impossible. Perhaps Matthew intends, therefore, to support Paul's contention that righteousness cannot come by Law. Perhaps Matthew seeks to show there is a higher Law than Torah and Jesus came to reveal it for the few people who can keep it. The possibilities are many.

To put the problem in context is perhaps to find an answer. Matthew quotes Jesus as saying, "I tell you, unless you show yourselves to be far better men than the Pharisees and the doctors of the Law, you can never enter the kingdom of Heaven" (5:20). We can assume Matthew does not wish to argue with the theories of Law taught by the Pharisees who "sit in the chair of Moses" and so Christians should "do what they tell you;" he only wishes Christians to follow the Law more thoroughly than the Pharisees do. A Pharisaic theory of Law may help clarify the antitheses.

The antitheses as a hedge

Rabbinic Judaism evolved from Pharisaic Judaism and taught it was wise to establish a "hedge around the Torah." This phrase derives from imagery of a garden. Suppose a Law exists forbidding one to eat the fruit of a certain tree. It would be possible to live in the garden and not eat that fruit, but temptations might arise if the tree were always right nearby and always easy to reach. Suppose a gardener, determined not to eat that fruit, plants a thick hedge, bush by bush, all around the tree to wall himself away from it so that, even to come near the tree, he would have to push and hack his way through the hedge. Once the gardener plants the hedge he has decreased the possibility of eating the forbidden fruit; he is no longer anywhere near it. He has made a hedge he chooses not to cross. But if he crosses it, he has not broken the Law he is determined not to break. Rather, he has broken through a hedge he created.

This is, essentially, what the hedge around the Torah means. Regulations are established by Jewish teachers, Pharisees, and later, rabbis, to ensure that none of the laws of God, the Torah, are broken. One well-known example is the rules of kosher. The Torah Law not to be broken is "Do not boil a baby goat in its mother's milk." Regulations came into being to hedge that Law. Do not boil the meat of any baby goat in the milk of any mother goat. Do not boil the meat of any animal in the milk of any animal. Do not cook milk and meat together in any way. Do not mix milk and meat in any way. Today many Jewish families have separate dishes, separate sinks, and separate refrigerators for milk and meat. Their likelihood of breaking the Law approaches zero. These kosher practices developed after the time of the New Testament, but the theory of a "hedge around the Torah" was present then.

Mark 7:9–12 gives an example of the controversy caused by the hedge around the Torah. Here Jesus is said to argue, rather technically, that the donation of all of one's property to the temple (that is, corban) might mean one's mother and father would be penniless, for they would have no legal access to that property. This is said to contradict the commandment "Honor your father and mother." Here a technicality of Law, part of a hedge, is condemned on the basis that the Torah Law always should come first. Another such passage is from Q and can be found in Matthew 23:23–24. Here the Pharisees are accused of focusing so much on the hedge they have created that they have more concern for tithing mint and dill and cumin than they have for Torah Law requiring justice, mercy, and good faith.

In both instances the Torah is upheld by Jesus in cases where conflict occurs between it and the traditions (or hedges) created to enforce it. Jesus argues with Pharisees but often does so in a manner agreeable to Pharisees, for the primacy of the written Torah over oral tradition was a commonly accepted principle in Pharisaic circles.

Arguments between Pharisees are the essence of the Pharisaic method of determining truth. To put it more formally, the Pharisees believed that only through dialogue and the exchange of considered opinion could truth be found. The early and important Oral Law text known as the Mishnah was written after the time of Jesus, but it probably represents the style of legal argumentation of his time. It primarily consists of arguments between one legal authority and another. When Jesus argues Law with the Pharisees, he is not contradicting their entire approach to Law. Rather, he is acting as a Pharisee would act. The principles he invokes in his arguments, such as the primacy of the Torah, are principles most Pharisees would accept.

If we look at the antitheses found in Matthew's Sermon on the Mount and regard them as hedges around the Torah, we have an approach showing Jesus neither "abolishing the Law" nor that he "set aside even the least of the Law's demands." Suppose the statements of Jesus introduced by "But what I tell you is this" mean "But I tell you also to work earnestly to do this," where *this* refers to regulations constituting a hedge around the Torah passage quoted. The antitheses would then mean:

1. If you earnestly strive never to be angry you will surely never commit murder.
2. If you earnestly strive never to look lustfully you will surely never commit adultery.
3. If you do not get divorced at all (except in cases of adultery) you will certainly not break any of the Law regarding divorce.
4. If you do not swear any oaths at all it will be impossible for you to break your oath.
5. If you do not seek revenge, ever, you will not ever try to get more revenge than the Law allows. (Incidentally, the Law does not require an eye for an eye but sets that as the maximum revenge allowed. The Pharisees would not demand that a person willing to be merciful to one who blinded him should be compelled to take the eye of his adversary.)
6. If you work hard to love everyone, even your enemies, you will be far more able to love your neighbor.

One passage does not fit this theory of the hedge: "love your enemies" is the opposite of "hate your enemies," not a way of fulfilling that demand. But "hate your enemies" is not in the Torah at all, nor is it in the books of the prophets. The explicit command "hate your enemies" is found nowhere in the authoritative writings of the Jewish religion. Whether Matthew mistakenly believes this is a commandment of Torah, or whether he finds it implied in the Hebrew Scriptures (for instance, in Joshua) and seeks to cancel it out, is unclear. But it is significant that only in this non-Torah passage do the sayings of Jesus contradict a quoted passage rather than establish a hedge around it.

The concept of hedge means the demands of Jesus can be both impossible and reasonable. The demands are not "never be angry, never look lustfully, never swear," as though these were new Law, but "never be angry, never look lustfully, never swear," as something to strive for (without hope of complete success) in order not to break the old Law. They are impossible as Law; they are reasonable as approaches to Law. When they are overstated, for example, "If one sneers at one's brother one will answer for it in the fires of hell," they should be seen as literary devices, not as statements of facts; such statements have never been regarded as facts by the later Christian church.

There is no way of knowing for certain if Jesus himself created the antitheses. Some scholars believe he did, arguing that only a man who believed he came from God could directly alter the commands of Torah. But others believe the antitheses were created by Matthew, and this is probably the more reasonable approach. For one thing, from the perspective that the antitheses are a hedge, they do not alter the Torah at all. Furthermore, the antitheses are unique in the New Testament. No other book or letter mentions anything like them, although many of the sayings of Jesus included in the antitheses are found elsewhere. The Gospel of Thomas also contains no antitheses. It is likely that Matthew, confronted with the need to understand and explain traditional sayings of Jesus to his audience, put them in the context they have in his Gospel and that it was Matthew who sought to instruct his readers how to achieve righteousness greater than that of the Pharisees through the creation of a hedge. While many of the sayings may be Jesus', their context, and therefore the interpretation we find of them in Matthew's Gospel, is Matthew's creation.

To avoid hypocrisy

Following the antitheses come three passages written with the Pharisees in mind. Like the antitheses they tend to take a principle to an extreme, in this case advocating the avoidance of self-promotion by performing religious activities in complete secrecy. Pharisees, in Matthew's opinion, are hypocrites more interested in making a good show and impressing people with their righteousness than in being obedient and attaining righteousness. Christians should avoid this tendency, and one way to avoid it is to withdraw one's religious activities from the public arena altogether. If one performs one's religious obligations in private they are just as valid as if performed publicly, but they do not win the admiration of the crowd. From

Matthew 6:1 to 6:18 instructions are given for how to do an act of charity, how to pray and how to fast: do these things in secret, quietly, out of the public eye. This will cut down the temptation to do such acts for the purpose of public approval and thus lead one away from hypocrisy.

These, like the antitheses, are probably constructions by Matthew based on sayings of Jesus. Matthew's interpretation of sayings, his redaction of them, is his own, even if many of the included sayings are from Jesus himself. These passages have a perspective similar to that of the antitheses if we assume they are not intended always to be obeyed literally; should one strive earnestly to perform religious activity in secret one may fail on occasion, but one will almost certainly not be guilty of behaving religiously in a flamboyant and hypocritical manner.

Christian obedience

The Sermon on the Mount concludes with 7:21–29, where Jesus insists that calling him Lord but failing to do what he commands is insufficient. This could be a comment regarding Christians who might declare that faith in Jesus as Lord is sufficient and obedience is thereby made unnecessary. From Matthew's perspective obedience is crucial.

Matthew believes that faith not accompanied by obedience will lead to disaster; even the ability to do miracles (which in the first century was thought often to accompany faith) does not validate faith without obedience to Law. Some Christians may say, "Lord, Lord, did we not prophesy in your name, cast out devils in your name, and in your name perform many miracles?" but if they are not obedient, Matthew believes Jesus will say to such people, "I never knew you; out of my sight you and your wicked ways" (7:22–23). Remember, this is directed toward people who call Jesus Lord. As Matthew's early and key passage in the Sermon on the Mount begins with criticism of Christians who believe Jesus came to abolish Law or to set aside some of the Law's demands, so the Sermon on the Mount ends with the repudiation of Christians who, while calling Jesus Lord and doing miracles in his name, do not obey Torah Law as Jesus interprets that Law.

To fulfill the prophets

More frequently than the other evangelists, but in the same manner, Matthew shows Jesus doing things various prophets of the Hebrew Scriptures supposedly predicted the Messiah would do. The logic of this approach is as follows: God, through the prophets, declared what the Messiah would do. Jesus was the Messiah. Jesus, therefore, did those things. Anyone wishing to know what Jesus did can refer to the prophets to find out, and anyone wishing to know why certain things happened in Jesus' life can safely presume they happened because the prophets declared they would happen. The predictions of the prophets, therefore, are fulfilled when Jesus does what they predicted the Messiah would do.

Matthew used the prophets in two ways in his Gospel. First, Matthew evidently used the writings of the prophets as a biographical source for Jesus. If, for example, a prophet declared, "I called my son out of Egypt" (Hosea 11:1) and this is assumed to refer to the Messiah, then Jesus must at some point have come out of Egypt. Matthew, therefore, writes an account of a childhood journey to Egypt from which Jesus returns in order to "fulfil what the Lord had declared through the prophet" (Matt 2:15). Second, the prophets can explain why Jesus acted as he did. For example, in order to explain why Jesus taught in parables Matthew writes, "That is why I speak to them in parables; for they look without seeing, and listen without hearing or understanding. There is a prophecy of Isaiah which is being fulfilled for them: 'You may hear and hear, but you will never understand; you may look and look, but you will never see. For this people's mind has become gross; their ears are dulled, and their eyes are closed. Otherwise, their eyes might see, their ears hear, and their mind understand, and then they might turn again, and I would heal them'" (Matt 13:13–15, referring to Isaiah 6:9–10). Matthew here revises Mark. Matthew is understandably disturbed by Mark's statement that Scripture (in Isaiah 6:9–10) anticipated that the parables deliberately would be designed to keep people from turning to God and being forgiven (Mark 4:12). Thus Matthew turned back to the original source (always a commendable idea) and discovered it does not say what Mark believed it did. In Isaiah 6:9–10 the people are to blame for their lack of comprehension; they are not deliberately being kept from comprehending. Accordingly, Matthew changed the meaning of the passage in Mark and quoted the Isaiah passage at greater length. The idea that Scripture or prophecy provides a key to understanding the activities of Jesus the Messiah is common to Mark and Matthew, but their interpretation of those activities is not the same. Therefore, their use of Scripture (even the same passage) to back up their interpretations differs.

Isaiah and the virgin birth

Let us examine the first prophecy Matthew declares that Jesus fulfilled. In the Gospel an angel of the Lord appears to Joseph in a dream and says, "'Joseph son of David . . . do not be afraid to take Mary home with you as your wife. It is by the Holy Spirit that she has conceived this child. She will bear a son; and you shall give him the name Jesus (Saviour), for he will save his people from their sins.' All this happened in order to fulfil what the Lord declared through the prophet: 'The virgin will conceive and bear a son, and he shall be called Emmanuel,' a name which means 'God is with us'" (Matt 1:20–23).

Matthew has quoted Isaiah 7:14. Isaiah's prophecy is as follows: "The Lord himself shall give you a sign: A young woman is with child, and she will bear a son, and will call him Emmanuel. By the time that he has learnt to reject evil and choose good, he will be eating curds and honey; before the child has learnt to reject evil and choose good, desolation will come upon the land before whose two kings you cower now'" (7:14–16). Some historical background is necessary to understand this.

Prophets in the Hebrew Scriptures do not often predict events in the distant future. Most commonly they interpret contemporary political events theologically, and they offer theologically supported political advice. In the passage quoted above, Isaiah is speaking to King Ahaz of Judah in the year 734 B.C.E.

Since the end of the reign of King Solomon (922 B.C.E.), two states have existed in the region of Palestine: Israel to the north and Judah to the south. Often they have gone to war against each other; sometimes they have made alliances against greater powers threatening them. In 734 B.C.E. Judah's King Ahaz is refusing to join an alliance of small states, including Syria and Israel, against the powerful Assyrian Empire. The alliance intends to go to war against Judah to force it to join; King Ahaz intends to call upon the Assyrian Empire for military assistance against the alliance. It is in this context that Isaiah speaks to Ahaz, urging him not to declare his kingdom an ally of the Assyrians.

The child is a sign, a symbol, for a period of time. The time between birth and moral maturity (when the child will have learned to reject evil and choose good) was considered to be twelve or thirteen years. Isaiah predicts that before that time desolation will come to the lands of Israel and Syria, due to Assyrian invasion. In about twelve or thirteen years the child will "eat curds and honey," the food of people living on a subsistence level, symbolically indicating that Ahaz's kingdom of Judah will be considerably weakened. The predicted events did occur. Ahaz, against Isaiah's advice, allied Judah with Assyria. Assyria swept through the kingdoms of Syria and Israel in 734 B.C.E., defeating them completely. The kingdom of Judah, although not devastated, was reduced in power and prestige to the level of a vassal state to Assyria.

This prophecy apparently has little to do with the birth of Jesus of Nazareth to the virgin Mary. In fact the word *virgin,* the key term in Matthew's use of the prophecy, does not occur in the Hebrew prophecy at all. Matthew, however, is not using the Hebrew version of Isaiah but a Greek translation known as the Septuagint, where the word *virgin* does appear. To understand the discrepancy, we must trace the translation of

Isaiah's passage into Greek. In Isaiah 7:14, the Hebrew word for a young woman, *almah,* is used. If virginity had been specified, the Hebrew term used would have been *bethulah.* In Greek the term for virgin is *parthenos,* and the term for young woman is *neanis.* Greek translations of Isaiah 7:14 frequently use the word *neanis,* but one translation, the Septuagint, instead uses *parthenos.* Matthew, therefore, read Isaiah in that translation, discovered that "the virgin will bear a child," presumed this referred to Jesus, and entered the passage in his Gospel as a prophecy of which the virgin birth of Jesus is the fulfillment. The origin of the story of the virgin birth may be due to this action on Matthew's part, for he did use the writings of the prophets as a biographical source. It is more likely, however, that Matthew received the account of the virgin birth from tradition and wanted to show that Jesus fulfilled a prophecy in the manner of his birth.

In paying no attention to the historical context of prophecies, Matthew and the other New Testament writers followed the practice of other Jewish interpreters of that time. They presumed the prophets spoke God's words to all people and not to any particular person. Therefore, prophets' words are as applicable in the present as they were when first delivered. The question then is not what a prophet's words meant at a particular time in the past but what they can be understood to mean in the present. If one believes that the prophets primarily spoke of a Messiah to come in the future (which, actually, they very rarely did), and Jesus was the Messiah (as the evangelists believed), it stands to reason that most passages in the prophets are open to interpretation as references to Jesus even if, in their own context, they have nothing to do with Jesus or the Messiah.

The belief that Jesus fulfilled the prophets is not based on reading the prophets and discovering they refer to Jesus. It is based on the belief that Jesus is the Messiah and then reading the prophets with the understanding that they must be referring to him.

Jesus the Messiah

Matthew understands the prophets to be foretelling the coming of the Messiah. Jesus, for him, is the Messiah. Therefore the Messiah, Jesus, is the Son of David (and Matthew supplies a genealogy to demonstrate he is) and the Son of God. Mark's difficulties with the term *Son of David* are not shared by Matthew.

Jesus the Messiah is still present in the church, according to Matthew. He promises to remain with his people until the end of time (28:20) and declares, "Where two or three have met together in my name, I am there among them" (18:20). This saying emphasizes community. The Spirit in other parts of the New Testament is said to come to individuals, but, in this text, Jesus is said to come to people who have met together, not to isolated individuals. To Matthew, therefore, Jesus is more than a historical figure who came to fulfill the Law and the prophets. Having been raised from the dead he continues to be present in his community, and the community should act accordingly.

Topics

Sources

Matthew used Mark as his primary source for Jesus' life and death, even though he disagreed with elements of Mark's interpretation. The only substantial portions of Jesus' life for which Mark was not his source are Jesus' birth and his appearance to the disciples after his resurrection.

Matthew's Gospel contains many sayings of Jesus absent in Mark's Gospel. He took the majority of them from the Q source and modified them in accordance with his own point of view.

Many of the sayings classified as Special Matthew come from oral tradition. Other sayings, usually interpretive, were composed by Matthew. Finally, the books of the prophets found in the Hebrew Scriptures constitute a kind of source for Matthew, for in some instances he seems to have thought they revealed biographical data; the story of Jesus' family's exile to Egypt and return is one example.

Jesus

Jesus' life is important to Matthew. He believes that Jesus was both a miracle worker and a teacher. Jesus' miracles functioned as evidence for the truth of his teachings, and they were validated by the positive response of multitudes of common Jewish people. The Pharisees and other Jewish leaders were supposedly too concerned with maintaining their own status to support Jesus. Matthew believes Jesus' teaching activities were extremely important, hence his addition of Q sayings and the sayings called Special Matthew to Mark's basic Gospel narrative.

Jesus was the Christ, the Messiah of God, for whom Matthew also uses the terms Son of God and Son of Man. There is no clear evidence that Matthew believes these terms to be anything other than synonyms. The main goal of Jesus the Messiah during his life was to teach proper obedience to God's Law and to ensure (through his interpretation of the Law) that both Jews and Gentiles would be able to win God's approval by acting more righteously than the Pharisees.

Matthew does not see *Jesus' death* and his suffering as the key events in his life, as do Mark and Paul. Matthew expands Mark's section on Jesus' life but not Mark's interpretation of Jesus' death. He agrees with Mark that the Son of Man was destined to suffer and die and rise, and he agrees that

God ordained those events. But in his Gospel these are not the central motifs.

Matthew is more prone to blame Jesus' enemies for Jesus' death and use it as an example of the hardness of the Pharisees' hypocritical hearts than he is to regard it as an element in God's mysterious plán. In Mark some of those who contribute to Jesus' death are praised as persons who understand the necessary death of the Son of Man; in Matthew those who contribute to his death do so because they reject him. While Mark has the centurion declare Jesus a Son of God "because of the way he died," in Matthew that declaration comes from the centurion's subordinate troops as well as the centurion himself, and it is based, not on the way he died, but on the awe-inspiring, miraculous events accompanying his death: "There was an earthquake, the rocks split and the graves opened, and many of God's saints were raised from sleep; and coming out of their graves after his resurrection they entered the Holy City were many saw them" (27:52–53). For Matthew the miracles of Jesus and the amazing events at his death convince the doubtful he was Son of God.

Eschatology

Matthew believes this world will soon come to an end and be replaced by the Kingdom of God. Here he basically agrees with the other authors we have studied. His concern with the church and the eventual creation of a community from "all nations" indicates he does not expect the end to come immediately. Matthew is convinced that when Jesus the Son of Man returns he will judge all people, those within the church as well as outside; "the sheep will be separated from the goats," and the goats will be thrown into the place of wailing and gnashing of teeth.

A reading of Special Matthew reveals that Matthew frequently adds to his sources references about the place of wailing and gnashing of teeth. In Mark, imagery of hell is present only once, in 9:43–48. Luke deletes that passage; Matthew uses it twice (5:29–30, 18:8–9). Q contains no mention of hell (nor does the Gospel of Thomas). Neither John nor Paul believed in hell; the idea is absent in their writings. Were it not for the work of Matthew it is questionable whether a belief in hell would have become a doctrine of the Christian Churches.

Torah Law

In Matthew's opinion Jesus came to complete the Law and to assist all people in following it. To be a Christian, he believes, is to follow the Law of Moses while accepting the interpretations of Pharisaic Judaism guided by the interpretation brought from God by the Messiah Jesus. The Law for Jews and for Gentiles is identical.

Community

The people of Matthew's community considered themselves Jewish, although many or most of them may formerly have been Gentiles. In the fourth discourse section of the Gospel some rules and procedures for community discipline are outlined, but in Matthew the church is not a bureaucratic entity nor does it have a tightly controlled structure. Still, the church in Matthew is more structured than the communities evident in Q, Paul, and Mark. Significantly, the only place in the Gospels where the Greek word for "church" occurs is in the Gospel of Matthew.

Matthew's Gospel is evidence for a later stage in the evolution of the Christian movement from wandering itinerant preachers to self-contained and organized churches. His revision of the Beatitudes found in Q, to which he added several, tells us something about the social background of his community. Matthew's version of the Beatitudes is probably further from the original than is Luke's version. We know this for three reasons. First, Matthew seems to have rewritten Mark somewhat more extensively than did Luke, and so he probably also did more rewriting of Q. Second, the version of the Beatitudes in Luke corresponds to the social situation of most of the Q sayings wherein people are impoverished and worried about their daily bread. Third, the version of Beatitudes in Luke is similar to the version in the independent source, the Gospel of Thomas. Matthew's versions are not present in Thomas. We can therefore safely assume that Matthew made changes in order to make the Beatitudes relevant to the people for whom he was writing, the people of his community. The parallels with Luke are these:

Luke 6:20	How blest are you who are in need (i.e. the poor); the kingdom of God is yours
Matt 5:3	How blest are these who know their need of God; the kingdom of Heaven is theirs
Luke 6:21	How blest are you who now go hungry; your hunger shall be satisfied
Matt 5:6	How blest are those who hunger and thirst to see right prevail; they shall be satisfied
Luke 6:21	How blest are you who weep now; you shall laugh
Matt 5:4	How blest are the sorrowful; they shall find consolation"
Luke 6:22	How blest are you when men hate you, when they outlaw you and insult you, and ban your very name as infamous, because of the Son of Man
Matt 5:11	How blest you are, when you suffer insults and persecution and every kind of calumny for my sake

Matthew makes systematic changes. References to those in need and those who weep are, in Q, directed to poor, hungry, and unhappy people of the lower economic class. Matthew's references can be applied to any person regardless of class. The poverty of those financially in need is transformed to the need to know God, or poverty of Spirit. Hunger for food becomes hunger and thirst for righteousness. Weeping is transformed to sorrowing or mourning, more moderate expressions of emotion. Matthew leaves out the clause about hate in the final beatitude. Evidently he addresses an audience of people who are not poor or hungry, who do not often find themselves weeping, who do not wish to believe themselves hated. Matthew also adds to the Q list of beatitudes several others, all applicable to people who are not poor. This indicates Matthew was addressing people of what today would be called the middle-class.

Controversy

Matthew's chapter 23 and other passages in his Gospel prove animosity existed between Matthew (and, presumably, other members of his community) and the Pharisees who were leaders of the Jewish synagogues of his day. He regards them as hypocrites in the performance of the Law but respects them as authorities in the teaching of the Law.

Matthew is also in conflict with other Christians, some of whom apparently taught that Jesus came to abolish the Torah or at least to reduce the number of Torah commandments. These people, he claims, have the lowest place in the Kingdom of Heaven. Some Christians known to Matthew held the view that, although Jesus is Lord, they do not need to obey his interpretation of the commands of the Torah; that view is thought by Matthew to be so inadequate that Jesus upon his return will repudiate such people completely despite their ability to do signs and wonders (Matt 7:23).

Interactions

Miracles sources

Matthew, unlike Mark, believes faith based on the evidence of Jesus' miracles is not misleading. In this he is closer to the point of view contained in Mark's miracles sources than he is to Mark. He probably does not know many more miracles than those in Mark (and the one in Q), for if he had known others he surely would have used them. Significantly, while Matthew feels free to modify the stories he receives from tradition, he does not feel free to invent new stories.

Matthew often reduces the miracle stories in length, while at the same time heightening the miraculous elements in them. In Mark 10:46 Jesus brings sight to one blind man; in Matthew's version of that passage (Matt 20:29), he brings sight to two blind men. In Mark 5:23 the daughter of

Jairus is close to death when Jesus revives her; in Matthew's version (matt.
9:18), she is dead and Jesus raises her from the dead. Matthew adds accounts of an earthquake and the resurrection of many dead saints to Mark's
story of Jesus' death and attributes the proclamation of the centurion (and
his soldiers) to those astonishing events.

All of this indicates Matthew believes Jesus' miracles provide reliable
evidence that he is the Christ and that people who believe on the basis of
miracles are correct. He would, of course, insist that such belief is inadequate if it is not accompanied by obedience. Matthew knows of people
whom he does not believe to be obedient to Jesus' teachings but who do
prophesy in Jesus' name, who do cast out devils in Jesus' name, and who do
call upon Jesus as Lord (7:23). He does not approve of them, for obedience
takes precedence over miraculous power. Jesus for him is the perfect example of a miracle worker absolutely obedient to the will of God; Christian
miracle workers who are not obedient will be repudiated by Jesus.

The Q source

Matthew uses Q extensively and he generally agrees with its perspectives.
Matthew (and also Luke) respect the disciples of Jesus and use the Q source
to supplement the reports of Jesus' teaching found in Mark. This indicates
that, from their perspective at least, sayings from the Q source were the sort
of things taught by Jesus' disciples.

Both the thesis statement and the concluding passage of the Sermon on
the Mount (Matt 5:17 and 7:21–27) are derived from Q. Although not
addressing people who are from the same social strata as the Q people,
Matthew's perspective on obedience and judgment is more like that of Q
than is that of any other evangelist. Matthew supplements several Q passages with conclusions saying that Jesus judges the good and the wicked
both within and outside the church. This does not contradict Q, for it is
difficult to believe the people of the Q community would have insisted that
Jesus would not judge all people. Matthew is emphatic about the need to
obey Torah, whereas Q takes the necessity for obedience for granted; this
may not reflect a difference of opinion but differences between the communities the texts addressed. Q was directed toward Jews who would assume
obedience to Torah to be required; Matthew's Gospel seems directed
mainly toward Gentiles converted to Judaism who would not necessarily
take the need for obedience for granted. Matthew's relatively well-to-do
community contrasts with the people revealed in the Q sayings. While
Christianity may have originated as a movement among the very poor, it
soon spread, and as it spread it appealed increasingly to more wealthy
individuals, some of whom, evidently, were the intended audience for
Matthew's Gospel.

Paul

Matthew cannot be proven to have known Paul's teachings. He possibly has Paul, or Paul's followers, in mind when he writes, "If any man therefore sets aside even the least of the Law's demands, and teaches others to do the same, he will have the lowest place in the kingdom of Heaven." More probably he was thinking of Mark, whose Gospel he had in front of him as he wrote. If Matthew had known of Paul's teachings about the Law, he would have profoundly disagreed with them. Matthew upholds Torah obedience for Gentiles, unlike Paul, who believes not only that it is unnecessary, but that it contradicts the spirit of the gospel.

Mark

Matthew both knows and uses the Gospel of Mark. In several respects he disagrees with Mark; we know this by comparing the original Mark with Matthew's revision of it. Matthew respects the disciples and regards them as authoritative teachers. While they may have had trouble understanding Jesus at various points, he believes that in the long run they came to understand and were commissioned by the risen Christ to be his apostles. Matthew does not believe faith based on the evidence of miracles is misleading; he encourages such faith. He believes that all of the Torah, including the Laws respecting clean and unclean foods, is in force. He does not focus on the suffering and death of the Son of Man as the main point of Jesus' life, but he does not deny its importance as evidence that Jesus would obey God regardless of consequences.

Bibliography

Betz, Hans Dieter. *Essays on the Sermon on the Mount.* Philadelphia: Fortress Press, 1984.

Bornkamm, G., G. Barth, and H. Held. *Tradition and Interpretation in Matthew.* Philadelphia: Westminster Press, 1963.

Crossan, John Dominic. *In Parables: The Challenge of the Historical Jesus.* Sonoma, CA: Polebridge Press, 1992.

Davies, W. D. *The Setting of the Sermon on the Mount.* New York: Cambridge University Press, 1964.

Funk, Robert, ed. *New Gospel Parallels,* 2 vols. Philadelphia: Fortress Press, 1985–86. (available from Polebridge Press)

Gardner, Richard B. *Matthew.* Scottsdale, Pennsylvania: Herald Press, 1991.

Kingsbury, Jack Dean. *Matthew.* Proclamation Commentaries. Minneapolis: Fortress Press, 1988.

Jeremias, Joachim. *The Parables of Jesus*. London: SCM Press, 1954.

Meier, J. P. *Matthew*. Wilmington: Glazier, 1983.

Stanton, G. N. *The Interpretation of Matthew*. Philadelphia: Fortress Press, 1974.

Thompson, William G, *Matthew's Story: Good News for Uncertain Times*. Mahwah: Paulist Press, 1989.

Throckmorton, B. H., ed. *Gospel Parallels*. Nashville: Thomas Nelson Publishers, 1979.

Seven

The Gospel of Luke
and the Acts of the Apostles

The Growth of the New Testament

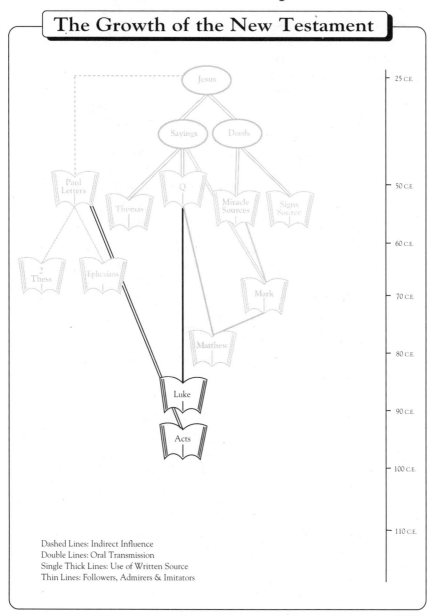

Dashed Lines: Indirect Influence
Double Lines: Oral Transmission
Single Thick Lines: Use of Written Source
Thin Lines: Followers, Admirers & Imitators

More than 25 percent of the New Testament was written by the author known as Luke. His two books, the Gospel of Luke and the Acts of the Apostles, are one book divided into two sections. The first section tells the story of Jesus' life up to the time of the resurrection. The second section begins with Jesus' ascension, continues through the period of the early church in Jerusalem and the spread of Christianity through the empire, and concludes with Paul's mission to Rome. The books are optimistic in tone; although their principal characters are subject to persecution, they ultimately triumph. The books conclude with Paul in Rome "proclaiming the kingdom of God and teaching the facts about the Lord Jesus Christ quite openly and without hindrance" (Acts 28:30–31). *Read the Gospel of Luke and underline the references made in stories and sayings to women and to people of evident wealth.* Luke's Gospel is unique in the extent of its concern for women and wealthy people, and later in this chapter many of the passages you will have underlined will be the subject of discussion.

Author, date, and place of origin

We know no more about the identity of the author of these books than we do about the authors of the Gospels of Mark and Matthew. Legend has it Luke was "the beloved physician" who accompanied Paul during some of his journeys. However, the author of Luke/Acts does not seem to have had firsthand knowledge of Paul, nor is there any evidence he was a physician.

Luke/Acts was written late in the first century, somewhere between C.E. 85 and 100. The date C.E. 90 is reasonable, although it is only an approximation. We do not now where Luke/Acts was written; somewhere in Asia Minor is a reasonable guess, but it is only a guess.

The beginning of the Gospel

Luke's first two chapters tell the story of the births of Jesus and John the Baptist. The style of writing in these chapters differs from that of the remainder of Luke/Acts, being more influenced by Hebrew constructions,

---

Luke

The tradition that Luke the physician and companion of Paul was the author of Luke-Acts goes back to the second century C.E. The Luke in question is referred to in Col 4:14, Phlm 24, 2 Tim 4:11, where he is identified as a physician. It is improbable that he author of Luke-Acts was a physician; it is doubtful that he was a companion of Paul. Like the other attributions, this one, too, is fanciful.

although still bearing substantial traces of Luke's writing style. It is possible they were written at a different time, but whether they were written earlier or later than the rest of Luke/Acts is difficult to say.

John the Baptist

One can only speculate why John the Baptist has such prominence in the opening chapters of Luke or, indeed, why his birth story is told at all. It is possible Luke's account of John's birth came from sources Luke received from John's followers. John's disciples did not disband after his execution. While some became followers of Jesus, others, probably the majority, remained loyal to John's memory. A small and isolated group of people called the Mandaeans, who live today in the nation of Iraq, believe themselves to be descendants of the followers of John the Baptist. Unfortunately, their extensive literature has become so altered over time that it adds nothing to our historical knowledge of John.

The poem John's father Zechariah recites, 1:67–69, may have circulated first among disciples of John, for it has no direct connection to specifically Christian teaching. John's followers would have understood the phrase *the Lord's forerunner* to mean that John announced the coming of the Lord God, while followers of Jesus would have thought it referred to the Lord Jesus. Mary's poem, 1:46–55, also contains nothing specifically Christian and it too may have been used originally by followers of John and first attributed to John's mother, Elizabeth. Despite their lack of specifically Christian themes, the two poems in no way contradict Christian teaching. Although both poems are written in Greek, they exhibit the style of, and use language influenced by, ancient Hebrew poetry. They may be Greek translations of Hebrew originals.

Like Mark and Matthew, Luke depicts John as inferior to Jesus. Luke wishes to make it clear John is not speaking of the future coming of God but of the immediate appearance of the Messiah, Jesus. Therefore, when John says, "I baptize you with water; but there is one to come who is mightier than I" (3:16), the statement is made in the context of people asking him whether or not he is the Messiah.

Matthew and Mark were content to have John play down his own importance before his baptism of Jesus. For Luke this is insufficient; he is also careful *not* to say John baptized Jesus. Luke moves Mark's account of John's imprisonment to the beginning of his Gospel (3:19–20) and subsequently writes about Jesus' baptism. "And when Jesus too had been baptized and was praying, heaven opened, and the Holy Spirit descended on him . . ." (3:21–22). At the time John is presumably in prison. Locating Jesus' baptism after John's arrest is not a mistake on Luke's part but a deliberate decision.

The ending of the Gospel

Luke's Gospel concludes with Jesus' appearances to his disciples in and near Jerusalem. In Matthew's Gospel Jesus' appearance takes place in Galilee. Apparently, the risen Christ did not look the same as he did previously, for Matthew informs us "when they saw him, they fell prostrate before him, though some were doubtful" (Matt. 28:17), and Luke (24:16) writes that the disciples who first met him did not recognize him until he later broke bread and offered it to them. Then "they recognized him; and he vanished from their sight" (24:31). Later in Jerusalem, suddenly "there he was, standing among them. Startled and terrified, they thought they were seeing a ghost" (24:36–37). John's Gospel will repeat the same themes: Jesus' appearance is substantially changed. Mary Magdalene does not recognize him at the tomb (John 20:14), nor do his disciples (John 21:4), and he can appear instantaneously. "Although the doors were latched, he came and stood among them" (John 20:26).

It was only after the resurrection that the disciples, in Luke, begin to think the Messiah was bound to suffer before entering his glory. The disciples had previously believed "he was the man to liberate Israel" (24:21), but apparently his execution proved to them this was not the case. The risen Jesus, however, "opened their minds to understand the scriptures. 'This,' he said, 'is what is written: that the Messiah is to suffer death and to rise from the dead on the third day, and that in his name repentance bringing the forgiveness of sins is to be proclaimed to all nations'" (24:46–47).

From a historical perspective the sequence of events in Luke's final chapter gives insight into the earliest development of Christian thought. It is likely, as Luke implies, that Jesus' disciples believed during his lifetime that he was a political messiah or a miracle-working prophet destined to liberate Israel from Roman occupation. They did not, Luke indicates, think before hand that he would rise from the dead. The Gospels' reports that he told them this in advance are probably based on later ideas and on Mark's ideas of what he would have said. Although Jesus is reported to have told his disciples about his resurrection, both Luke's and Mark's final chapters suggest they were unprepared for it. Luke reports that when certain women came from Jesus' tomb to tell his disciples they believed him to be risen from the dead, "the story appeared to them [the apostles] to be nonsense, and they would not believe them" (24:11). Soon, however, rather than assuming that Jesus' mission had been a failure, his followers came to the conclusion that Jesus' death did not contradict the idea of his messiahship, but confirmed it. They then looked for and discovered passages in the Hebrew Bible useful in supporting that claim and believed Jesus had "opened their minds to understand the scriptures." Finding only limited success in convincing Jews of their theory, as the book of Acts reports, some of Jesus' followers turned to Gentile people with their message and had much greater success.

Pontius Pilate

Luke, like Mark and Matthew, shifts the responsibility for Jesus' execution from Pilate onto the Jewish people. Pilate first denies there is a case to be made against Jesus (23:4). Luke then adds a paragraph stating Pilate turned over Jesus' case to Herod (technically in charge of the Galilean region) to demonstrate Pilate had no wish to execute Jesus and to imply Pilate did not even have legal jurisdiction in the matter (23:6–12). After Jesus' return from Herod, "Pilate called together the chief priests, councillors, and people, and said to them, 'You brought this man before me on a charge of subversion. But, as you see, I have myself examined him in your presence and found nothing in him to support your charges. No more did Herod, for he has referred him back to us. Clearly he has done nothing to deserve death" (23:13–15). Repeatedly, throughout the book of acts, Jews are stated to have used Pilate to execute Jesus, as though Pilate were acting under their instructions. Responsibility for Jesus' death belongs entirely to the Jews, according to Luke, although ultimately they were carrying out the will of God (Acts 2:23).

Luke's efforts to show that Pilate was not responsible for Jesus' death reflects one of his main themes, that the Christian movement is loyal to and supportive of the Roman Empire. Where official persecution of Christians is mentioned in Acts, from the execution of Jesus to the imprisonment of Paul, persecution is said to have originated with Jews and not with Romans. If anything, the Romans are shown to be defenders of Christians against persecution. Pilate finds Jesus innocent, although he eventually executes him. Later, in Acts, Paul escapes persecution by Jewish opponents by appealing to Caesar, a privilege of his Roman citizenship.

Salvation History

Some scholars believe Luke 16:16 is a key verse for understanding Luke's purpose: "Until John, it was the Law and the prophets: since then, there is the good news of the kingdom of God, and everyone forces his way in." From their perspective, the first third of history, contained in the Hebrew Scriptures, is the period of the Law and the prophets. This period came to an end when the ministry of John the Baptist concluded. The second period of history, related in the Gospel of Luke, is the time of Jesus' ministry. These scholars believe Luke regarded this era as the middle of time, a special period when the Kingdom of God was beginning to break into the world and during which Satan was gone. The Acts of the Apostles is the account of the third period of history, the time of the church. Both the Gospel and Acts indicate a time will come when history ends, judgment occurs, and the Kingdom of God arrives on earth. The arrival of the kingdom will be the culmination of history. Stephen's speech in Acts 7:1–53 traces the first period of history and concludes with a prophetic vision of history's eventual end. "Look," Stephen said, "there is a rift in the sky; I can see the Son of Man standing at God's right hand!"

Luke, more than any other evangelist, writes in the style traditional among ancient historians. His concept of history, however, is focused on history's implications for salvation, which was then a uniquely Jewish idea. Salvation, Luke believes, does not come all at once but as a process stretched out over centuries, a process centered on the time of Jesus' life.

Luke's teaching about Jesus

Read the Acts of the Apostles. Underline or highlight each section you find summarizing the life and significance of Jesus. Most of those sections will appear in speeches or preaching attributed to Peter and Paul. It is in the passages you will have underlined that Luke's ideas and conception of Jesus and his mission are most clearly set forth. When you read Acts do so as you would read a popular novel; Luke intended the book to be full of adventures, conflicts, miracles, arrests and trials and escapes from prison, long journeys, shipwreck and so forth. It's supposed to be fun!

The speeches attributed to Paul in Acts do not contain his particular vocabulary, his style of expression, or his unique ideas. This we know by comparing them to his letters. Therefore, most scholars conclude that while Luke knew something of Paul's life and influence, when writing speeches attributed to Paul, Luke is giving his conception of what Paul would have said rather than what Paul actually said. Historians in the ancient world often wrote speeches for the subjects of their books, speeches giving more information about the opinions of the historians than about the opinions of the persons who supposedly spoke. Thus, the apostles' speeches in Acts give Luke's opinions, not Paul's or Peter's or the other apostles he quoted. The best source of information about Paul is the letters Paul wrote. Acts is a much better source for information about the opinions of Luke than about the opinions of Paul.

Little is known of the teachings of the historical Peter. The style and content of speeches attributed to him in Acts are nearly the same as those attributed to Paul, although we have reason to believe the two were in disagreement (see Gal. 2:11). But this should not be surprising, as Luke wrote for both Peter and Paul. Except possibly for the lengthy speech of Stephen in Acts 7:1–53, all of the speeches in Acts were created by Luke. Luke's Gospel is filled with detail, as are the Gospels of Mark and Matthew, but the speeches Luke wrote in Acts are short, concise summaries. These speeches can save us much intellectual effort for, rather than going through Luke's Gospel and making our own summary of his ideas about Jesus, we can use the summaries Luke himself wrote in Acts.

The Gospel was probably written before Acts was written. Still, it is conceivable Acts was written first, for Acts contains few details about Jesus' life. The virgin birth, for example, is never mentioned. An author who previously wrote an extensive book about Jesus might be expected to give substantial information about him in a later book written to present the teachings of his followers about him; yet Acts does not do this.

Two of the more lengthy speeches in Acts are found in 2:22-45 and 10:34-43. They show limited interest in the events of Jesus' life. These events can be summarized quickly:

1. Jesus was anointed by God with the Holy Spirit and with power.
2. After the baptism proclaimed by John, Jesus started from Galilee, went to the Jewish countryside, and, eventually, arrived in Jerusalem.
3. He went about doing good and healing all who were oppressed by the devil, doing miracles, portents, and signs as evidence of the fact he had been chosen by God.

That is about all. No specific miracle stories are told, nor are Jesus' teachings or parables mentioned. No detailed stories of his life are given. This is true for all of the speeches in Acts.

Jesus' death, on the other hand, is of particular importance in Acts' speeches. In those speeches claims are made that Jesus' death was planned beforehand by God, announced beforehand by prophets, and brought about by the leaders of the Jewish people. Luke does not wish the authorities of the Roman Empire to bear any blame, so he portrays the Jews of Israel as having "used heathen men [Romans] to crucify and kill him" (2:23). The Romans are only tools in the hands of others. If there is blame for Jesus' death, and the language of Acts certainly implies there is, it should be borne by Jews and not Romans. The idea of blame, however, is difficult to justify by Luke's principles, for he states categorically that Jesus' death came about "by the deliberate will and plan of God" (2:23). Perhaps we should separate the questions of political and final responsibility for Jesus' death. From the perspective of Luke's books, Jewish people are politically responsible, not the Roman authorities. But final responsibility rests with God, who ordained that those things should happen. If you read Acts' speeches carefully you can see Luke is quite definite that everything in Jesus' life, including his death and his resurrection, was empowered by God. God chose Jesus' God sent the Holy Spirit to him; God worked miracles through him; God arranged for his death; God brought him back to life; God exalted him.

The speeches in Acts focus primary attention on Jesus' role after his resurrection. It is as though the purpose of his life was to give evidence that after his death he would receive exalted responsibility. Then God made him both Lord and Messiah, and God designated him judge of the living and the dead. Everything that happens within the church happens through him or is empowered by him, including the power of the apostles to do miracles and, most importantly, the coming of the Holy Spirit to all who have faith. To an extent, Jesus is to the apostles what God was to Jesus.

Luke draws deliberate parallels between the people of the church and Jesus during his life. He received the Holy Spirit; they receive the Holy Spirit. He did signs and wonders; they do signs and wonders. Their regard for money is the same as his; he advocated that the wealthy give to the poor, and all wealth is equally distributed within the community of the apostles. In the Gospel of Luke Jesus is the paradigm, or the prime example, of how a person possessed of the Holy Spirit should behave. The way he lived is the way his apostles and other followers should live. The Gospel presents Jesus' way of life; Acts shows it being carried out by others.

The Holy Spirit

The factor linking Jesus and his followers is not so much belief, although faith is important, but the Holy Spirit. Luke's two books might be conceived to be a history of the activity of the Holy Spirit, not various histories of the activities of certain famous individuals.

At the time of Jesus' conception, the Holy Spirit brings about Mary's pregnancy. Jesus receives the Holy Spirit at his baptism and it stays with him throughout his life. Through the Spirit he performs signs and wonders. At his death the Spirit returns to God. (That is Luke's meaning in 23:46 of Jesus' last words, "Father, into thy hands I commit my Spirit.") Risen from the dead, Jesus again receives the Spirit, and through it he speaks to the apostles (Acts 1:2). After his ascension he sends the Spirit to his followers beginning at Pentecost. Through their ministry the Spirit comes to multitudes of people. Jews and Gentiles alike. Luke is careful throughout his two books to trace the presence of the Spirit from the birth of John the Baptist to the time of the annunciation, through the time of Jesus' ministry to the time of the early church. Luke believes the Spirit to be the central and crucial link binding all these times together.

The Gospel of Luke

Much of what was said about the origin of the Gospel of Matthew could be said about the origin of the Gospel of Luke. Like Matthew, Luke revised Mark. Like Matthew, Luke used the written sayings source Q. Like Matthew, Luke added to Mark an extended beginning discussing the birth of Jesus and an extended ending discussing Jesus' appearances to his disciples after his death. Finally, like Matthew, Luke added sayings and stories to the Gospel, some from Q, some found in no other New Testament Gospel.

The stories and sayings found only in Luke, thus not in Matthew, Mark, or John, are called Special Luke. Some scholars believe many of these were previously written in a document they call L, which, like Q, was a list of sayings with a particular perspective of its own. But this theory does not convince all scholars; the sayings in Special Luke may have been taken from oral tradition or perhaps were composed by Luke. *The following are Special Luke, and you should underline each of them.*

Luke 1:1–3:2	Luke 14:12–14
Luke 3:5–6	Luke 14:28–33
Luke 4:17–22a, 25–30	Luke 15:8–32
Luke 5:1–11	Luke 16:1–12
Luke 7:11–16	Luke 16:19–31
Luke 7:36–50	Luke 17:12–19
Luke 8:1–3	Luke 17:20–21
Luke 9:51–56	Luke 18:1–8
Luke 10:29–37	Luke 19:2–10
Luke 10:38–42	Luke 19:40
Luke 11:27–28	Luke 19:42–44
Luke 12:15	Luke 21:34–36
Luke 12:16–21	Luke 22:31–32
Luke 12:32	Luke 22:35–38
Luke 12:35–38	Luke 23:4–16
Luke 12:47–48	Luke 23:27–34
Luke 13:1–17	Luke 23:39–43
Luke 13:31–33	Luke 23:46
Luke 14:1–10	Luke 24:8–53

After you have underlined these Special Luke passages, read them carefully several times. They reveal many of Luke's special perspectives and concerns.

Travel in Luke/Acts

One of Luke's main thematic and organizational structures is based on travel. Evidently Luke does not regard Mark's Gospel as a useful guide to Jesus' journeys; they are substantially reorganized. In Luke's Gospel Jesus is depicted as beginning his mission in Galilee and then journeying through Judea to the city of Jerusalem where he dies, rises, and appears to his disciples. Luke emphasizes this frequently: "As the time approached when he was to be taken up to heaven, he set his face resolutely towards Jerusalem, and sent messengers ahead" (9:51–52). "I must be on my way today and tomorrow and the next day, because it is unthinkable for a prophet to meet his death anywhere but in Jerusalem: (13:33). "In the course of his journey to Jerusalem he was travelling through the borderlands of Samaria and Galilee" (17:11). For more than half the Gospel Luke depicts Jesus as going toward Jerusalem, traveling exclusively in Jewish territory.

In Acts Jerusalem serves as the starting point for a pattern of travel that fans out through the regions of Judea and Samaria and beyond into regions increasingly populated by Gentiles. Paul, after his conversion, becomes the prime example of this expansion as he travels throughout the northeastern Mediterranean area devoting himself to a mission predominantly focused on Gentiles.

As Jesus' journey led to Jerusalem, so Paul's journey leads to Rome. At the end of Acts Paul is preaching the gospel in Rome "quite openly and without hindrance" (28:31). The Gospel of Luke begins its story of Jesus' ministry in the outlying Jewish region of Galilee and concludes in the Jewish capital, Jerusalem; the book of Acts begins in an outlying region of the empire, Jerusalem, and concludes in the empire's capital, Rome. Evidently Luke designed the two books to show the Christian movement continually expanding toward increasingly influential areas.

As the Christian movement expands outward, embracing Gentiles, it seems increasingly alienated from Jewish people. However, Luke does not wish to suggest the apostles were forced to appeal only to Gentiles for support because all Jews rejected the Messiah, Jesus. Many passages in Acts show Jews as well as Gentiles becoming Christian: "At Iconium similarly they went into the Jewish synagogue and spoke to such purpose that a large body of Jews and Greeks became believers. But the unconverted Jews stirred up the Gentiles and poisoned their minds against the Christians" (14:1–2). James and the elders in Jerusalem say to Paul, "You see, brother, how many thousands of converts we have among the Jews, all of them staunch upholders of the Law" (21:20). Acts' message is that the mission to the Gentiles followed upon the mission to the Jews. Gentiles only began to predominate because relatively few Jews chose to become Christians. Neither in Acts nor in history is there a point in the first century when the Christian movement gave up altogether on the conversion of Jewish people and focused exclusively on Gentiles.

Luke's perspective is in agreement with that of modern scholars. At first the Christian movement reached out to Jewish people. This effort was somewhat successful, but limited. The movement then began to attract Gentile converts and, largely through Paul's efforts, began to achieve great success among Gentiles. Luke's two books tell the story of how Gentiles began to predominate in the movement.

Jesus' mission to the Jews

According to the Gospel of Luke, during his lifetime Jesus spoke virtually only to Jews. Luke is quite careful to show Jesus traveling only within Jewish areas. This may help to answer a problem in Luke's use of Mark for, curiously, Luke omits everything from Mark, 6:45 to 8:26. Some scholars believe Luke possessed a copy of Mark from which those passages were missing and so Luke did not know of the passages he did not use. Others look at the passages in Mark and find most of them redundant or not in accord with various of Luke's main themes. They suspect Luke found them to be inappropriate for several reasons:

First, those passages Jesus traveling in non-Jewish regions (Tyre and Sidon, the Decapolis) and speaking to Gentile people. Luke sought to portray Jesus as devoting himself to Jewish territory and to Jewish people.

Second, Luke gives an account of the miraculous multiplication of loaves and fishes in 9:10–17 (using Mark 6:30–44) and may have thought it unnecessary to repeat the story as Mark did in 8:1–10. Luke's omissions begin after the first multiplication story and end shortly after the second. He also may have chosen not to repeat Mark's story of the blind man of Bethsaida because he found it to duplicate Mark's account of blind Bartimaeus, which he did use.

Third, Mark 7:1–23 does not support the necessity for Jewish people to follow all the Law of Moses. Luke believes the Jewish people remained obliged to follow the Law. An examination of Luke's use of Mark by means of Gospel parallels will reveal that Luke tends to omit material with which he disagrees. Luke is quite seriously concerned with Jews and Gentiles and the different responsibilities of each group. Other New Testament writers do not distinguish between people of Jewish or Gentile origin; for them the same expectations are in force for Christians regardless of origin.

Fourth, Luke believes Mark went too far in his criticism of Jesus' disciples, and so, like Matthew, Luke modified many of the passages in Mark critical of them. One of the harshest criticisms in Mark is found in Mark 8:14–21. Matthew's version tones down this criticism (Matt. 16:5–12); Luke omits it altogether.

The responsibilities of wealth

Luke may have received an expensive education for the Gospel is written well. For those who assume Christians of the first century were all poor and needy people it may come as a surprise to learn that Luke categorically states, in Acts, that many worshippers were wealthy. Paul and Silas are said to have converted "a great number of godfearing Gentiles and a good many influential women" (Acts 17:4). "Women of standing as well as men" were converted, Acts says a little later (17:11). Among those who were Christian but fell away were some "women of standing who were worshippers" (13:50). Ananias and his wife Sapphira, who did not give all they possessed to the community, are depicted as well-to-do landowners (5:1–12). Lydia, a Christian woman prominent in chapter 16 of Acts, is an independent business woman, a dealer in purple fabric, a luxury material. Like these people, Luke probably came from a wealthy background.

Many passages in Luke, particularly Special Luke, are directed toward wealthy persons. Such sayings contrast with Q sayings directed toward the poor.

The Special Luke parable found in 16:1–8 is told from the perspective of a landlord's agent, not from the perspective of the debtors who owe that landlord money. The conclusion Luke composed, "So I say to you, use your worldly wealth to win friends for yourselves, so that when money is a thing of the past you may be received into an eternal home" (16:9), assumes the audience has worldly wealth to use. The parable of the prodigal son in Special Luke (15:11–32) discusses events in a wealthy household. Those who hear the parable in 14:7–10 are people who ordinarily would take place of honor at a wedding feast. The audience addressed in 14:12–14 is able to invite rich neighbors to a party; those who hear the parable in 17:7–10 are people who have servants to do their plowing and to mind their sheep. The wealthy people addressed in the Special Luke sayings are those who financially controlled the destinies of the people addressed in Q sayings.

And yet Luke uses Q sayings and does not substantially revise them. He does not make them reflect the point of view of the wealthy but allows them to continue to reflect the point of view of the poor. Matthew, on the other hand, seems to have revised some of the Q sayings to make them more acceptable to people who were not poor.

There is nothing contradictory in Luke's approach. One must distinguish between his probable audience and his sympathies. Luke's audience was probably rather well-to-do (Theophilus, for whom the Gospel was written, and who may well have been expected to pay for the privilege of receiving it), is addressed as "Your Excellency" [Luke 1:3]), but Luke's sympathies are with the poor. Jesus, as Luke's Gospel presents him, urges the wealthy to share their wealth with the poor, to use their worldly wealth to win friends for themselves. Luke gives a compromise portrayal of Jesus, not as one who addresses only the poor and hungry, but as one who also addresses wealthy audiences. His primary sympathy, however, remains with the poor.

Women in Luke

Perhaps more striking than Luke's interest in the responsibilities of wealthy Christians is Luke's interest in demonstrating Jesus' concern for women. Remarks favorable to women appear in other Gospels (for example, Mark 14:1–9, John 4:1–30), but there we find nothing like the careful, sustained attention paid to women in the Gospel of Luke.

The first two chapters of Luke's Gospel tell the story of Jesus' birth and of the birth of John the Baptist. The principal characters in the story are Elizabeth and Mary. Jesus' name occurs only three times in those two chapters. Joseph is mentioned only occasionally and is a minor character. In contrast, Matthew's account gives Joseph more prominence than Mary. Zechariah, the father of John the Baptist, is portrayed negatively by Luke. He is made unable to speak because he does not believe the angel Gabriel. He is directly contrasted to the women who do accept Gabriel's messages.

The stories in chapters 1 and 2 of Luke are the stories of Mary and Elizabeth. These women, especially Mary, are portrayed as willing servants of God who happily accept the special roles God gives them. In doing so they are similar to the apostles whose stories are told in Acts. If Christians can be defined in the Lukan sense as persons who receive the Holy Spirit through their relationship with Jesus, then Mary, to whom the Holy Spirit came, and Elizabeth, who was filled with the Holy Spirit (1:41), are the first Christians mentioned in the Gospel of Luke. John the Baptist may be filled with the Holy Spirit from the moment of his birth (1:15), but this does not derive from a relationship with Jesus.

Two others who are filled with the Spirit appear in chapters 1 and 2: Simeon (2:25–35) and Anna (2:36–38). The Holy Spirit is said to have disclosed to Simeon that he would not die until he saw the Messiah. So, guided by the Spirit, he came to the Jerusalem temple and there he circumcised Jesus. Anna was an elderly widow, a prophet guided by the Spirit. She talked about the child Jesus to all who were looking forward to the liberation of Jerusalem. These are the first examples in Luke's Gospel of his tendency to pair characters and stories so as to ensure stories about men are paired with stories about women. These are a remarkable number of paired sayings and stories, one in reference to women and one in reference to men. The following list is revised from Mary Rose D'Angelo's article "Women in Luke-Acts: A Redactional View," published in the *Journal of Biblical Literature* in the Fall, 1990 issue.

2 annunciations
    to Zechariah   1:5–23
    to Mary   1:26–38

2 songs	
of Mary	1:46–55
of Zechariah	1:68–79
2 prophets	
Simeon	2:25–35
Anna	2:36–38
2 miracles	
Gentile widow	4:25–26
leprous Syrian man	4:27
2 first miracles	
possessed man	4:33–37 (Mark 1:23–28)
Peter's mother-in-law	4:38–39 (Mark 1:29–31)
2 lists of named disciples:	
men apostles	6:12–19 (Mark 3:13–19)
women associates	8:1–3
2 rescues from death:	
the centurion's servant	7:1–10 (Matt 8:5–13)
the widow's son	7:11–17
2 penitents:	
the paralytic	5:18–26 (Mark 2:1–12)
the penitent woman	7:36–50 (Mark 14:3–9?)
3 miracles	
the Gerasene man	8:26–39 (Mark 5:1–20)
the daughter of Jairus	8:40–42, 49–56 (Mark 5:21–24, 35–43)
the hemorrhaging woman	8:43-48 (Mark 5:25-34)
3 questions about discipleship	
the scribe	10:25–37 (Mark 12:28–34)
Martha	10:38–42
the disciple	11:1–13
2 Gentile accusers of Israel	
the Ninevites	11:29–30
the queen of the south	11:31 (Matt 12:38–42)
2 "releases":	
the bent-over woman	13:10–17
the dropsical man	14:1–6 (Mark 3:1–5?)
2 parables	
man planting mustard	13:18–19 (Matt 13:31–32)
woman hiding leaven	13:20–21 (Matt 13:33)
2 finder parables	
man with sheep	15:1–7 (Matt 18:12–14)
woman with coin	15:8–10

2 taken

men in a bed	17:34 (Matt 24:40)
women grinding	17:35 (Matt 24:41)

2 examples of prayer

widow	18:1–8
Pharisee, publican	18:9–14

2 attitudes to worship

scribes	20:45–47 (Mark 12:38–40)
widow	21:1–4 (Mark 12:41–44)

2 followers

Simon of Cyrene	23:26 (Mark 15:21)
women	23:27–29

2 groups of watchers

women and all

his associates	23:49 (Mark 15:40–41)

2 kinds of resurrection witnesses

women and Peter	24:1–11 (Mark 16:1–8).

Acts also inludes a number of references to women paired with men.

2 groups waiting	1:13–14
Menservants and maidservants, sons and daughters	2:17–18
Ananias and Sapphira	5:1–11
a crowd of both men and women added	5:14
Paul as persecutor of both men and women	8:3
both men and women added	8:12
Paul as persecutor of both men and women	9:2
Peter cures lame man and Tabitha	9:32–43
Rhoda recognizes Peter	12:12–17 (cf.
Others do not	Luke 24:8–11)
worshiping women and first men of the city	13:50
Paul driven from Lystra by cure of lame man	14:8–18
from Philippi by cure of mantic girl	16:16–34
a great crowd of worshiping Greeks and not a few of the first women were persuaded	17:4
not a few respectable Greek women and men	17:12
Dionysius and Damaris converted at Athens	17:34
Paul received by Priscilla and Aquila	18:1–4
Paul as persecutor of both men and women	22:4
Felix arrives with Drusilla	24:24
Agrippa and Bernice	25:13, 23; 26:30

As you can see many pairs of stories—one featuring a woman, one featuring a man—are found in Luke's Gospel and in Luke's Acts. One, found only in Special Luke, occurs in Jesus' remarks about widows (4:25) and leprous men (4:28) during the commentary on a passage from Isaiah in the Nazareth synagogue; these are among the first words of his ministry. Another is Luke's pairing of a story taken from Mark (Luke 5:17–20) about Jesus' forgiving the sins of a paralyzed man (and thereby scandalizing Pharisees and teachers of the Law) with a Special Luke story in 7:36–50 where Jesus astonishes Pharisees by forgiving the sins of a woman. Luke pairs the Q miracle about Jesus healing the centurion's servant who was near death (7:1–10) with a Special Luke story about Jesus raising the dead son of a widow to life (7:11–17).

Luke pairs Mark's story about Jesus curing a man with a withered arm and receiving criticism for doing that on the Sabbath (6:6–11) with a Special Luke story about a crippled woman cured on the Sabbath, and here too Jesus is criticized for healing on the Sabbath (13:10–17). The parable of the shepherd who sought his lost sheep, taken from Q (15:4–7), is followed immediately by a Special Luke parable about a woman with a lost silver coin (15:8–10). Significantly, the Q parable is about a man at the bottom of the social order, while the Special Luke parable is about a woman with what was, in those days, considerable wealth.

A parable in 18:1–8, making the point that constant crying out to God will bring about God's response, has as its central character a widow; the story paired with it occurs in 11:5–8. It has the same point but features a man. Many of the stories in Luke featuring women are from Special Luke; most of the stories featuring men come from Mark and Q.

These pairs occur too frequently to be coincidental. Luke consciously and deliberately supplements the sources Q and Mark by using or composing complementary stories about women.

Perhaps the most significant point Luke's Gospel makes about women is the Special Luke passage about Martha and Mary (10:38–42). Martha works at domestic chores while Mary sits and listens to Jesus. The story concludes strongly, "The part that Mary has chosen is best; and it shall not be taken away from her." From Luke's perspective Christian women are not servants to be kept in the background but should be disciples of Jesus.

Luke distinguishes between "the Twelve" and Jesus' other disciples. Although the Twelve have a special place, they are not his only disciples. To make this very clear, toward the end of his Gospel Luke repeatedly asserts women had accompanied Jesus all the way from Galilee to the end. At the crucifixion, "his friends had all been standing at a distance; the women who had accompanied him from Galilee stood with them and watched it all" (23:49). After the crucifixion, "the women who had accompanied him from

Galilee followed; they took note of the tomb and observed how his body was laid" (23:55). At Jesus' tomb "Mary of Magdala, Joanna, Mary the mother of James, and the other women" (24:10–11) heard two men in dazzling garments say, "Remember what he told *you* while he was still in Galilee, about the Son of Man: how he must be given up into the power of sinful men and be crucified, and must rise again on the third day. Then *they* recalled his words and, returning from the tomb, they reported all this to the Eleven and all the others" (24:6–11). Luke is following Mark's account here, but it is significantly changed. In Mark the youth in white clothes tells only "Mary of Magdala, Mary the mother of James, and Salome" (Mark 16:1) to "go and give this message to his disciples and Peter" (16:7).

In the first place, the number of women in Luke's account is significantly greater. In the second place, what the women are told is directed to them rather than to the Eleven and Peter; in Luke they are not ordered to tell the disciples, they choose to do so. Finally, the message they are given, and which they recall Jesus teaching, is the one Mark especially reserved only for Jesus' twelve disciples (Mark 8:31). According to Luke, Jesus previously taught it to the women.

The women go to tell the apostles but "the story appeared to them [the disciples] to be nonsense, and they would not believe them [the women]" (24:11). For a short period, until the apostles finally do believe (24:45), the only human beings with faith in Jesus' resurrection are women, women who act as apostles to the apostles.

From the beginning of the Gospel and the stories of Elizabeth and Mary, to the end of the Gospel and the story of the women at the tomb, Luke emphasizes the part women played in Jesus' ministry. Jesus' first public words refer to widows (4:25); his last public words are addressed to the women of Jerusalem (23:27–31). Luke emphasizes that women were with Jesus from the beginning of his ministry in Galilee to the end of his ministry in Jerusalem.

It appears odd then that the one story in Mark's gospel that shows Jesus fulsomely praising a woman is missing in Luke's gospel (cf. Mark 14:3–9). But one must bear in mind that Mark's point is to make a contrast between that one wise anonymous woman and the well-meaning but misunderstanding women who accompanied Jesus but who went to his tomb to anoint him ignorant of the fact that he would be risen. Unlike Mark, Luke intends to praise the women who accompanied Jesus and so deletes Mark's story. Perhaps, Luke transformed Mark's story to become the story of the repentant woman who annointed Jesus' feet in 7:36–50. She is favorably contrasted with Pharisees there.

Luke states, quite clearly, how the ministry of Jesus was financed, and this interesting point links Luke's themes of the responsibilities of wealth and of the discipleship of women. The other Gospels leave us to assume he and his followers were supported by donations from the common people and the hospitality of various associates, but Luke's does not. While allowing that Jesus was invited to dine with both friends and opponents, Luke tells us categorically that when Jesus went from town to town, village to village, proclaiming the good news of the Kingdom of God, he was accompanied by "the Twelve and a number of women who had been set free from evil spirits and infirmities: Mary, known as Mary of Magdala, from whom seven devils had come out, Joanna, the wife of Chuza a steward of Herod's, Susanna, and many others. *These women provided for them out of their own resources*" (8:1–3). This passage, naming those women, precedes Jesus' parables sermon in Luke. This is a stylistic literary parallel with a passage that names Jesus' male disciples and that immediately precedes the sermon on the mount (6:12–19).

Luke's theme that the wealthy should contribute their resources to the poor has its high point in 8:1–3, for the wealthy are contributing their resources to the support of Jesus' personal mission. The wealthy, in this instance are, all of them, independently wealthy women.

Two theories may account for Luke's emphatic and sustained emphasis on women. The first is conventional, and virtualy all analytical scholars are in agreement with it. The second is unconventional, but it also is worthy of attention.

The first is this: Luke was a man who, believing Jesus to be the Messiah for all people, wished to portray him as Messiah for both men and women. Because he noticed that women were not prominently mentioned in his sources, Luke decided to write a Gospel emphasizing their presence and their support of Jesus' mission. Luke, then, was a man with great respect for and admiration of Christian women, a man determined to see that Christian women received a place of respect in his church.

The second is this: the anonymous author of the Gospel called Luke was a woman. We have reason to believe the author of the Gospel and Acts came from a relatively wealthy background and so may have been either male or female. In many regions of the empire both the boys and the girls of well-to-do families received education. In some regions women's education was discouraged, but as we do not know where the Gospel was written, it may just as well have been written in a locale where well-to-do girls were educated as in a locale where their education was restricted.

We may assume that Luke held a leadership position in a church. Acts tells us some women had churches in their homes (Acts 12:12 and Acts 16:40), and we can assume such women held leadership positions in those churches. Acts also indicates that widowed Christian women sometimes associated, lived, and worked together (9:36–43). In such associations women presumably held leadership positions. Accordingly, the leader of a church who wrote "Theophilus" who then, presumably, paid to have books copied, and circulated may have been female

It might be argued that common sense supports the thesis that the author of the Gospel and Acts was a woman, for rarely in the early history of the Christian movement have men been known sympathetically and emphatically to argue for the important place of women in the church. But this is exactly what the author of Luke does.

A woman author of a Gospel might have resembled Lydia, whose story Luke tells in Acts 16:11–40. Lydia was an independent business woman and, as a retailer selling luxurious purple cloth, she was wealthy, the head of a considerable household. She was a "worshipper of God," meaning that although she was born a Gentile she was sympathetic to Judaism and, even before accepting Christianity, worshiped the Jewish God. Therefore, presumably, she knew something of the Greek translation of the Hebrew Scriptures. She was converted to Christianity by Paul and, through her influence, so was her household. She knew Paul personally and also the author of the "we passages," as Acts' text indicates. At this time a household would have included her nuclear and extended family, her employees, and slaves. A church apparently met in her house, and it surely would have continued to meet after the departure of the apostles responsible for the conversion of its members. Presumably Lydia would have led a church that met in her house and that was composed in large part of members of her household.

No method exists for conclusively proving the gender of anonymous authors. It is still customary for scholars to presume, without further discussion or argument, that anonymous authors must be male. But if, as feminist scholars have argued, women played more important roles in early Christianity than they have received credit for, it may well be that we will discover that the custom of assuming male authorship of Luke/Acts needs to be re-examined.

Compromises in Luke/Acts

Luke accepts the tradition, probably transmitted by the Jerusalem church, that Jesus came to Jewish people and traveled in Jewish territory. The Gospel of Luke takes this point of view. So also does the Gospel of Matthew, where Jesus is quoted as saying, "Do not take the road to Gentile lands, and do not enter any Samaritan town; but go rather to the lost sheep of the house of Israel" (Matt. 10:6).

Luke also accepts the tradition that the gospel should be preached to all nations (to Gentile people), a tradition that, if not begun by Paul, certainly had Paul as a major advocate. The book of Acts takes that point of view, as does the concluding passage in Matthew's Gospel. But we should remember that not everyone in the first century agreed with this perspective. First-century Christians disagreed about whether the gospel was for Jews or whether it was for everyone. Luke's books present a compromise by turning an apparent conflict into a matter of a change in time and circumstance: in the beginning the gospel came to Jews in Jewish territory; later it came to Gentiles in the whole of the empire. This point of view is historically valid, but it grew out of an attempt to harmonize two different perspectives. Luke's compromise eventually was accepted throughout the Christian church, but in the first century it was a compromise and not a universally accepted opinion.

Luke was confronted with another problem. Some Christians, and Paul is an example, believed the Law of Moses was no longer in force for Christians. Other Christians, and Matthew is an example, believed the Law of Moses did remain in force for Christians. These are not easily reconcilable positions. Luke sought to reconcile them, believing Peter and James and Paul all taught the true gospel.

In Acts Luke reports a compromise in regard to the Law. James and the elders of Jerusalem say to Paul, "'You see, brother, how many thousands of converts we have among the Jews, all of them staunch upholders of the Law. Now they have been given certain information about you: it is said that you teach all the Jews in the Gentile world to turn their backs on Moses, telling them to give up circumcising their children and following our way of life. What is the position, then? They are sure to hear that you have arrived. You must therefore do as we tell you. We have four men here who are under a vow; take them with you and go through the ritual of purification with them, paying their expenses, after which they may shave their heads. Then everyone will know that there is nothing in the stories they were told about you but that you are a practising Jew and keep the Law yourself. As for the Gentile converts, we sent them our decision that they must abstain from meat that has been offered to idols, from blood, from anything that has been strangled, and from fornication.' So Paul took the four men, and next day, after going through the ritual of purification with them, he went into the temple to give notice of the date when the period of purification would end and the offering be made for each one of them" (Acts 21:21–26).

Here the Law is different for Christians of Jewish background and Christians of Gentile background. The Torah Law is necessarily to be obeyed by Jewish Christians *including Paul himself*. Gentile Christians, on the other hand, must obey precisely four of those laws, a decision found also in Acts 15:19 and 15:29. The four may derive from passages in Leviticus chapters 17 and 18 where they are designated for both the non-Jews and the Jews who live in Jewish territory.

According to Acts, this compromise is agreeable to Paul, but would the Paul who wrote Galatians and the other letters have agreed that his Gentile converts must keep a section of the Law? Paul thinks in black-and-white terms; either one seeks salvation through Law or one receives salvation through faith. To seek salvation through faith and a little bit of the Law if you are Gentile and through faith and all the Law if you are Jewish is a compromise Paul could not possibly have accepted.

Socially such a compromise would have led to the division between Jewish and Gentile Christians at meals, and Paul fought against all such sources of division. Luke seems to have recognized this problem, so he portrays Peter, one of the disciples who usually supported the observance of Law, as having a revelation that changed his mind. Peter, Luke twice informs us, saw a vision from God. "He saw a rift in the sky, and a thing coming down that looked like a great sheet of sail-cloth. It was slung by the four corners, and was being lowered to the ground. In it he saw creatures of every kind, whatever walks or crawls or flies. Then there was a voice which said to him, 'Up, Peter, kill and eat.' But Peter said, 'No, Lord, no: I have never eaten anything profane or unclean.' The voice came again a second time: 'It is not for you to call profane what God counts clean.' This happened three times; and then the thing was taken up again into the sky" (Acts 10:11–16). According to Luke, by this means God made all foods clean, and so the social divisions the food laws would bring about, and which so worried Paul, were to be avoided. We know from Paul's eyewitness account of a meeting with Peter (Gal. 2:11–14) that although Peter sometimes dined with Gentiles, he agreed to stop when ordered to stop by James, an action Paul regarded as treachery. It is difficult, therefore, to believe Luke's account that Peter received a message from God announcing that all foods are clean.

Luke's books are, in part, compromises made necessary by the various developments of first-century Christianity. Luke conceded to Jewish Christians that Jesus upheld the whole Law. He therefore omitted the portion of Mark where Jesus is said to have made all foods clean. Instead, he established the principle later by attributing it to Peter's vision. From that point on, the food laws are suspended for Jewish and Gentile Christians alike, while all other laws, apparently, remain in effect for Jewish Christians.

Luke's compromise position—that Gentiles keep only a limited portion of the Law—would not have satisfied either Paul or his opponents. Matthew and James surely would not have agreed that the food laws were no longer in force, and Paul would not have agreed that Christians, especially Gentile Christians, should be required to follow any of the Law.

Luke's compromise did ultimately prevail, but in a different form. Rather than the four laws for Gentiles specified in Acts, most Christians believe ten laws to be required: the Ten Commandments.

Luke, in the later first century, faced some of the problems analytical students of the New Testament face today. How is it that traditions say Jesus came only to Jews and yet the church is composed primarily of non-Jewish people? How can we reconcile Paul's teachings of freedom from the Law with teachings that Law must be obeyed strictly? Luke's answers appear in his books or, rather, his books are his answer.

Topics

Sources

Luke's Gospel is based on the Gospel of Mark. His Gospel begins to follow Mark at Luke 3:3 and ceases to do so at Luke 24:5. He supplements Mark at the beginning with a birth narrative and at the end with an account of Jesus' resurrection appearances. As discussed previously, Luke omits Mark 6:45–8:26. The remainder of Mark he uses in sections. He alternates sections dependent on Mark with sections derived from his other two major sources, Q and Special Luke.

Luke uses Q extensively and evidently regards it as a reliable source for Jesus' teachings, since he seldom revises either its sayings or the order in which the sayings are presented. Matthew, on the other hand, often revises Q sayings and ignores Q's order of sayings, rearranging them into his five sections of discourse.

Many of the passages in Special Luke (meaning material found only in Luke's Gospel) probably existed in oral tradition before Luke wrote them down. Some scholars have tried to identify a written collection of sayings, similar to Q, from which much Special Luke material may have come, but their theories have not been widely accepted. Some of the sayings and stories in the Special Luke material may have been composed by the author Luke, as were many transitions, scene settings, and commentaries on sayings in his Gospel.

For his story of the births of Jesus and John the Baptist, Luke may have used oral and written traditions from followers of John the Baptist. The two poems in chapter 1 perhaps came from John's followers; they contain no specifically Christian themes.

It is relatively easy to discuss the sources of the Gospel of Luke, because we can compare it with the other synoptic Gospels and, to a limited degree, with the Gospel of John. Because Acts is unique, however, our ability to determine what sources Luke used for it is very limited.

Most speeches in Acts were written by Luke and convey his idea of what the apostles would have said; he does not use written speeches of Peter or Paul as sources. There is no evidence Luke was familiar with Paul's letters. The long historical account attributed to Stephen (7:1–53) is written in a style more directly influenced by Hebrew constructions than are other sections of Acts and so was probably not composed by Luke.

Luke probably had a variety of sources of information to work with, some from followers of Peter and James, others from followers of Paul and Paul's associates. No two scholars now agree on which passages came from which sources, with one exception. On one source scholars agree; it is called the "we" source.

Most of Acts is written in the third person: "They did this, they went there," and so forth. But occasionally passages appear written in the first person: "We did this, we went there." Although this may be a literary device used by Luke to make his book more interesting and give it more immediacy, it is more likely Luke had access to the travel diary of someone who journeyed with Paul. The "we" passages contain many details, but few are important in either a theological or a historical sense. The "we" passages are: Acts 16:10–18, 20:4–21:18, 27:1–28:16. The details they contain give the "we" passages a definite ring of eyewitness truth. For example, Acts 27:4–8, part of the account of Paul's journey to Rome, reads, "Leaving Sidon we sailed under the lee of Cyprus because of the head-winds, then across the open sea off the coast of Cilicia and Pamphylia, and so reached Myra in Lycia. There the centurion found an Alexandrian vessel bound for Italy and put us aboard. For a good many days we made little headway, and we were hard put to it to reach Cnidus. Then, as the wind continued against us, off Salmone we began to sail under the lee of Crete, and, hugging the coast, struggled on to a place called Fair Havens, not far from the town of Lasea." It is difficult to imagine that such interesting but insignificant details were invented.

Jesus

For Luke *Jesus' life* is an important introduction to his exalted role as risen Messiah. Jesus' teachings and activities are so significant to Luke that he substantially supplements Mark's account of them. Nevertheless, Acts shows that Luke believes Jesus' primary powers and responsibilities were given him after his death.

Jesus, during his life, was Son of Man and, in Luke's opinion, a prophet capable of doing miracles to provide evidence of his messianic role. His life is a model for the lives of later followers, especially apostles, who are expected to live as he did and do what he did. Acts shows them doing this even to the point of death; Jesus' last words are echoed, with slight alteration, by Stephen's last words (Acts 7:59–60).

Jesus' death does not itself bring salvation, in Luke's opinion. He omits the key element in the crucial Mark passage, "For even the Son of Man did not come to be served but to serve, and to surrender his life as a ransom for many" (Mark 10:45), altering it to read, "For who is greater, the one who sits at table or the servant who waits on him? Surely the one who sits at the table. Yet here am I among you like a servant" (Luke 22:27). For Luke Jesus is the servant of God and of humanity; his death is ordained by God and serves as the prologue to his resurrection and exaltation. Jesus is shown by Luke always to be obedient to God. His death is his greatest act of obedience.

Jesus' main role comes after his death. Here Luke's ideas differ from those of Matthew (who believed Jesus' teaching during his life to have been crucial) and Paul (who believed his death to have been of cosmic significance). Although both Matthew and Paul would agree Jesus remained active in the church and present among his people after his ascension, it is in Luke that we find that idea most strongly stressed. Jesus, in Acts, sends the Holy Spirit to all who receive it (Acts 2:33). Until the ascension, the Holy Spirit had always been sent, and received back, by God. After his death people are healed "in Jesus' name," and sins are forgiven "in Jesus' name." In the future he will return on clouds of glory to usher in the Kingdom of God.

Eschatology

Luke's understanding of the end of this world and its replacement by the Kingdom of God is not very different from that of his sources. He alters Mark's chapter 13 only in details and does not seriously modify Q sayings about the end. But Luke does not expect the end to come immediately. First there will be a time for the church, a period of history when the Christian movement will spread throughout the empire. The very fact Luke wrote Acts indicates he believes a period of some considerable duration will take place between the crucifixion and the return of the Son of Man. Still, Luke, like Matthew, quotes Mark 13:30 without significant alteration, "Truly, I say to you this generation will not pass away before all these things take place." The two later evangelists apparently did sometimes believe the end to be as immediate as did the Q people, Paul, and Mark, who believed it likely to occur during their own lifetimes.

Torah Law

In Acts Luke reports that various factions in the early church agreed that the Torah Law was in effect for Christians of Jewish origin. There was one exception, the food laws, which were suspended in accord with a vision supposedly granted to Peter. Christians of Gentile origin, however, were required to obey only four laws: not to eat blood (that is, meat with blood still in it), not to eat the meat of creatures strangled (and which, therefore, would still contain blood), not to eat meat offered to idols, and not to engage in sexual intercourse outside of marriage. Luke depicts these compromises regarding Law arising during the period of the church and depict Jesus, during his lifetime, wholly upholding the Law.

Community

By the time of Luke's writing, the Christian church had become a widespread and successful movement. Churches met in private houses in many places. A central authority structure existed in Jerusalem under the leadership of James and his associates. Paul and a host of other apostles successfully spread the message about Jesus to many areas. People as diverse as wealthy Greek women, priests of the Jerusalem temple (Acts 6:7), the treasurer of the kingdom of Ethiopia (8:27), and some leaders of the Jewish community in Rome (28:24) are reported to have joined.

Luke portrays the Christian church as diverse but ultimately united, as a widespread movement capable of finding ways to handle problems arising from differences of background and of belief. Acts indicates that although Hellenistic and Palestinian Jewish Christians initially quarreled about financial support for widowed women, they came to a satisfactory agreement (Acts 6:1–16). Although there was some mutual distrust between the mission to Jews led by James and the mission to Gentiles led by Paul, Acts reports that a compromise regarding the Law was successfully worked out (21:21–26).

These successful compromises may be an ideal vision rather than matters of historical record, but they say something significant about Luke and his books. He was tolerant of diversity and sought pragmatic solutions to conflict rather than demanding one side or the other give in. Such an attitude was essential if the church was to prosper as an empire-wide social institution. Its eventual success was largely due to the tradition of compromise evidenced in Luke's books.

Controversy

Both the leaders of the Jewish people and multitudes of Jewish people are repeatedly depicted as actively hostile to the Christian movement. It was, so Luke reports, Jewish people who caused the death of Jesus, who killed Stephen, who sought Paul's death. This attitude has caused some to label Luke anti-Semitic.

Luke is not anti-Semitic. He is, rather, pro-Roman. He does not want the Roman Empire to believe it has anything to fear from the Christian movement, or that Jesus was in any way a traitor to the empire, or that Paul was anything but a good and loyal citizen of Rome. The conflict depicted in

Luke/Acts is between Jewish authority and Christian teachers. This apparent conflict is a reinterpretation of the real conflicts existing between both Jewish and Roman authority and Christian teachers.

Roman authorities did persecute and even execute Christians (the prime case being the execution of Jesus). This demonstrates that Christians were perceived as threats to the empire by various imperial officials. Luke denies the truth of this perception. As he could not deny the fact of persecution or the fact of the crucifixion, he shifts blame from Roman authority to Jewish authority. His motive may have been that while Jewish antagonism did not endanger the lives of Christians living outside of Palestine, Roman antagonism did. Rather than reveal that some persecution came from Roman and some from Jewish authority, Luke's books portray all persecution coming from Jews.

Interactions

Miracles sources

Jesus, Luke writes in one of the speeches in Acts, was a man chosen by God and "made known to you through miracles, portents, and signs, which God worked among you through him" (Acts 2:22). This is the attitude toward miracles held by those who compiled the miracles sources. Throughout the Gospel of Luke and Acts, Jesus, and subsequently his apostles, brings faith to people through miraculous actions. Miracles are evidence of the Holy Spirit's presence in both Luke's and Paul's (see Gal. 3:5) opinion. Although the Spirit is not mentioned prominently in the miracles sources, it is difficult to imagine their compilers would have denied that the Holy Spirit empowered Jesus.

Luke includes a few stories of miracles in addition to those he took from Mark, but he seems to have used no extensive sources. The Special Luke miracle stories are 5:1–6, 7:11–16, 13:10–17, 14:1–6, and 17:12–19. Luke may have had a source for part of Acts listing miracles done by Peter (for example, Acts 3:1–10, 5:1–11, 9:9–25, 10:36–43), but this is uncertain.

The Q source

Luke supplements Mark by extensive use of sayings from the Q source. He modifies them little, apparently sympathizing with the impoverished people to whom the sayings are directed. The way of life of the Q people is mirrored in the lives of the apostles in Acts, who are itinerant and dependent upon the conversion of strangers for food and shelter. The apostles in Acts, however, are rarely seen to go hungry and thirsty, to be penniless or without a place to lay their heads and rest. Thus, Luke is less realistic about the difficulties of the itinerant life than Q is. The way of life of those converted in Acts who are not apostles is not radical, and their former social networks remain intact. So, despite his use of Q and his sympathy for much of what is contained in its sayings, Luke would not wish the rejection of family and normal social life to be practiced by the majority of Christians.

Paul

To Luke Paul is a hero. Although Acts begins with accounts of the ministries of Peter, Philip, and others, it eventually focuses exclusively on the ministry of Paul. As Luke presents it, parallels exist between the career of Paul and that of Jesus. Paul began in Jerusalem, and his mission culminated in Rome, the capital of the empire; Jesus began in Galilee and his mission culminated in Jerusalem, the capital of Judea. Both, unlike John the Baptist, received the Holy Spirit as adults, and both performed miracles. Like Jesus, Paul was persecuted by Jewish leaders and, like Jesus, did nothing to offend Roman authority. As Jesus was found innocent by Pilate (Luke 23:13–15), so Paul found protection by appealing to Caesar. As King Herod found Jesus innocent, so the king found Paul innocent (Acts 26:31).

Luke does not know Paul's teachings well. What Paul is said to be accused falsely of doing (Acts 21:21), he probably did do. The compromise presented in Acts, that Jews follow all Law but the food laws and that Gentiles follow four of the laws, would not have satisfied Paul. Paul was not a compromiser: "When you seek to be justified by way of law, your relation with Christ is completely severed: you have fallen out of the domain of God's grace" (Gal. 5:4). Although Paul describes a compromise he reached with James in Jerusalem (Gal 2:1–8), it was only in regard to spheres of influence and not matters of central doctrine.

In Paul's letters we read Paul's view of Jesus; in Acts we read Luke's view of Paul's view of Jesus; in this book, the author's view of Luke's view, and so forth. This kind of interpretive transmission is inevitable in human communication. Your view of what you read in this book constitutes another step in the same transmission.

Mark

Luke's Gospel depends for its biographical outline on the Gospel of Mark. Like Matthew, Luke revises Mark to eliminate perspectives he did not share and to add perspectives he found missing.

Luke's respect for the disciples of Jesus leads him frequently to diminish the criticism of them found in Mark. Although Luke agrees the Son of Man was destined to suffer, die, and rise again, he does not emphasize that suffering and death as strongly as Mark did. For Luke the miracles Jesus did are valid grounds for faith; Mark's Gospel seems skeptical of this.

The resurrection appearances in Luke show that before the resurrection Jesus' disciples understood him differently than they did after the resurrection. Before it they believed "he was the man to liberate Israel" and "a prophet powerful in speech and action." Although Luke and Mark seem to agree that the disciples initially misunderstood Jesus, Luke alone indicates that after Jesus' resurrection his followers came to understand correctly. Mark's Gospel gives us no reason to think they ever understood.

Luke revises Mark's account of Jesus' travels so that he is shown always to have remained on Jewish territory and usually to have spoken to Jewish people. Mark, especially in chapter 7 of his Gospel, shows Jesus traveling in Gentile regions and speaking to Gentile people and reports that Jesus canceled the food laws. In Luke's account, Jesus suspends none of the Law. Such differences of opinion seem to have led Luke to omit much of Mark's chapters 6, 7, and 8.

Matthew

Luke and Matthew agree that the disciples of Jesus were reasonably loyal and reasonably responsive to Jesus' teachings during his life. Both agree they ultimately understood him. Despite differences of approach, both agree Mark's Gospel should substantially be revised.

Luke does not believe, as Matthew does, that one of Jesus principal purposes was to ensure the Torah be followed fully. Luke assumes his readers agree that Jewish Christians should follow Torah Law, so he does not stress obedience.

Luke agrees with Matthew that the miracles of Jesus are good evidence for his special status. Both supplement the miracle stories they find in Mark. Matthew heightens them; Luke adds others from his special sources.

Although Luke's and Matthew's Gospels are structurally different, conceptually they are similar. In their own ways, both restructure Mark. Both add Q sayings, birth narratives, and stories of resurrection appearances. The differences are matters of emphasis rather than of central opinion. Luke's emphasis on women is missing in Matthew; Matthew's emphasis on the fulfillment of prophecy is greater than that in Luke's Gospel (although Luke's emphasis on fulfillment of prophecy is strong in Acts). Matthew revises Q sayings to make them acceptable to middle-class people; Luke does not revise them much but adds sayings from another source that are directed specifically toward the wealthy.

Matthew would have disagreed strongly with one important aspect of Acts. The suspension of the food laws through the vision of Peter and the position attributed to both James and Paul that Gentile Christians need keep only a small portion of the Law would absolutely have contradicted the thesis found in Matthew that "so long as heaven and earth endure, not a letter, not a stroke, will disappear from the Law until all that must happen has happened. If any man therefore sets aside even the least of the Law's demands, and teaches others to do the same, he will have the lowest place in the kingdom of Heaven" (Matt. 5:18–19). Otherwise, however, much of what we read in Acts is summarized in Matthew's quotation of the commandment of the risen Christ: "Full authority in heaven and on earth has been committed to me. Go forth therefore and make all nations my disciples; baptize people everywhere in the name of the Father and the Son and the Holy Spirit, and teach them to observe all that I have commanded you. And be assured, I am with you always, to the end of time" (Matt. 28:18–20). All the apostles in Acts acted accordingly.

Bibliography

Conzelmann, Hans. *The Theology of St. Luke*. Philadelphia: Fortress Press, 1982.

Dupont, D. J. *The Sources of Acts*. London: Longmann and Todd, 1964.

Edwards, O. C., Jr. *Luke's Story of Jesus*. Philadelphia: Fortress Press, 1981.

Ellis, E. E. *The Gospel of Luke*. Grand Rapids: Eerdmans, 1981.

Fitzmeyer, Joseph A. *The Gospel of Luke*. New York: Doubleday, 1981. Westminster Press, 1971.

Hengel, Martin. *Acts and the History of Earliest Christianity*. Philadelphia: Fortress Press, 1980.

Jervill, J. *Luke and the People of God*. Minneapolis: Augsburg Publishing House, 1972.

Johnson, Luke Timothy, *The Acts of the Apostles* (Sacra Pagina, Volume 5). Collegeville: Michael Glazier Books 1992.

Keck, Leander E., and J. Martyn, eds. *Studies in Luke-Acts*. Philadelphia: Fortress Press, 1980.

Kingsbury, Jack Dean, *Confict In Luke*, Minneapolis: Fortress Press, 1991.

Powell, Mark Allen, *What Are They Saying About Acts?* Mahwah, NJ: Paulist Press, 1991.

Tiede, David L. *Prophecy and History in Luke-Acts*. Philadelphia: Fortress Press, 1980.

Eight

The Gospel of John

The Growth of the New Testament

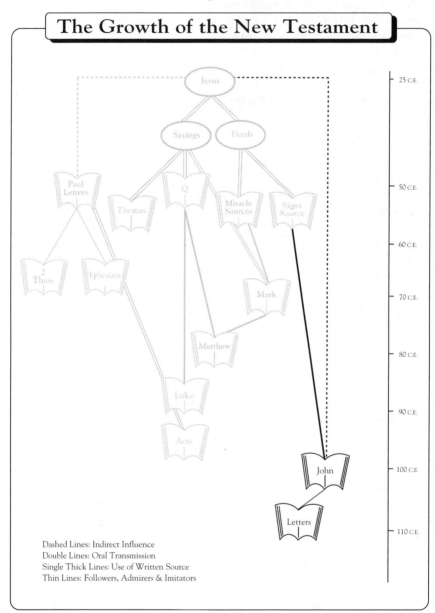

25 C.E.

50 C.E.

60 C.E.

70 C.E.

80 C.E.

90 C.E.

100 C.E.

110 C.E.

Jesus

Sayings   Deeds

Paul
Letters

Q

Thomas

Miracle
Sources

Signs
Source

2
Thess

Ephesians

Mark

Matthew

Luke

Acts

John

Letters

Dashed Lines: Indirect Influence
Double Lines: Oral Transmission
Single Thick Lines: Use of Written Source
Thin Lines: Followers, Admirers & Imitators

The Gospel of John is very different from the synoptic Gospels. The ministry of Jesus takes place over a three-year period rather than for only one year. The style of speech attributed to Jesus is not at all the same as it is elsewhere. In John we frequently find long discourses continuing on for many paragraphs, whereas in the synoptics Jesus' speech (even when collected into discourse sections) consists of short parables, debates, proverbs, and comments. While the order of events in Jesus' life differs to some extent from that in the synoptics, the overall biographical outline is the same. Most scholars divide the Gospel into two major parts: a Book of Signs (1:19–12:50) and a Book of Glory (13:1–20:31), preceded by an introductory poem and followed by a chapter of resurrection appearances. In the Book of Signs Jesus reveals himself primarily through miracles, signs, and wonders. In the Book of Glory revelation comes primarily through his words and his resurrection.

Read the Gospel of John. Underline the passages in which Jesus says "I am, . . ." for example, "I am the light of the world.' Also underline the passages in which Jesus claims to have come from above, or from the Father, and those in which Jesus declares he will return above, or return to the Father. The "I am" passages you underline will highlight an important and unique feature of John; the others will enable you to see more clearly the most important themes in John's Gospel.

Author, date, and place of origin

After a century or more of study and debate, scholars who analytically study the New Testament find themselves in general agreement on one point: the Gospel of John is the product of a complex process of creation involving the work of several individuals over a period of years. The Gospel seems to have been edited and reedited. Various passages seem to have been shifted from their original location to other locations. For example, it is likely that chapter 7 originally followed chapter 5, for it continues the thought of 5

John

The Fourth Gospel was composed by an anonymous author in the last decade of the first century. About 180 C.E. Irenaeus reports the tradition that ascribes the book to John the elder who lived at Ephesus, and still others to the beloved disciple (John 13:23–25, 19:25– 27, 20:2–10, 21:7, 20–23). The Fourth Gospel was opposed as heretical in the early church, and it knows none of the stories associated with John, son of Zebedee. In the judgment of many scholars, it was produced by a "school" of disciples, probably in Syria.

and takes place in the same region. Chapter 6 seems to have been inserted between them at some later time. Other passages seem to have been written as additions to earlier material. It has been suggested, for example, that John 3:31–36; 5:51–58; 8:1–59; 12:44–50; 15:1–17:26; and 21:1–18, 20–22 were added by a later author to sections he found already in existence. At the end of chapter 14 for example, Jesus says, "So up, let us go forward!" (14:31) but the discourses continue to 18:1 when, "after these words, Jesus went out with his disciples, and crossed the Kedron ravine." Apparently 15:1–17:26 was inserted right after 14:31. Chapter 17, an extended prayer by Jesus, may have been written independently and then added to the end of the section 15:1—16:33. The passage John 7:53–8:11 is out of place in its context and is written more in the style of Luke's author than of John's. Today some translations place that passage at the very end of the Gospel.

Some scholars, recognizing John's original order has been altered, have attempted to reorganize the Gospel, but they do not agree on what the proper order should be. Many scholars, recognizing the Gospel has gone through a complex set of stages to arrive at its present form, have offered theories about what those stages were, but in this matter too there is no agreement.

John's is the only Gospel to make any claim to eyewitness evidence. Shortly after Jesus' death, "one of the soldiers stabbed his side with a lance, and at one there was a flow of blood and water. This is vouched for by an eyewitness, whose evidence is to be trusted" (19:34–35). This person is evidently not the author of the Gospel. Rather, he is someone whom the author uses to validate his own non-eyewitness account of this particular event. Chapter 21, at the very end of the Gospel, may have been written separately, by an individual who had little or nothing to do with writing the other parts of the Gospel, and later added to the Gospel. In chapter 21, "the disciple whom Jesus loved" is reported to be "this same disciple who attests what has here been written. It is in fact he who wrote it, and we know that his testimony is true" (21:24). The passage is probably meant to refer to chapter 21, rather than to the whole Gospel.

The disciple whom Jesus loved is also referred to as "the Beloved Disciple." John's author depicts the Beloved Disciple closest to Jesus during the Last Supper (13:23) and is careful to show him arriving at the tomb of Jesus first, beating Peter to the site in a race (20:4). But we know nothing of him apart from what John's Gospel tells us. There are no convincing reasons to believe the Beloved Disciple's name was John or that he wrote the Gospel. He may, however, have been the source for the traditions appearing in chapter 21.

The Gospel goes by the name John, but this does not tell us anything about its author. Whoever he was, he was not the same person who is responsible for the New Testament's last book, the Revelation of John, although the author of the Gospel may also have written the three Letters of John. At least it may be said that those letters are quite similar to the Gospel in their ideas and style and probably were written by members of the same community as the Gospel's author. Because the Gospel was written over a period of years by several persons it is misleading to use one name for its author. But to do otherwise would lead to great confusion. We shall refer to John as the author of the Gospel of John just as we call the unknown author of the Gospel of Matthew "Matthew," but in this case John refers to more than one person.

The Greek in which John is written seems often to have been influenced by Semitic linguistic constructions. Therefore, most scholars believe it was written in an area where Semitic languages were commonly used, perhaps Syria.

The date of John is debated. The earliest fragments of any Gospel yet found are fragments of John, fragments dated to the first half of the second century, yet the fact that John came into being through the work of a sequence of editors may indicate it was only toward the end of the first century that it finally was completed. Because it contains an exalted view of Jesus, as the Word of God come from God, some believe it must have been written a considerable time after the life of Jesus. But, on the other hand, Paul's view of Jesus is quite exalted, and his works are the earliest we have.

The Gospel contains few sayings of Jesus from oral tradition and so many scholars assume it was written after the period of oral transmission was nearly over. But it could be argued that emphasis on orally transmitted sayings was a later development in Christianity, and sayings of Jesus received through spiritually inspired individuals were found satisfactory in very early Christian communities. Paul, for example, depends more on personal inspiration than on oral tradition, a fact he seeks to make clear in the first part of Galatians. The Gospel of Thomas begins by declaring that it contains the words the living Jesus spoke, which may be intended to contrast with traditions carrying forth words the risen Jesus spoke.

The fact is, we do not know when the gospel was written. Although the date C.E. 95 is frequently used for John, it is uncertain even in comparison with the inexact dating of the other Gospels. Some scholars have argued it may even have been the first Gospel written, and, while this is a minority view, it cannot be dismissed out of hand. Even if the Gospel went through a series of revisions, they may have taken far fewer years than the decades many scholars believe were required.

The beginning of the Gospel

The Gospel of John begins with a poem that probably existed long before the Gospel was written. Possibly it was written before the time of Jesus. As it stands, the poem is divided by inserted passages about John the Baptist. The following passages probably constitute the original: 1:1–5, 10–14, 16–17. The poem begins the Gospel, and so we know it was important to the Gospel's author, but it is possible to stress its importance too much. Many of the themes of the poem, that Jesus is the Word, for example, are never mentioned again.

The Greek term usually translated *word* is *logos*. *Logos* is a complex term with broader meaning than the English term *word*. Logos can mean reason, organizing principle, saying, or even philosophical position. Teachings about the nature of life, for example, would be *bios* (life) *logos*, which gave rise to the word *biology*.

The term *logos* (Word) has various meanings in Greek and was a key word in Greek philosophy of the first century. It is likely, however, that the poem at the beginning of John does not derive from Greek philosophical speculation. It probably stems from Jewish speculations about the nature of the Wisdom of God.

In the book of Proverbs, especially in chapter 8, the Wisdom of God is treated as a semi-independent aspect of God who was present at the creation and before creation, and who descends to earth to call human beings to live morally and to seek understanding. Often, Proverbs reports, Wisdom's call is ignored. Nearly all of the attributes of the Word in the first chapter of John are attributes of Wisdom in Proverbs.

The term for Wisdom in Greek is *sophia*, a noun of feminine gender. The term *logos* is a noun of masculine gender. It is possible that because Jesus was male the masculine term *logos* was substituted for the feminine term *sophia*. If we experimentally substitute *Wisdom* for *Word*, the following statements from John's introductory poem correspond with pre-Christian Jewish speculations about Wisdom:

"When all things began, Wisdom already was. Wisdom dwelt with God, and what God was, Wisdom was. Wisdom, then, was with God at the beginning, and through her all things came to be; no single thing was created without her. All that came to be was alive with her life, and that life was the light of men. The light shines on in the dark, and the darkness has never mastered it. . . . Wisdom was in the world; but the world, though it owed its being to her, did not recognize her. She entered her own realm, and her own would not receive her."

The idea that "Wisdom became flesh" is absent from previous speculations. It is not, however, unique to John's Gospel, for it is found in the Christian tradition as early as Paul's first letter to the Corinthians, where he declares Christ is the Wisdom of God (1 Cor. 1:24). The concept of Jesus as God's Word is unique to the community of John; the concept of Jesus as God's Wisdom can be found in several other New Testament texts and in the Gospel of Thomas.

Like the Gospel of Mark and the letters of Paul, John contains no story of Jesus' birth. One passage, however, implies he was born in Nazareth instead of Bethlehem and that his father was not a descendent of David (7:41–42); another passage assumes his father was Joseph (1:45). On these matters John and the synoptic Gospels seem to disagree.

Jesus' mission begins during the time of John the Baptist (not after John's arrest as other Gospels report) and continues for three years. This number can be derived from the fact that the Gospel mentions three Passover festivals.

At its beginning the Gospel takes care to make clear who Jesus is and asserts that at least some individuals recognized him correctly. In 1:29 John the Baptist declares he is "the Lamb of God," and in 1:34 he is "God's Chosen One." Andrew and an unnamed associate call Jesus "Rabbi" (1:38) and then inform Simon Peter he is "Messiah" and "Christ" (1:41). Philip declares he is "the man spoken of by Moses in the Law, and by the prophets" (1:45), and Nathanial says he is "Son of God" and "King of Israel" (1:49). Finally, Jesus publicly implies he is Son of Man (1:51). The gradual revelation of the mission of the Son of Man, which characterizes Mark, and the delayed discovery of the testimony of the prophets Luke reports (24:27) are absent here; Jesus' full complement of titles is announced immediately.

John the Baptist

Like the Gospel of Mark, John's Gospel begins its story of Jesus' ministry with an account of his interaction with John the Baptist and even inserts passages referring to John into its introductory poem. More directly than in any other Gospel, John the Baptist states his inferiority to Jesus and, indeed, denies he has any significant purpose other than announcing the coming of Jesus. According to this Gospel, John was "sent from God; he came as a witness to testify to the light, that all might become believers through him. He was not himself the light; he came to bear witness to the light" (1:6–7). When asked who he was, John the Baptist "confessed without reserve and avowed, 'I am not the Messiah.' 'What then? Are you Elijah?' 'No,' he replied. 'Are you the prophet we await?' He answered 'No'" (1:19–20). He declares Jesus to be the lamb of God who takes away the sin of the world, that he is God's Chosen One, and that he has seen "the Spirit coming down like a dove and resting upon him" (1:29, 32–34).

John does not baptize Jesus, nor is his mission of baptizing given much significance in itself. Instead, his baptizing "in water" seems only to be a prelude to Jesus' baptizing "in Spirit."

According to this Gospel, at least two of Jesus' disciples formerly were disciples of John: Andrew and another who is unnamed. This report is quite probably true, at least insofar as it leads us to believe some of the Baptist's followers became followers of Jesus.

The ending of the Gospel

Like Matthew and Luke, John concludes his Gospel with accounts of Jesus' appearances to his followers after his resurrection. The accounts of Jesus' trial, death, and empty tomb in John are sufficiently similar to the accounts in the synoptics to prove John depends on established tradition for his version of these events.

There appear to be two separate accounts of the appearances of the risen Jesus. One is John 20:14–31; its final passage is a suitable conclusion for the whole Gospel. The second, 21:1–25, was written at a different time by a different author.

One of the most interesting aspects of the resurrection appearance stories in John is that they alternate between elements affirming the physical body of Jesus and elements that do not. For example, Jesus mysteriously enters a locked room and, immediately, gives evidence to Thomas of his solid physical existence (20:26–27). The diverse nature of these accounts testifies to a diversity of opinion in the John community.

Pontius Pilate

In the Gospel of John Pilate not only tries to avoid executing Jesus but even declares Jesus innocent. These efforts culminate in Pilate's declaration that Jesus is King of the Jews and imply his belief that his own authority derives from the Jewish God.

At first Pilate urges the Jewish leaders to "take him away and try him by your own law" (18:31). After their refusal and an interview with Jesus, he declares, "I find no case against him" (18:38). He repeats this two times subsequently (19:4, 19:6). Having heard from Jesus that his (Pilate's) authority derives from God, "from that moment Pilate tried hard to release him" (19:12). This seems to imply Pilate concurs with Jesus' statement.

"The Jews" use political pressure to force Pilate to agree to the execution, arguing they will tell Pilate's superior, Caesar, that Pilate refused to execute someone who defied Caesar. Pilate gives in "to satisfy" them. But, at the end, he writes an inscription reading, "Jesus of Nazareth King of the Jews" and has it fastened to the cross. The Jews protest, wishing it to read "'He claimed to be' King of the Jews," but Pilate refuses, saying, "What I have written, I have written" (19:19–22). This implies that Pilate concurs with the claim. In writing the account this way, John absolves Pilate of responsibility in Jesus' execution at least as strongly as any of the other Gospels.

Instead of Pilate, "the Jews" are blamed. Only in John are Jesus' opponents called "the Jews." In other Gospels various factions of the Jewish leadership oppose Jesus: Pharisees, Chief Priests, Sadducees, but the inclusive term *the Jews* is not used. It bears repeating that the accounts in the Gospels do not give an unbiased historical view of the trial and execution of Jesus. They seek to absolve those who owe their position to Rome (Pilate and Herod) and to shift the blame to others; the only others present are Jewish. While it is conceivable there may have been a kind of grand jury inquisition into Jesus' case by the Sanhedrin, a Jewish court dominated by priests and Sadducees, it is not possible that they or any other Jewish people could have forced Pilate to execute a person whom he declared to be innocent. Pilate, should he have done this, would have been guilty under Roman law of a serious crime and would have been subject to removal from office.

John's central theme

The Gospel of John contains two crucial, interrelated statements about Jesus: he came from the Father into the world; he will leave the world and return to the Father (see 13:3, 16:25–30). In a sense, these are John's main gospel message. The Gospel elaborates on those statements in substantial detail. The elaborations make seemingly complex claims about the nature and mission of Jesus, but they are based on quite a simple system of ideas. Much of the apparent complexity of the Gospel derives from two factors: first, the Gospel went through various hands in its composition and so contains the perspectives of a number of people; second, its relatively simple underlying ideas are expressed in a wide variety of ways.

The basic system of ideas in John presupposes two aspects to reality. One is valued positively, the other negatively. These aspects may be thought of in a variety of ways: two realms or two dimensions or two levels or two forms of human existence. The primary image in John is of two levels, one above and one below, but it would be naive to think of them as a heaven up there and a world down here.

The realm above is the place of God, light, life, truth, love, peace, unity, and other positively valued aspects of existence. The realm below, the world, is the place of the devil, darkness, death, lies, hatred, conflict, disharmony, and other negatively valued aspects of existence. Initially human beings are in the realm below and Jesus in the realm above. Jesus comes into this realm, and enables those who believe in him to become members of the realm above. At times the Gospel states the distinction between the two realms very directly. Jesus is quoted as having said to "worldly" individuals who oppose him, "You belong to this world below, I to the world above. Your home is in this world, mine is not" (8:23).

The physical world itself is not rejected by God. In John's most famous passage we read (in the often-quoted King James Version), "God so loved the world, that he gave his only begotten Son, that whosoever believeth in him should not perish but have everlasting life" (3:16). The world as this physical place is loved, but the world as a realm contradictory to the realm above is repudiated. In most of the passages in John the second, negative, sense of *world* is meant.

Even more than Paul, who believes that people made perfect through Christ remain subject to temptations of the flesh, John is dualistic, black and white, without shades of gray. One is either of this world or of the world above; there are no alternatives.

Salvation

Although the Gospel states Jesus knows about the elements of the higher world and speaks of them and reveals them, the primary fact is that he *is* those elements. The "I am" sayings in John, found in no other Gospel, do not simply speak poetically. When Jesus says, "I am the light of the world" (8:13) or "I am the way; I am the truth; I am life" (14:6), he does not merely claim to know about those things or to teach about those things; he claims to *be* those things. If one comprehends or "finds" Jesus, one finds the light, way, truth, life. But the proposition may be inverted: if you find the light of the world, or the way, the truth, life, you find Jesus. There are no halfway measures, no people who have a little light and some life and a general grasp of the way.

John's Gospel presents Jesus as one from above who has come below and, having gathered people to him, returns above. Those whom he gathered continue his mission and will join Jesus above. Thus, they have eternal life, light, and truth. Once Jesus has come, the possibility exists for people to come to Jesus. Even though he returned above, a new representative from the higher region has come down: the Holy Spirit, which unites and characterizes those with faith who are still in this world. In John, the Holy Spirit is called the *Paraclete,* meaning advocate, representative, or helper.

The characteristics of the higher realm are characteristics of persons who have attained it. You cannot gradually attain them. Either you have them or you do not. Those who have life, in this sense, have a different kind of life than those who simply are biologically alive. Their life is eternal, the variety of life appropriate to the higher realm.

Unity

Because unity is a characteristic of the higher realm, those in that realm (including people alive in this world who have attained that realm) are unified with each other and with God. Jesus, because he is that realm and because he presents that realm to people is, therefore, unified with God. Often Jesus' words in John 10:30, "My Father and I are one," are taken to mean Jesus uniquely is God. But, in another place, he said, "If you loved me you would have been glad to hear that I was going to the Father; for the Father is greater than I" (14:28).

Jesus is united with the Father—the Gospel leaves no doubt about that—but this unity is not unique to him; it is characteristic of all who have attained the higher realm. Chapter 17 stresses this overriding unity. In verses 20–23 Jesus prays "for those also who through their words put their faith in me; may they all be one: as you, Father, are in me, and I in you, so also may they be in us, that the world may believe that you did send me. The glory which you gave me I have given to them, that they may be one, as we are one; I in them and you in me, may they be perfectly one. Then the world will learn that you did send me, that you did love them as you did me." Since they are in a state of unity appropriate to the higher realm, they should act accordingly; action in accord with such unity is love.

Jesus is not one thing and his followers another. As he came from above, so they who dwell with him or who have faith in him now come from above. Here the saying "he who receives any messenger of mine receives me; receiving me, he receives the One who sent me" (13:20 and found also in Q [Luke 10:16 and Matt. 10:40]) is interpreted most literally. There is no distinction among those who are of the higher realm; to hear a messenger of Jesus years after his death is to hear Jesus and so to hear God. The ideas of 13:20 are restated in 16:15 when Jesus addresses his followers and says, "All that the Father has is mine, and that is why I said, 'Everything that he makes known to you he will draw from what is mine.'"

It is hard to imagine that persons born in this world and dwelling in it like everybody else can suddenly achieve the ability to declare they come from above. Yet the logic of John's Gospel leads one to believe this can be the case, for when one hears an individual claim to come from above, one does not hear that individual per se, but the Spirit of God speaking through the individual. After Jesus declares in chapter 10, "My Father and I are one" (10:30), the passage goes on to argue that Scripture (Psalm 82:6) demonstrates that those to whom the word of God is delivered, and who accept the word of God, are themselves Gods. Jesus declares in 8:42–47 that only those who listen to the words of God have the right to claim God is their father. The Gospel of John does not take the concept "children of God" lightly. Jesus is the preeminent child of God; those who have faith in him and continue his work are children of God as well.

Judgment

It seems, on the surface, that on the matter of judgment the Gospel of John is inconsistent or even contradictory. Some passages imply that Jesus came to pass judgment on the world and those who hear him. He says, "It is for judgment that I have come into this world" (9:39); "The Father does not judge anyone, but has given full jurisdiction to the Son . . . As Son of Man, [I have] also been given the right to pass judgment . . . I cannot act by myself; I judge as I am bidden [by the Father]" (5:22, 27, 30). On the other hand, other passages imply he did not come to pass judgment at all: "It was not to judge the world that God sent his Son into the world, but that through him the world might be saved" (3:17); "I pass judgment on no man, but if I do judge, my judgment is valid because it is not I alone who judge, but I and he who sent me" (8:16). In addition, we hear "the man who puts his faith in [the Son] does not come under judgment; but the unbeliever has already been judged in that he has not given his allegiance to God's only Son" (3:18).

The key passage is the last one quoted: John does not use the term *judgment* in the same way it is used in other New Testament books. Outside John, *judgment* means a decision rendered by God or the Son of Man on a person's fitness to receive eternal life. For John *judgment* refers to the *believer's* decision.

The Father sends the Son. All inhabitants of the lower realm must then either choose to have faith in him and to believe he came from above, or choose against him. The correct choice *is* eternal life; the incorrect choice leaves one in darkness and in the realm of death. The correct choice does not "lead to" eternal life, or "eventually result in" eternal life. Eternal life is the immediate consequence of belief. The judgment promised or threatened in the future in other Gospels and letters occurs in John in the present time. Your choice is your judgment. Eternal life is *promised* in other sources. In John it is *present* as soon as the right choice is made.

The Father, then, judges insofar as he sends the Son and thereby requires the judgmental choice to be made. The Son judges insofar as he is the determining factor concerning which choice must be made. But, really, individuals judge themselves, for it is their own choice. Clearly, judgment in John means something quite different than it means elsewhere in the New Testament. It is not judicial. There is no trial and no totaling up of sins, only the requirement that each individual choose to believe or not to believe. We may be reasonably confident the rather inappropriate term *judgment* would not have been used in John had it not been firmly established in previous Christian tradition.

The Gospel of John can, without contradiction, switch sentences in midsentence: "I tell you a time is coming, indeed it is already here, when the dead shall hear the voice of the Son of God, and all who hear shall come to life" (5:25). Here the "dead" are people without belief. Events that others assumed to be future are made present in this Gospel: "Now is the hour of judgment for this world; now shall the Prince of this world be driven out" (12:31). To those who believe, the future is now.

Obedience to Torah is not an important factor in John. Its legal sections are not relevant, although its authority as prophecy remains. Moses is not the lawgiver in John but an important prophet testifying to the coming of Jesus Christ. The most extended discussion of Law occurs in 7:19–24 where Jesus, with argumentation that would have been acceptable to some Pharisees, contends the act of healing on the Sabbath is acceptable under Mosaic Law. When it comes to Law in regard to Christians, a new commandment is given: "Love one another" (13:34). As salvation comes instantly with belief, and the only commandment specifically given is to love one another, Torah Law has little significance. Jesus says, "This is the work that God requires: believe in the one whom he has sent" (6:29).

According to the account in John's Gospel, Jesus came from the realm above, manifested himself so those who chose to believe might "dwell with him," ascended to the realm above, and, for a brief period, manifested himself to his followers after his death. Afterwards, in Jesus' absence from this lower realm, those dwelling in it can enter the realm above through the work of the Spirit. The term sometimes used for the Spirit is in Greek *Paraclete* or in English *Advocate*. This term has legal connotations and is possibly connected to the idea found in Mark 13:11 that "when you are arrested and taken away [to court], do not worry beforehand about what you will say, but when the time comes say whatever is given you to say; for it is not you who will be speaking, but the Holy Spirit." In John, the presence of the Spirit provides the continuing presence of the higher realm in the lower and, accordingly, the continuing possibility for people to enter that realm.

Baptism and the last supper

Only in John is it reported that Jesus baptized anyone, and only in John is Jesus not said to have been baptized: "Jesus went into Judaea with his disciples, stayed there with them, and baptized. John too was baptizing at Aenon, near to Salim, because water was plentiful in that region; and people were constantly coming for baptism. This was before John's imprisonment" (3:22–24). Later, however, the Pharisees hear "Jesus is winning and baptizing more disciples than John" (4:1). But the Gospel adds to this statement the comment "although, in fact, it was only the disciples who were baptizing and not Jesus himself." Evidently, at an earlier stage of the Gospel, the tradition that Jesus did baptize people was accepted and included to show that even during John's ministry he came to surpass John as a baptizer. Later the idea that Jesus baptized was retracted.

The passages on baptism are followed by a discussion between Jesus and a Samaritan woman at a well. Jesus declares he will give her "living water," which is "an inner spring always welling up for eternal life" (4:14). From John's perspective Jesus is the living water (as the Holy Spirit will be later).

It is typical of John's Gospel that a discussion of a historical event, the baptisms by John, shifts into a more metaphoric discussion of reception of "water and Spirit" and then into the identification of Jesus with the living water of eternal life. The discussion becomes increasingly abstract, but as it does so it moves increasingly close to the principal themes of the Gospel. Recognition that the true water is Jesus is akin to the recognition that the true air is the Spirit. One must know that *pneuma* is the term for both wind and for Spirit in Greek to understand 3:8, where a discussion of Spirit shifts suddenly, but not inappropriately, to quotation of a proverb about wind.

John's account of the Last Supper, 13:1–17:26, is extremely long, yet the incident for which the Last Supper is most famous—the precedent for all subsequent communion meals—Jesus' words "this is my body" and "this is my blood," do not appear. The most significant action Jesus performs is to wash his disciples' feet and command his followers to do likewise (13:15).

Earlier in the Gospel, following the signs source's account of the miraculous feeding of the five thousand (6:1–13), Jesus delivers a long discourse declaring himself to be the food of eternal life and the bread come down from heaven bringing life to the world (6:27, 34). (Recall that the miracles source in John is called the signs source because it uses the word *sign* instead of *miracle*.) This occurs in the context of a discussion of the incident where God sent manna from heaven to Moses' people in the desert (see Exodus 16:1–36). It is typical of John's Gospel to take a Torah passage, often one relating a miracle associated with the Exodus, and to reveal that it has principal symbolic reference to Jesus. The discourse in chapter 6 progresses to a passage probably reflecting speculations about the communion meal: "Unless you eat the flesh of the Son of Man and drink his blood you can have no life in you. Whoever eats my flesh and drinks my blood possesses eternal life, and I will raise him up on the last day. my flesh is real food; my blood is real drink. Whoever eats my flesh and drinks my blood dwells continually in me and I dwell in him" (6:53–56). Hearing this, many of his disciples exclaimed, "This is more than we can stomach! Why listen to such words?" (6:61). "From that time on, many of his disciples withdrew and no longer went about with him" (6:66). From the perspective of the Gospel of John, literal interpretations of Jesus' words, or of statements in the Hebrew Scriptures, will mislead. Many disciples, so the report goes, were literal in their interpretations and so were offended. The Gospel intends Jesus' words instead to be interpreted symbolically. Jesus is the bread of life and living water, and therefore eating and drinking him are the equivalent of recognizing he has come from God.

The origin of the discourses of Jesus

There are three alternative theories about whose words are being quoted in the majority of the passages in the Gospel of John:

1. Jesus spoke them in Aramaic during his lifetime, and they were subsequently translated into the Greek versions in John. Few if any analytical scholars accept this alternative. Most of the words attributed to Jesus in John are too far out of accord in style and substance with the words attributed to Jesus in all other sources (the synoptics, Paul, and Thomas) for them to have been produced by the same person. All evidence indicates the style of sayings in the synoptics is basically that of Jesus, even though there is great debate as to exactly which of those sayings derive from Jesus.
2. An author wrote the words in Jesus' name. This theory is held, implicitly, by many scholars. The idea that discourses in John's Gospel originated as written texts seems attractive at first. The Gospel, after all, is a written document. But given that the discourses so frequently contain defenses and arguments against *listeners* with contrary views and opposing opinions, it is not probable they were written down by individuals in the privacy of their studies.
3. Persons spoke the words in Jesus' name through the action of the Holy Spirit. This is the likely origin of many discourses in John. They originally were actual speech presented publicly to actual people, some sympathetic but many unsympathetic. The discourses were then transcribed, either on the spot or from memory, and finally edited into their present written form. The assumption that speech by later Christians would be the same as the speech of Jesus is inherent in the logic of John's system. To rephrase John 13:20, "He who writes down the words of a messenger of Jesus writes down the words of Jesus; writing down those words he writes down the words of the One who sent Jesus."

How should one in the community of John go about learning what Jesus taught? The writer of the Gospel does not recommend researching ancient documents or discussing matters with elderly eyewitnesses. The answer is contained in the following statement attributed to Jesus: "I have told you all this while I am still here with you; but your Advocate, the Holy Spirit whom the Father will send in my name, will teach you everything, and will call to mind all that I have told you" (14:26). In order to determine what Jesus said one can either ask him, during his lifetime in the world, or later, ask one to whom the Holy Spirit has been sent.

The discourses in John seem to derive from a period considerably after the crucifixion and from individuals who spoke Greek rather than Aramaic. Their origin, therefore, derives from people who spoke in the Spirit rather than from Jesus himself. Theoretically this should make no difference, for otherwise it would be senseless for the Gospel to declare that Jesus said the Holy Spirit would "teach you everything and call to mind all that I have told you." Insofar as people possessed of the Holy Spirit spoke what they heard from the Spirit, they would speak what Jesus spoke. In the community of John there presumably were people who had received the new Advocate, the Holy Spirit. If one accepted such people as messengers of Jesus, essentially one thereby received Jesus, and thus the One who sent Jesus. When such people spoke, their listeners heard God. That is asking a great deal of individuals. For them to claim to speak the words of God, to represent God, would lead inevitably to the kind of misunderstandings repeatedly evidenced in the Gospel. Those who are messengers of Jesus, who have received the Holy Spirit and belong to the higher realm and can claim Jesus dwells in them, are revealers of God, as Jesus was. But revealers who say that hearing their words is the same as hearing God will, obviously, be accused of self-glorification and claiming to be God. Time after time the speaker in the Gospel demands his listeners not confuse him with the originator of the words spoken. The words invariably are said to derive from the Father.

Imagine a Christian man of the John community on a street corner declaring that his listeners' eternal fate depends on accepting his words as those of God. He would immediately be accused of extraordinary self-glorification. His response would be that he, personally, did not claim to be God and that he, personally, did not offer private opinions as revelations. Rather, he would insist that what he spoke through the Spirit was delivered to him from above and that he laid no claim to any personal glory at all.

Many discourses in the Gospel of John contain such disclaimers. Here are several examples: "The teaching that I give is not my own. it is the teaching of him who sent me" (7:16). "I have not come of my own accord. I was sent by the One who truly is, and him you do not know. I know him because I come from him and he it is who sent me" (7:28). "I do nothing on my own authority, but in all that I say, I have been taught by my Father. He who sent me is present with me, and has not left me alone; for I always do what is acceptable to him" (8:28–29). "God is the source of my being, and from him I come. I have not come of my own accord; he sent me. Why do you not understand my language? It is because my revelation is beyond your grasp" (8:42–43). "When a man believes in me, he believes in him who sent me rather than in me; seeing me, he sees him who sent me. . . . I do not speak on my own authority, but the Father who sent me has himself commanded me what to say and to speak" (12:45, 49). "I am not myself the source of the words I speak to you; it is the Father who dwells in me doing his own work" (14:10). "The word you hear is not mine. it is the word of the Father who sent me" (14:24).

The very repetitiveness of these examples should add up to a solid impression: whoever is responsible for the words in the discourses in John is denying flatly, repeatedly, and emphatically that he is the source of his own words or authority. The discourses in the Gospel of John derive from Jesus, but *not* from the Jesus whose life story the Gospel relates; they derive from Jesus in the sense that Jesus is the source of the Spirit of God in whose name a Spirit-inspired Christian prophet might speak.

The previous few paragraphs discuss the orgin of the discourses of Jesus in John's Gospel. But one certainly must not lose sight of the fact that in John's Gospel Jesus is presented as an historical man who spoke specifically about himself. In John's Gospel Jesus is the light of the world, Jesus is the way and truth and the life, Jesus came from the Father into the workd and Jesus belongs eternally with the Father. Jesus is unique, a human being, to be sure, but a divine person sent to the world from God. Through faith in Jesus, and only by such faith, can one attain eternal life.

Topics

Sources

The principal source for the sayings and discourses of Jesus in the Gospel of John is, probably, the transcribed speech of Spirit-inspired prophets of the John community. In addition, the Gospel contains a few sayings from the same oral tradition used by the other evangelists. These few are usually edited to reflect the point of view of the Gospel.

At its beginning the Gospel contains a poem focused on the word *logos*, which probably, when first written, was intended to refer to the idea of God's wisdom, *sophia*. Whether the poem is pre-Christian or not is uncertain, but if we assume the ideas it contains refer to the Wisdom of God (identified, in John, with Jesus), then it at least contains ideas circulating prominently in Judaism prior to Christianity.

John apparently used a collection of miracle stories during one stage of the composition of the Gospel. This collection, referring to miracles as "signs," has come to be known as the signs source. It is discussed in some detail in chapter 3 of this book.

Despite John's substantial differences from the synoptic Gospels, its account of Jesus' trial and execution and the discovery of his empty tomb is similar in outline, but not in detail, to that of the synoptics. This similarity indicates John used a source in common with the synoptic authors. Possibly he was familiar with one of their versions; more likely both he and they were dependent on a passion narrative written in the early years of the Christian movement before any of the Gospels had been written.

Jesus

The phrase *Jesus' life* has two meanings in reference to John. In one sense it is Life with a capital letter, an aspect of God's higher realm. As such, Jesus' Life begins before the creation of the world, and it is Life the believer can receive. In this sense of the word, it is eternal Life, and it is either synonymous with or correlated with Light, Truth, and Unity, which are characteristics of the higher realm.

In the more ordinary sense, Jesus' life is significant in John primarily for the very fact that he came to the world. The particular events of his life testify to the fact of his presence in the world and to the fact he came from God; in themselves they are of little importance.

His life is his presentation of himself to the world with the demand the world recognize him for what he is. All else is detail.

Jesus' death is not the essential element in salvation for John. Jesus is once called "the Lamb of God" who "takes away the sin of the world" (1:29). This language reminds us of Paul's concept that Jesus' death is sacrificial. Although the Gospel deliberately places Jesus' death on Passover (in contrast to the synoptic accounts), there are no other indications that he was thought to have died as a sacrifice for sin.

Jesus' death is his return to his original place, the higher realm. Therefore it is not a tragic or even problematic death; it is a journey home. John reports Jesus said, "No one ever went up into heaven except the one who came down from heaven, the Son of Man whose home is in heaven. This Son of Man must be lifted up as the serpent was lifted up by Moses in the wilderness, so that everyone who has faith in him may in him possess eternal life" (3:13–15). Many scholars assume the "lifting up" of the Son of Man refers to his crucifixion, resurrection, and ascension. It seems odd that this should be likened to the raising up of a serpent. The reference is to Numbers 21:4–9, where the story is told of the Israelite people, disrespectful of God, being punished by a plague of serpents. They come to Moses for help. "And the Lord told Moses to make a serpent of bronze and erect it as a standard, so that anyone who had been bitten could look at it and recover." The connection between this and John's image of Jesus is clear: Jesus is one sent by God upon whom anyone in the realm of death might look and subsequently believe and thereby attain life. Understood in this way the image of the uplifted serpent refers to Jesus' whole mission rather than to his crucifixion, resurrection, and ascension.

Eschatology

The technical term for the variety of belief in the end of this world found in John is *realized eschatology*. The future has already become present. The end of this world, understood as a world of darkness, lies, and death, has already come. Jesus brought a potential end of the world with his arrival in it. For some the end has come; they believe Jesus came from the Father. For others the end has not yet come; they may believe at some time in the future. In one sense, therefore, the end time is coming; in another sense, it is already here. But, in any case, the potential for the end is here. Those who believe now have eternal life and now have passed through judgment. In the other texts we have examined, these characteristics are reserved for those who successfully survive the trials of the end and enter the Kingdom of Heaven.

Torah law

The system of ideas in John's Gospel contains no room for the idea that one must be obedient to detailed laws. Salvation comes to those who believe, although they are expected subsequently to act in accord with their belief and thus to obey the command to love one another. This command is not a law in the sense found in Torah, nor is it a revision or alteration of the Mosaic Law such as can be found elsewhere in the New Testament. It is a command along the lines of "live eternally," and as such it is, or should become, a characteristic of those in the higher realm.

Moses' role in the Gospel is that of a prophet, the most important of the prophets. "If you believed Moses, you would believe what I tell you, for it was about me that he wrote. But if you do not believe what he wrote, how are you to believe what I saw?" (5:46). Here the reference is not to Moses the lawgiver but Moses the prophet. When Moses is said to be a lawgiver, no particular implications are drawn from the fact. "Did not Moses give you the Law? Yet you all break it" (7:19); this statement may imply the people's disregard for the Law is not surprising considering their disregard for Moses' testimony to Jesus Christ. It does not imply that obedience to Moses' Law is necessary for salvation or even that one who never breaks it will be saved. From the point of view of John's Gospel the Torah is important as a prophetic document, but as a legal document it has little significance.

Community

Many members of the community of John were probably Jewish by birth. The Gospel is oriented significantly to Jewish festivals, concerning which Gentiles would have been ignorant, and the arguments it contains regarding the temple and Mosaic prophecy probably would not have been devised by

Gentile Christians. John is sympathetic to Samaritans, and the Gospel's community probably had Samaritan members. The Gospel portrays Samaritans as capable of anticipating and recognizing the Messiah, Jesus, even though he comes from the Jews (4:1–42).

Some members of the community were probably Gentile by birth. There is nothing to exclude Gentiles from recognizing Jesus came from God, and the principle that one must be born again through the Spirit means Jewish birth would be no decisive factor in community membership.

Controversy

The community is in serious conflict with what it calls "the Jews." As the Gospel shows substantial numbers of Jewish and Samaritan people correctly recognizing Jesus, the phrase *the Jews* cannot mean all Jewish people. It must be a subset of some sort, a subset probably including members of the leadership of the synagogues.

Three times the Gospel indicates the members of its community were expelled from synagogues. This expulsion is not depicted as a temporary crisis but as a permanent condition and may mark the beginning of the permanent break between the Jewish and the Christian religions. In 9:22 we are told the parents of the man born blind "were afraid of the Jews; for the Jewish authorities had already agreed that anyone who acknowledged Jesus as Messiah should be banned from the synagogue" (see also 12:42 and 16:2). Conflict between the John community and "the Jews" is emphasized in the Gospel.

Interactions

Miracles sources

John probably used a list of miracle stories to provide a narrative structure for the Gospel. It is called the signs source because it uses the term *signs* (in Greek, *semeia*) to indicate the miraculous actions of Jesus (see 20:30). The list was evidently written down to provide evidence Jesus was the Christ.

The Gospel of John retains from the signs source the idea that the signs do lead to belief, but at the same time it denies that those seeking truth should seek signs. Jesus says to the officer in the royal service whose son was ill and who came wishing him to help, "Will none of you ever believe without seeing signs and portents?" (4:48). Later (6:30), when he is asked by the people, "What sign can you give us to see, so that we may believe you?" rather than conjuring manna from heaven (as they seem to expect), he informs them, "I am the bread of life." In another place, however, Jesus is reported to have said, "If I am not acting as my Father would, do not believe me. But if I am, accept the evidence of my deeds, even if you do not believe me, so that you may recognize and know that the Father is in me, and I in the Father" (10:37–38). The ambiguity in John between, on the one hand, rejecting the practice of seeking signs and, on the other hand, believing in signs as evidence (along with the use of a source providing stories of signs), shows the various stages through which the Gospel passed. The signs source stems from a period when signs were an important way of communicating about Jesus; the rejection of signs, or their transference into metaphor, as with "the bread of life," is from a later period when asking for signs was regarded as evidence of a lack of faith.

Q Source

John did not use the Q source and probably did not know of its existence. It is more surprising that both Matthew and Luke used two of the same documents (Mark and Q) than it is that John did not have them (or did not choose to use them). John's realized eschatology is in direct contrast with the future eschatology of Q. Whereas Q tends to regard the judgment at the end time as a judicial trial, John regards it as the event of belief whereby the end of this world is made present.

Q predicts the second coming of the Son of Man, but for John there is no second coming. The Spirit will come after Jesus, but nowhere is it stated Jesus will come again. What Q thought the second coming would produce —the Kingdom of God on earth—John thought had been produced already in the first and only coming of Jesus. Where Q thought Jesus would usher in the Kingdom of God, John believes Jesus to be the Kingdom of God.

John seems to have relied upon persons inspired by the Spirit rather than on traditional sources, oral or written, for the sayings of Jesus. If John was the earliest Gospel (as is possible, but not probable), the later Gospels may have been written in reaction to its tendency to rely on Spirit-inspired prophetic information. The use of traditional oral and written sayings provides some control over the attribution of sayings to Jesus. The sayings of prophets would have had an unfortunate tendency to vary widely from prophet to prophet, a difficulty discussed in the First Letter of John, where "false prophets" and "antichrists" seem to be synonymous. They are contrasted with authentic "prophets" who presumably would be authentic "christs."

The Gospel of Thomas, a collection of sayings similar in format to Q, contains many ideas close to those of John. There we find sayings from the perspective of realized eschatology and the statement by Jesus that "I am the light." Thomas, like the poem introducing the Gospel of John, believes Jesus to be the Wisdom of God, who has come to earth to call humanity but who frequently finds rejection. Although Thomas is not a literary source for John, it may well reflect an earlier stage of development in the literature of the community that later produced John.

Paul

There is no evidence that John knew of Paul's letters or was directly influenced by Paul's teachings. Nevertheless, interesting relationships between the two exist. These relationships probably derive more from the similar working out of common themes than from a historical connection. As John's Gospel seems to rely heavily on the speeches of inspired Christian prophets for knowledge of Jesus' teachings, so Paul relied on inspiration for his teachings, as did his communities (see I Cor. 12:1–14:40). Neither John nor Paul felt obliged to seek what we would call historically accurate quotations.

Most striking is their common conception that, through Jesus, humanity received the ability to be totally transformed. How they speak of the transformation differs, but Paul almost certainly would have agreed with John's emphatic claims that anyone who believes in Jesus has (or will receive) eternal life, walks in light, and enters the realm of God. Paul, however, includes an "eschatological reservation" in nearly all of his comments about transformation: he believes that total transformation must await the return of Christ. John's "realized eschatology" requires no return.

Much that Paul wrote is intended to deny that the Law will bring salvation. John never discusses the matter but, implicitly, he agrees with Paul. From John's standpoint, to keep the Law but not to believe Jesus came from the Father and returned to him would not be a successful means of seeking salvation.

The major difference between the two is the difference in their interpretation of Jesus' death. For Paul, Jesus' death was the dividing line between the old order and the new, between the time when people sought salvation through Law and the time when salvation was achieved through faith. For John, Jesus' coming to earth is the dividing line; Jesus' death is his return to God that opened a way to God for those people who already had found eternal life. For Paul his death brought the opportunity for eternal life.

Mark

John and Mark seem to agree on the inadequacy of believing that because Jesus could do miracles and signs he was, therefore, Christ. Neither deny the miracles occurred. Both include them in their books, but neither wishes them to be the principal image their readers have of Jesus.

John does not share Mark's focus on the suffering, death, and resurrection of the Son of Man. In John, Jesus is glorified in his death and resurrection. His death and resurrection should be sources of revelation, but not the primary source of revelation; during his life Jesus revealed himself and brought eternal life to those who understood. For Mark the revelation of Jesus the Son of Man through his suffering, death, and resurrection was the essential element of his mission.

At times John, in a style reminiscent of Mark, shows some of Jesus' disciples seriously misunderstanding him. In chapter 6, Jesus' statements about eating flesh and drinking blood alienate some of them permanently. Shortly thereafter we hear "even his brothers were not believers in him" (7:5), but this is followed by the implicitly optimistic statement to his brothers, "The right time for me has not yet come, but any time is right for you" (7:6).

On the whole, however, John's Gospel gives a positive impression of the disciples. At the Gospel's very beginning, Andrew tells his brother Simon Peter, "We have found the Messiah" (1:41). Peter's statement in John 6:69 is possibly a version of the tradition we find in Mark 8:30 and reads: "We have faith, and we know that you are the Holy One of God." It is correct from John's perspective. At the end the disciples do encounter him raised from the dead, in contrast to the ending of Mark, where they all have fled and learn nothing of the resurrection.

Matthew

Few of Matthew's primary interests are reflected in John. For Matthew the Law is crucial, and Jesus came, in large part, to interpret it and bring it to completion. There is no good evidence that Christians of John's community were expected to follow the Law. The one command given is "love one another," but even that may be a command with which Matthew would disagree. The saying in Matthew, "love your enemies" (Matt. 5:44), includes people inside and outside the Christian community. In John "love one another" refers only to those who believe and have faith. It does not include those who are in the "world" and live in darkness.

In John the Law is prophetic, testifying to the coming of Jesus the Christ. On this point Matthew would agree, while insisting the Law must be obeyed.

Luke

Luke's Gospel has a "low Christology," which is a technical theological term meaning the humanity of Jesus is more strongly emphasized than his divinity. According to Luke, during his life Jesus revealed what he would be after his death, when God would give him unique and important tasks. He remains, however, a human being whom God chose for these special tasks. There is no implication in Luke's Gospel that Jesus and God are one. This contrasts, of course, with John's "high Christology," or emphasis on Jesus' divinity. In John, Jesus says, "I and the Father are one," and, according to the *logos* poem beginning the Gospel, Jesus was with God from the beginning and was God.

Luke's Gospel has the lowest Christology of any New Testament text we have studied; John's Gospel has the highest. The fact that both survive in the New Testament and are equally counted as Scripture is both a testimony to the diversity of interpretations of Jesus in the first century and a cause of the diversity of interpretations of Jesus in this century. The New Testament's diversity of interpretations is the greatest intellectual resource Christianity has.

Bibliography

Brown, Raymond E. *The Community of the Beloved Disciple.* New York: Paulist Press, 1979.

Brown, Raymond. *The Gospel According to John.* Anchor Bible, vols. 29 and 29A. New York: Doubleday, 1966. 1972.

Culpepper, R. Alan. *Anatomy of the Fourth Gospel.* Philadelphia: Fortress Press, 1983.

Fortna, Robert. *The Fourth Gospel and Its Predecessor.* Philadelphia: Fortress Press, 1988.

Haenchen, Ernst. *The Gospel of John.* Volumes 1 and 2. Philadelphia: Fortress Press, 1984.

Jervell, Jacob. *Jesus in the Gospel of John.* Minneapolis: Augsburg Publishing House, 1984.

Kysar, Robert. *John, the Maverick Gospel.* Louisville: Westminster/John Knox, 1993.

_____. *The Fourth Evangelist and His Gospel.* Minneapolis: Augsburg Publishing House, 1975.

Lindars, Barnabas. *The Gospel of John.* London: Oliphants, 1972.

MacRae, George. W. *Invitation to John.* Garden City, NY: Doubleday, 1978.

Perkins, Pheme. *The Gospel of John: A Theological Commentary.* Chicago: Franciscan Herald Press, 1978.

Sloyan, Gerard S., *What Are They Saying About John?* Mahwah: Paulist Press, 1991.

Smith, D. Moody, *John Among the Gospels.* Minneapolis: Fortress Press, 1992.

Talbert, Charles H. *Reading John.* New York: The Crossroad Publishing Company, 1992.

Nine

The Concluding Letters

The Growth of the New Testament

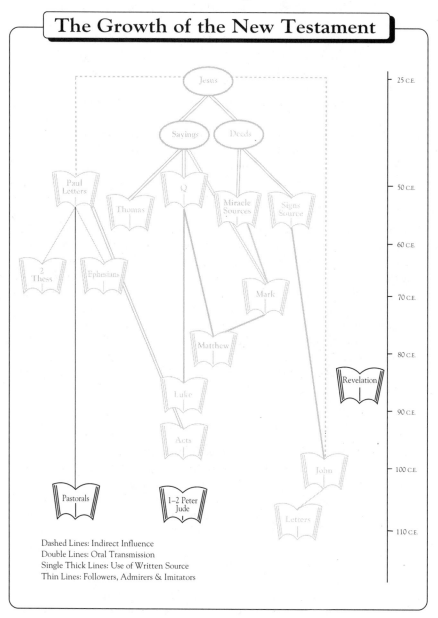

Jesus

Sayings   Deeds

Paul Letters   Q   Miracle Sources   Signs Source

Thomas

2 Thess   Ephesians

Mark

Matthew

Revelation

Luke

Acts

John

Pastorals   1–2 Peter Jude   Letters

25 C.E.

50 C.E.

60 C.E.

70 C.E.

80 C.E.

90 C.E.

100 C.E.

110 C.E.

Dashed Lines: Indirect Influence
Double Lines: Oral Transmission
Single Thick Lines: Use of Written Source
Thin Lines: Followers, Admirers & Imitators

In this chapter we will survey briefly the New Testament's concluding texts: the letters known as James, 1 John, 2 John, 3 John, Hebrews, 1 Timothy, 2 Timothy, Titus, 1 Peter, Jude, 2 Peter, and the Revelation to John. All in one way or another present themselves as letters, but some are not letters, as we shall see. The Revelation to John begins as a series of seven letters and then becomes a description of visions. We shall not consider any of the concluding letters in the detail with which we treated earlier texts, for, with the exception of the Revelation to John, they are relatively straightforward and easy to understand. The consensus of scholars is that they were written toward the end of the first century or during the first part of the second century. They provide us evidence of the consolidation of Christianity into an organized and structured religious movement.

The canon

A canon of Scripture is a collection of specific texts. The Hebrew Bible is the Jewish canon and is also part of the Christian canon. The authors of the New Testament texts did not regard their writings as sacred Scripture; the creation of the Christian canon happened many decades later, well after the authors of the texts had died. We know little of the "who, what, where, when" of the canon's creation, but we do know something of the "why," which involved responses to problems of several sorts, many of which are mentioned or implied in the concluding letters. Since the origin of the Christian canon is of interest to many people, we will discuss in greater detail those passages from the concluding letters that are most relevant to its creation.

The letter of James

Read the Letter of James paying attention to the separate units: 2:1–13, 2:14–26, 3:1–12. The Letter of James is written in good Greek by a person familiar with the forms of thought and argument commonly found among educated, Greek-speaking people. Since its author was thoroughly familiar with the traditions and teachings of Judaism we may be reasonably confident he was a Hellenistic Jew. Although Jesus' brother James is sometimes said to have written this letter, the letter nowhere claims or implies its author is Jesus' brother, and it is unlikely that he would have been educated in the manner of the letter's author.

Although known as a letter, James is really a collection of teachings or short sermons about how to live and how not to live. Three self-contained, short sermons are easily isolated: 2:1–13, 2:14–26, 3:1–12. The remainder of the letter, while not inconsistent with these sections, does not show any logical development of idea from idea. It probably circulated originally as a collection of separated teachings and was later combined into the form we now have.

It is questionable whether the Letter of James was originally Christian. The addition of two phrases (James 1:1, 2:1) could have adapted a collection of Hellenistic Jewish teachings for Christian use. There is nothing in the letter that could not have been accepted by most Jews. "Faith," for example, is not necessarily faith in Christ but faith in God, faith like Abraham's. "The coming of the Lord" (5:7) could refer to the coming of the Lord of Hosts (5:4). The letter insists faith must be accompanied by good works. This has troubled those who most firmly adhere to Paul's gospel of salvation through faith.

In its insistence that action must accompany faith the letter is reminiscent of Matthew's Gospel (Matt. 7:21). If the letter was originally Christian in origin it might have been written, as Matthew might have been written, in part to argue against those Christians who, following Paul, believed they were free from the obligation to follow the Law. James is uncompromising about the Law: "If a man keeps the whole law apart from one single point, he is guilty of breaking all of it" (2:10). Paul would agree with that statement, but would conclude that because all will break some point of the Law sooner or later, the Law cannot bring about salvation. But James concludes that therefore people must earnestly strive to keep the Law, arguing, "A man is justified by deeds and not by faith in itself" (2:24).

Both Paul and James appeal to Genesis 15:6 to demonstrate their points. James 2:18–24 uses that passage, along with the story in Genesis 22:1–19 of Abraham's obedience to God's command to sacrifice his son Isaac, to prove that faith must be combined with obedience to the Law. For Paul (Rom 4:1–25), Genesis 15:6 proves faith alone is essential.

While taking a strong stand on a variety of matters, the letter seems most strongly to object to improper behavior by wealthy people. When the Lord comes their wealth will do them no good, and, insofar as it tempts them to oppress the poor, their wealth will lead to their condemnation (5:1–6). This perspective, like many found in James, can be discovered in other New Testament letters and Gospels. The reason for this is not that the author of James used those writings as sources, but that many moral positions taken in James's letters and elsewhere, including the letters of Paul, were moral positions common in the ancient world and were taught by philosophers and religious leaders from many different traditions including, especially, Judaism.

Hebrews

Read Hebrews. Note the comparisons made between Christian beliefs and practices and Jewish beliefs and practices. Scholarly comments on the New

Testament document sometimes called "the Letter of Paul to Hebrews" usually contain the quite valid observation that the document is not a letter, is not by Paul, and is not written to Hebrews. It is an essay written for Christians by a Christian whose name we do not know. The author has substantial knowledge of the Greek translation of the Hebrew Bible, the Septuagint. His discussion of Judaism and of practices in the Jewish temple derive from his reading of biblical texts rather than from firsthand experience.

Hebrews has one main purpose, but the many details used to achieve that purpose make it seem complex. The main purpose of Hebrews is to demonstrate through biblical examples that Christianity is superior to Judaism. This does not mean Judaism is totally rejected, only that in the author's opinion it is inferior. By choosing to compare Christian ideas favorably with Jewish ideas, the author adopts Judaism as a fit standard of comparison. But, however, he finds item after item in Judaism and in Jewish priestly practice to have been superseded by Jesus Christ. The following are examples:

God formerly spoke through prophets; in Jesus he speaks through a Son who is "heir to the whole universe," who is "the effulgence of God's splendor and the stamp of God's very being and sustains the universe by his word of power" (Heb. 1:2–3).

"Moses . . . was faithful in God's household; and Jesus, of whom I speak, has been deemed worthy of greater honor than Moses, as the founder of a house enjoys more honor than his household" (3:2–3).

"The high priests made by the Law are men in all their frailty; but the priest appointed by the words of the oath which supersedes the Law is the Son, made perfect now forever" (7:28).

"The first covenant indeed had its ordinances of divine service and its sanctuary, but a material sanctuary" (9:1). "But now Christ has come, high priest of good things already in being. The tent of his priesthood is a greater and more perfect one, not made by men's hands, that is, not belonging to this created world; the blood of his sacrifice is his own blood, not the blood of goats and calves. . . ." (9:11–12).

Examples could be multiplied. Hebrews especially stresses the excellence of Jesus' priesthood. Jewish priests were born in to a special caste, the Levites, of which Jesus was not a Member. Hebrews makes a sustained argument that there is a priesthood, that of Melchizedek, superior to the priesthood of the Levites. In Genesis 14:18–20 Abraham encounters Melchizedek, the king of Salem, who is called "priest of God Most High." Melchizedek brings out food and wine and blesses Abraham, who gives him a tenth of everything. This passage intrigued Jewish interpreters because Melchizedek is given no genealogy, is not related to Abraham, and is never again mentioned in the Torah. Only once more in the Hebrew Bible is there a reference to him. Psalm 110, written to be sung on the occasion of the enthronement of a king of Israel or Judah, contains the line "The Lord has sworn and will not change his purpose, 'you are a priest forever in the succession of Melchizedek.'" The author of Hebrews comments extensively on Psalm 110 and finds in that Psalm evidence that Jesus is a priest in the succession of Melchizedek and that Jesus' priesthood is superior to Levitical priesthood. Jesus' priestly role takes place in the temple in heaven, not in the temple on earth. Therefore, Hebrews argues, he is the ideal prototype on which all earthly priests should be modeled.

In conceiving of Jesus as sacrificial victim and as high priest of the sacrifice and as the Son of God enthroned with God who receives the sacrifice, Hebrews has had a powerful influence on later Christian theology and liturgy. The Jewish practice of sacrifice ended with the destruction of the temple in C.E. 70, but, due largely to the influence of Hebrews, the theory and symbolic practice of sacrifice continue to exist in Christianity to the present day. Because Hebrews discusses the ritual of the Jewish temple in detail, but never mentions its destruction, it may have been written prior to C.E. 70.

The first letter of John

Read the First Letter of John. On what issues do the author and the Christians he calls antichrists disagree? Three letters attributed to John appear in the New Testament. All reflect the ideas and the style of language found in the Gospel of John, and some scholars assume the author of the Gospel and the author of the letters were the same person. Others believe the letters were written much later than the Gospel, probably by someone else. Either way scholars generally agree that the letters and the Gospel derive from the same community.

The First Letter of John is not really a letter at all but a sermon directed to the author's congregation. In addition to restating basic principles found in John's Gospel, the sermon focuses on other, more specific matters. It repeatedly insists that loving behavior is required of Christians. The language of the sermon contrasts realms of life and death in a typically Johannine way. Those who do not love are metaphorically termed murderers. The sermon does not advocate adherence to the Torah Law but it does argue against the idea that those who have faith are thereby free to behave in a sinful fashion.

First John addresses a disagreement within the Johannine community. Some individuals believe the Spirit of God has revealed to them that Jesus' appearance on earth was more spiritual than physical and that it would be a mistake to believe he came in the flesh. Others believe the Spirit of God has revealed to them that Jesus' appearance on earth was physical and it is

essential to believe he came in the flesh. The sermon's author is a member of
the latter group.

Disagreement in John's community over the nature of Jesus' appearance
illustrates a problem faced by many early Christian groups, especially young
ones. At first the group relies for its direction on verbal information from
individuals who are inspired by the Spirit. Eventually they discover that
some persons who believe themselves inspired are saying things others in the
group find entirely wrong. The group then must decide how to proceed.
The group may stop seeking verbal information from inspired individuals
and rely instead on inspired written texts. Precedent for this had been set in
Judaism, where reliance on Spirit-inspired prophets had ceased among the
official Jewish leadership. Instead of living prophets, written prophetic
books such as those of Isaiah and Jeremiah became the principal sources of
information. Among the ordinary Jewish people, however, respect for prophetic books was coupled with continued belief in living prophets. During
their lifetimes John the Baptist and Jesus were considered prophets by many
ordinary people but by few Jewish leaders.

Similarly, from the beginning of the Christian movement, followers of
Jesus used Hebrew Bible texts, including prophetic books, to support
Christian teachings. At the same time, the Christian movement continued to
receive information from the Spirit through Christian prophets. As time
went on, however, Christian groups had trouble deciding which prophets
were reliable and which were not. This difficulty is evident as early as the
time of Paul, who condemns those who teach a gospel differing from his
own (Gal. 1:6–7) and of Mark, who refers to impostors who "will come
claiming to be messiahs or prophets, and they will produce signs and
wonders to mislead God's chosen" (Mark 13:22). We may suspect that any
time a Christian called another Christian a false prophet the accusation was
returned in kind. The increasing diversity of teachings coming from people
who believed themselves inspired by the Spirit led Christians to begin
choosing a canon of written Scripture. Written texts of Scripture may be
diversely interpreted, but they at least provide an unchanging set of data
from which to start.

Although the Johannine community did not yet possess a canon of
Scripture, nevertheless it had to confront the problems arising from contradictory information from Spirit-inspired individuals. In this situation a
group may declare that some people who believe themselves inspired by the
Spirit of God are, in fact, inspired by another spirit, presumably a demonic
spirit. The question then will be how to tell which is which.

In 1 Corinthians 12:10 Paul had suggested a possible solution: appealing
to people in the church who have the gift of discernment. That is, some
people are possessed by the Spirit of God so that they can tell which people
are similarly possessed and which are possessed by other spirits. This pro-

cess would lead to difficulty, of course, should two spiritually inspired persons mutually declare the other is possessed by a demonic spirit.

In 1 John a different solution is proposed. To determine whether a person is inspired by God's Spirit or another spirit, a doctrinal test is established. The test is whether persons will declare "Jesus Christ has come in the flesh." "Every spirit which acknowledges Jesus Christ has come in the flesh is from God, and every spirit which does not thus acknowledge Jesus is not from God" (1 John 4:2–3).

Over time, of course, more and more doctrinal requirements would be needed to test the validity of spirits, and more and more rival groups would appear, each regarding different doctrines to be true. One solution to the problem of myriad lists of doctrines would be to select a canon of written texts, which could then be used to control the potentially unlimited number of possible doctrines. Doctrines consistent with the texts would be acceptable; those clearly in conflict with the texts would be unacceptable. In the absence of a canon of Christian texts, the author of 1 John must rely upon his own authority to insist his congregation should believe "Jesus came in the flesh."

The second letter of John

Read the Second Letter of John. This, the New Testament's shortest text, is a personal letter written in the same style as 1 John, probably by the same person. Here the author takes the title "the Elder," which presumably is a title of authority in the church. As it deals in much the same words with the same problem (rival Christians called "antichrists"), it was probably written at about the same time as 1 John. The purpose of the letter is to tell its recipient not to welcome or even greet anyone who does not "acknowledge Jesus Christ as coming in the flesh" (1:7).

Many scholars of the New Testament declare that the lady referred to in the letter's opening passage and the sister referred to in the letter's close are two churches. This is not likely. That a letter would be addressed both to a church and also to the collectivity of its members, "her children," would be unlikely. First John uses *children* as a favored term for church members. But nowhere in 1 John is the church considered feminine; when the author refers to church members it is to "brothers" (3:13) and "fathers" and "young men" (1:13–14). As 2 John was, more likely than not, written by the same author, it is improbable that that author would think of the church as a lady or a sister. Furthermore, the term *lady* is not used for a church in any other first- or second-century text. It is more reasonable to assume the words *lady* and *sister* mean what they say, that the letter addressed a woman with responsibility for a church, and that she is greeted by her real or metaphorical sister, the author of the letter. Women did on occasion have responsibility for churches, which we infer from texts such as Acts 12:12, where Peter comes to "the house of Mary, the mother of John Mark, where a large company was at prayer." The fact that "Elder" is masculine in gender does not mean necessarily the author was male if the term "Elder" was a technical term for an established church office. Today, for example, the Presbyterian church does not usually distinguish elders from eldresses. There are instances of female deacons (masculine gender) mentioned in texts of the early church.

The third letter of John

This short personal letter was probably written by the Elder, author of the other two letters of John. Addressed to Gaius, it encourages him to show hospitality to certain itinerant Christian teachers of whom the author approves. It may have been carried by Demetrius (3 John 1:12) as a letter recommending him to Gaius. Gaius and Demetrius are otherwise unknown.

The author is apparently in serious conflict with Diotrephes, who may be the leader of Gaius's congregation (3 John 9). Diotrephes is making charges against the author and refuses to receive his or her representatives. It is unfortunate we know nothing of Diotrephes' charges. For all we know they may have had some foundation.

The three letters of John taken together reveal considerable conflict. The author in 1 John encourages love among those who agree with him or her and despises other Christians with whom he or she disagrees and whom he or she calls "the antichrist." It is conceivable that among Diotrephes' "baseless and spiteful charges" against the Elder was the accusation that the Elder is an antichrist, since that seems to have been the preferred term of abuse in that community. In 2 John the lady is urged not to receive the itinerant representatives of an opposing group, while in 3 John, the author is furious with Diotrephes, who will not receive representatives friendly to him or her. As both the second and third letters conclude with the comment that the author has much to say that he or she does not wish to put into writing, there was much more to the disputes than the letters reveal. In these letters, as in the letters of Paul and elsewhere in the New Testament, the pleasant vision of the primitive church as a place of love and brotherhood among all Christians can be seen to be false. That was an ideal, perhaps, but not a reality.

The Pastorals

Read the First Letter to Timothy, the Second Letter to Timothy, and the Letter to Titus. These letters, collectively called The Pastorals, are attributed to Paul, but they were written around C.E. 120 by someone writing in Paul's name. Each letter uses vocabulary Paul is not known to have used; each has a different concept than Paul had of key matters such as faith; and each refers to Paul's close friends Timothy and Titus in formal rather than friendly terms. They are commonly known as the Pastoral Epistles or Pastoral letters. The name comes from their purpose, which was to instruct Christian pastors in how to live and in what to teach their congregations. The Pastoral Epistles assume that Christian churches are governed by the kind of carefully organized authority structures that developed decades after Paul's time. They are similar in style and in content and in the issues they raise. Scholars generally believe them to have been written by the same person. Therefore, the three Pastoral Epistles will be considered together in this section.

The Pastoral Epistles provide evidence for the evolution of authority structures in Christian churches. At the time Paul wrote his letters (the late 50s), authority in his churches was unstructured. Itinerant Christian teachers and prophets, like Paul and others mentioned in his letters, traveled from town to town establishing churches and preaching to already established churches. The churches had people who worked in them (the Greek word for worker or servant, *diakonos,* is the origin of the term *deacon*) and probably were led by more or less informal groups of elders (the Greek word for older man, *presbyteros,* is the origin of the term *presbyter* and is often translated "elder"). In Paul's day such people were probably in charge only of housekeeping, finances, and so forth. The ultimate spiritual authority for doctrine and teaching came, it appears, primarily from Spirit-inspired persons within the congregations and from occasional visits and letters from prophetic itinerants like Paul who felt responsibility for the congregations.

Several decades later the situation had changed. Rather than relying primarily upon the inspiration of the Spirit, fixed principles of doctrine and behavior began to be established. These principles the Pastorals call "the faith," and so they use the term *faith* in a way differently than Paul used it. For Paul faith is a dynamic and transforming trust in God; it is not simple adherence to correct principles. In the Pastorals, those who are entrusted with teaching "the faith" constitute a church hierarchy. Deacons are subordinate to elders; elders select a general overseer to provide leadership (the Greek word for overseer, *episkopos,* is the origin of the term *bishop*). First Timothy gives instructions for bishops (3:2), elders (5:19), and deacons (3:8). Authority in the Christian church, initially charismatic and based on Spirit inspiration, has become institutional, based on formal elected or appointed positions. Decades after the writing of the Pastorals, bishops assumed almost complete responsibility for churches, and elders became assistants to bishops. Eventually the role of the elder became the role of the priest.

The Pastorals address questions about various subdivisions of Christian congregations. For example, in 1 Timothy rules are established to specify persons who may be considered destitute Christian widows and thus receive financial support from the church. The letter insists that anyone who could support elderly relatives but does not do so "has denied the faith and is worse than an unbeliever" (5:8). This charge seems to derive less from concern for the commandment to honor father and mother than from concern that church financial resources not be consumed needlessly. The letter does, however, advocate double pay for elders who do a good job (5:17).

Women, according to the Pastorals, are to be subordinate to men. Paul's teaching that in Christ there is no male or female (Gal. 3:28) is now laid aside. Directions for women's dress are provided (1 Tim. 2:8–9), and then we read, "A woman must be a learner, listening quietly with due submission. I do not permit a woman to be a teacher, nor must woman domineer over man; she must be quiet" (2:10–12). The reason given for these commands is that it was not Adam who first sinned but Eve (2:13–14). Paul himself never blamed Eve separately for the fall.

The Pastorals are *pseudepigraphal* writings; they were written in the name of a revered figure from the past. One might ask why individuals chose to write in the name of James or Peter or Paul. One answer is they felt only by using those names would their letters or essays be taken with enough seriousness. Another related answer is that by the end of the first century the Christian churches had developed the principle of apostolic authority, which is that doctrinal and moral teaching may be trusted only if it has been transmitted directly from Jesus' apostles.

We can now list various ways Christian teachers legitimized their teachings.

1. Personal authority: Jesus' parables and other sayings were based on his personal authority. Paul's letters usually appeal to his personal authority as a community's founder.
2. Apostolic authority: Those people whom the risen Christ authorized to teach were credited with apostolic authority. Paul writes in this regard that the risen Christ "appeared to Cephas [Peter], and afterwards to the Twelve. Then he appeared to over five hundred of our brothers at once, most of whom are still alive, though some have died. Then he appeared to James, and afterwards to al the apostles. In the end he appeared even to me" (1 Cor. 15:5–8). The titles of most New Testament texts appeal to apostolic authority.
3. Spiritual authority: Those people who believed themselves to be inspired by the Holy Spirit could claim the Spirit's authority for their teaching and writing. The author of Revelation does this.
4. Institutional authority: Those people with institutionalized authority based their claim on their position in the church hierarchy: deacons, elders, or bishops. The Pastorals' author has this kind of authority.

Toward the end of the first century those with a legitimate claim to apostolic authority had nearly all died. Spiritual authority continued to be asserted, but it was increasingly viewed with suspicion. Texts such as 1 John show some of the difficulties that claims to spiritual authority can cause. At the minimum, reliance on spiritual authority will lead to the almost impossible difficulty of deciding which of two conflicting spiritually inspired persons is truly inspired.

Most pseudepigraphal texts derive from attempts by individuals living after the age of the apostles to assert apostolic authority. However, unlimited multiplication of texts bearing the names of revered apostles would lead inevitably to chaos within the church. To counter this tendency churches began to select texts they regarded as having legitimate apostolic authority and to discard texts they thought did not have such authority. This process of selection was part of the process that led eventually to the creation of the New Testament canon.

We know nothing about how specific texts were chosen to be canonical, nor do we have very much knowledge of many of the rejected texts. Only a handful survive. It is dubious reasoning to argue that canonical New Testament texts were chosen because they contain correct teaching, for, over the centuries, Christians have come to define correct teaching as teaching in accord with the New Testament texts. So the argument becomes circular: "The New Testament canon was chosen because those documents contain teachings in accord with the teachings of the New Testament canon." It is equally odd to argue, "The New Testament is divinely inspired because the divinely inspired teachings of the New Testament say the New Testament is inspired." But even today such arguments are made.

All of the texts in the New Testament are attributed to figures from the apostolic age such as John, Peter, Paul, or Matthew. Likewise, many additional texts circulated in the late first and second centuries bearing the names of apostles and pretending to have been written by apostles. But it is not likely that texts were respected because they bore the name of an apostle. More likely, churches or groups of Christians thought a text authoritative and therefore assumed it derived from an apostle. The four Gospels were not authoritative *because* it could be historically proved that they derived from Matthew, Mark, Luke, and John. Rather, because they were considered authoritative *therefore* they were assigned to people who lived in the apostolic age.

Toward the end of the first century and for some time thereafter, any respected text, even if respected only by a minority of Christians, received an appropriate apostolic title. The Gospel of Thomas, the Gospel of Mary, the Gospel of Peter, the Apocryphon (secret book) of John, the Apocalypse of Peter, the Acts of John, and the Acts of Peter are examples. These texts still exist, some completely and some in fragmentary form. They provide almost no information about the people whose names they bear, but they are significant because they reveal the desires of Christians during the time of the formation of the canon to attribute their writing to apostolic persons and because they preserve Christian perspectives from very early times.

The first letter of Peter

Read the first letter of Peter. First Peter is an open letter to several churches located in Asia Minor. Its author uses the Greek translation of the Hebrew Bible. While not imitating Paul's thought and writing style, he seems familiar with Paul's ideas and may indirectly refer to Paul's Letter to the Romans. The Galilean fisherman whom Jesus called Peter is not the author of the letter. In the conclusion of the letter the author probably makes a personal reference: "Greetings from *her* who dwells in Babylon, chosen by God like you, and from *my* son Mark" (1 Pet. 5:13). It is entirely possible that the lady here, like the lady in Second John, is a real person, the author of the letter. The reference to the lady dwelling in Babylon is, however, usually said to mean the church in Rome. But, as in the case of Luke/Acts and the Letters of John, evidence of female authorship should be considered seriously and not simply wished away.

Scholarly opinion is divided as to whether 1 Peter is one or two letters. If it was once two separate letters, the first ends at 4:11 and the second consists of the verses from 4:12 to the end. Even if originally two letters, 1 Peter as it stands is consistent and can be read as a single text.

The letter is written to give encouragement to churches in Asia Minor suffering from persecution. It is more likely the persecution was informal, deriving from various groups antagonistic to Christians, than that it was imperially sponsored. The letter supports the authority of the government, as well as that of several seemingly repressive human institutions. It forthrightly condemns unsubmissive or rebellious behavior. Referring to the Roman government, the letter requires its recipients to "submit yourselves to every human institution for the sake of the Lord, whether to the sovereign as supreme, or to the governor as his deputy for the punishment of criminals and the commendation of those who do right" (2:13–14). Servants are to accept the authority of their masters even when the masters are perverse (2:18). Women must accept the authority of their husbands (3:1), and younger men must be subordinate to their elders (5:5). Jesus Christ is put forward as a model of obedience and of unresisting acceptance of suffering and injustice. In addition to submissiveness, 1 Peter requires loving and moral behavior and encourages its audience, who apparently were Gentile Christians, to refrain from behavior characteristic of pagans.

Twice (3:19–21, 4:6) this letter refers to Jesus preaching to the dead, the only times in the New Testament where that idea occurs. Here the idea that the gospel should be preached to all people has its most complete application.

Some scholars believe 1 Peter was designed originally as a sermon to be given on the occasion of the baptism of new Christians. This belief is based on a passage where baptism is likened to the flood in the days of Noah where a few persons "were brought to safety through the water. This water prefigured the water of baptism through which you are now brought to safety" (3:20–21). The common tendency of New Testament writers to claim events recounted in the Hebrew Bible are really symbolic references to Christian beliefs and traditions here finds a peculiar application, for the waters of the flood were not sent in order to bring people to safety.

The letter of Jude

Read the Letter of Jude. Mark 6:3 records the names of four brothers of Jesus: James, Joseph, Judas, and Simon. The author of Jude apparently claims to be James's brother Judas. Jude is an alternative spelling for Judas used to avoid confusion with Judas Iscariot. The name Judas was very common at the time. Jesus' brother James assumed leadership of the church after the crucifixion, a leadership disputed by such independently minded people as Paul (Gal. 2:9). It is possible that, after the death of James, Judas may have claimed authority. Christians who took literally the claim that Jesus was king of the Jews may have found it reasonable that the eldest surviving brother, in the absence of male children, would have authority, and thus they would try to link their views to this authoritative figure. Be that as it may, the Letter of Jude was actually written by someone living one or two generations later than Jesus' brothers.

The Letter of Jude is written to condemn certain Christians whose behavior the author believes to be scandalous. The language of Jude is so exaggerated it is difficult to tell what exactly his opponents were doing. The letter claims "they pervert the free favor of our God into licentiousness" (1:4), and it is possible that it refers here to people who took Paul's gospel of freedom from the Law to mean any behavior whatsoever was acceptable.

Jude refers to "the predictions made by the apostles of our Lord Jesus Christ" (1:17), a reference that could have been made only at a time substantially later than that of the apostles, a time when Christians were beginning to look to the teachings of the apostles for authority rather than to the immediate inspiration of the Spirit. The predictions of Jesus' apostles are given the same weight in Jude as the Scripture of the Hebrew Bible (1:4), and the author uses both as prophetic sources of evidence that his opponents are to be condemned. The tendency to regard apostolic teachings with the same respect as Scripture would culminate eventually with the creation of new Scripture based on apostolic authority, Scripture with equal or greater authority than the Hebrew Bible. That new Scripture is, of course, the New Testament. Although there is no evidence in Jude that the creation of a Christian canon of Scripture has begun, the principle of apostolic authority, advocated already in Jude, is one that came to govern the selection of Christian canonical texts.

It is interesting that Jude considers as authoritative two documents that do not appear in the present Hebrew Bible. Both are Jewish writings and thus give us good reason to assume Jude's author was a Jewish Christian. The text known as the Assumption of Moses is the source for the reported debate between Michael the archangel and the devil over possession of Moses' body (1:9). Jude quotes the text entitled Enoch in 1:14–15 and regards Enoch as an inspired prophet. During the first century Jews generally agreed on the inspired authority of most of the texts the Hebrew Bible would contain. The five books of Torah were certainly considered scriptural then. However, during most of the first century there was no complete agreement upon a canon of Jewish Scripture. Scholars believe the final authorized collection of Hebrew Bible texts began to be established in approximately C.E. 90, about the time the Letter of Jude was written.

The second letter of Peter

The letter called 2 Peter was not written by the person who wrote 1 Peter; it is considered by many scholars to be the latest of all New Testament writings. It may have been written as late as C.E. 130. The author makes a sustained effort to convince his readers he is Jesus' companion Peter. He frames his letter as a sort of "last will and testament." He writes, "I think it right to keep refreshing your memory so long as I still lodge in this body. I know that very soon I must leave it; indeed our Lord Jesus Christ has told me so" (1:13–14). The presentation of teachings in this last will and testament fashion was rather common in the ancient world, especially by Jewish writers.

Second Peter is similar to Jude in its condemnation of the beliefs and behaviors of Christians with whom the author disagrees. Indeed, much of Jude is incorporated into 2 Peter: Jude 1:4–16 can be found in Second Peter 2:1–18; Jude 1:17–18 appears in 2 Peter 3:1–3.

One interesting passage gives a description of a vision of the Lord, for the author claims to have seen Jesus in majesty when, at the hands of God, Jesus was invested with honor and glory. Upon the sacred mountain, he heard the voice of God declare Jesus to be "my Son, my beloved" (1:16–18). This seems at first to be an account of the transfiguration (Mark 9:2–8). But the general Christian belief was that God invested Jesus with honor and glory after his resurrection. The reference to the sacred mountain may be to Mount Zion, the location of the Jerusalem temple. Accordingly, some scholars believe the description in 2 Peter is of Jesus' resurrection rather than of the transfiguration and may come from a tradition independent of Mark's Gospel. In fact, some wonder if this resurrection account might not have been transformed by Mark into the transfiguration story. Mark, you will recall, does not choose to record any appearances of the risen Jesus.

In addition to condemning the behavior of his opponents in the manner of Jude, the author of 2 Peter protests against those who have lost faith in the second coming of Jesus: "They will say: 'Where now is the promise of his coming? Our fathers have been laid to their rest, but still everything continues exactly as it has always been since the world began'" (3:4). Christians throughout the New Testament period had awaited eagerly or fearfully the coming of the end of this world and the return of Jesus Christ. As time went on and these events did not take place, their failure to occur seemed to provide evidence Christian teachings were invalid. The apostles' most emphatic predictions, indeed, perhaps, Jesus' own predictions, were not, apparently, going to come true.

This dilemma was frequently recognized. Various solutions were offered. Some, such as Luke, believed the end would indeed come, but it would be a long time coming and prior to its coming there would be a period for the church to spread and for the gospel to be preached to all people. Others, such as John (and the Gospel of Thomas), suggested that in fact the end had already occurred and the opportunity for eternal life was already present. In the words of the Gospel of Thomas (saying 113), "The Kingdom of the Father is spread out on the earth, and men do not see it." Another solution, one adopted by various writers including the author of 1 Peter (1 Pet. 4:7), was to announce the delay was over and the end would occur immediately, thus rendering the question of delay irrelevant. The author of 2 Peter instead suggests that people have misunderstood the predictions; even if they seem to indicate the end will come in only a few months, "with the Lord one day is like a thousand years and a thousand years is like one day" (3:8). Presumably, therefore, many thousands of years could still pass without invalidating predictions of the end. Furthermore, he writes, the Lord is merciful in not returning for judgment, because, by delaying, he makes it possible for more people to repent.

To avoid an excessive number of interpretations of Scripture, the author of 2 Peter insisted that only authorized teachers may interpret Scripture: "No one can interpret any prophecy of Scripture by himself. For it was not through any human whim that men prophesied of old; men they were, but, impelled by the Holy Spirit they spoke the words of God" (1:20–21). But it is unclear in 2 Peter whether those authorized to interpret Scripture are to use established principles of interpretation or rely on inspiration from the Holy Spirit.

Second Peter is the only New Testament text to refer to any other New

Testament texts as Scripture, and so it stands at the beginning of the time when the New Testament canon began to form. The author writes, "Bear in mind that our Lord's patience with us is our salvation, as Paul, our friend and brother, said when he wrote to you with his inspired wisdom. And so he does in all his other letters, wherever he speaks of this subject, though they contain some obscure passages, which the ignorant and unstable misinterpret to their own ruin, as they do the other scriptures" (3:15–16). Evidently Paul's letters are regarded as Scripture similar to the Scriptures of the Hebrew Bible. It is interesting that in the early second century, just as in our time, readers of Paul's letters find "obscure passages."

As death depleted the ranks of apostles and others who were eyewitnesses to Jesus, the motivation to set certain Christian texts apart as inspired writing increased. Within a generation or so after the writing of 2 Peter the creation of a Christian canon of Scripture was well under way. Toward the end of the second century the four Gospels and Paul's letters were considered Scripture by most churches.

A Christian leader in Rome named Marcion, in about the year C.E. 150, established the first "New Testament" separate from the Hebrew Bible. Marcion rejected from his canon the Hebrew Bible and most of what is now considered to be Christian Scripture. He regarded as scriptural only Luke and certain letters of Paul, and he edited those to accord with his own ideas.

Marcion's ideas, particularly his notion that the God revealed in the Hebrew Bible was a secondary demonic god, proved unacceptable to most Christians. In response to Marcion's canon, churches whose members did respect the Hebrew Bible established canons of their own that were more extensive, canons usually containing all four Gospels. The earliest list we have of canonical books, a list called the Mutorian Fragment (ca. C.E. 180), includes the books of the present New Testament and one now outside the canon, the Apocalypse of Peter. Churches continued to disagree, however, whether such texts as Revelation, Jude, and 2 Peter should be included. Some included the Letters of Clement or the text called The Shepherd of Hermas. It was not until the fourth century that Western Christian churches agreed on the New Testament canon we now have.

Revelation or Apocalypse

As a general rule the documents in the New Testament occur in the order of the value placed on them by Christian leaders of the third century. The Revelation of God to John, commonly known simply as Revelation, is the New Testament's final text. The title of the work, in Greek, is the *Apocalypse* and that title is retained in some translations. The word "apocalypse" means here the disclosure of hidden divine secrets relating to events in the present and in the future. Revelation purports to show through symbols the events that will take place during the end of this world. Revelation is not unique in its apocalyptic approach. Other much shorter apocalypses appear in the New Testament: First and Second Thessalonians contain apocalyptic passages, and Mark's chapter 13 is apocalyptic. Some apocalyptic material may also be found in the Hebrew Bible and the author of Revelation was probably influenced by it.

Read Daniel 7–12, Zechariah 9–14, Ezekiel 39–44 to understand the style and content of apocalyptic writing.

Revelation's author is said to be named John, but he is not the author of the Gospel of John or of the letters of John. Revelation shares some ideas with the Gospel and the letters of John, for example the idea of Jesus as the Lamb of God, but it is written in a very different Greek style and lacks some of John's gospel's principal themes.

The author lives on the small Greek island of Patmos, exiled during a period of persecution. He writes, "It was on the Lord's day, and I was caught up by the Spirit; and behind me I heard a loud voice, like the sound of a trumpet, which said to me, 'Write down what you see on a scroll and send it to the seven churches . . .'" (Rev. 1:10–11). The seven churches named are located in cities of Asia Minor, in modern day Turkey. Chapters 2 and 3 of Revelation contain letters written to those specific churches and make accusations against members of those churches.

These letters might be contrasted with the letters of Paul in respect to the authority claim of the writer. Paul consistently appeals to his personal authority over churches despite the fact that he, like the author of Revelation, believes he can speak with the authority of the Spirit. Revelation's author does not seem to have personal authority and possibly was not known personally in all seven churches. He expects those who read the letters to acknowledge that they are the words of the Spirit, not his own personal words. In theory the author of the letters is the Spirit of God, not John, for we hear repeatedly "Hear, you who have ears to hear, what the Spirit says to the churches!" The letters sometimes praise, but more often condemn, the people of those churches. Scholars have sought to determine more specifically what the situations were in those churches, but the evidence in Revelation is so sketchy that opinions vary considerably.

It is entirely possible that the seven letters circulated, at first, independently of the remainder of our book of Revelation. The greater part of Revelation is directed toward the whole of Christianity, not to seven congregations only.

From 4:1–22:21 Revelation reports the author's visions of events in Heaven that are understood to symbolize events on earth. It symbolically details the devastations that will accompany the end of the present age and, with less emphasis, the glories that will accompany the age to come, the "new heaven and the new earth" (21:1).

This overall pattern of movement from extended devastation to predicted glory can be found also in smaller units of Revelation's organization. As any reading of the text will reveal, the author has made sustained use of an organizational pattern oriented around the number seven. There are seven seals, seven trumpets, seven bowls, and so forth. Often within the uncovering, "apocalypse," of these units the first four are forms of catastrophe to come upon the earth. The next two are often more richly detailed catastrophes to come. The last, the seventh unit, is often more affirmative, or at least ambiguous. The seventh seal is a time of silence preceded by a vision of the victory of God's people, the seventh angel gives a scroll as sweet as honey that turns the stomach sour, the seventh bowl is the final destruction of Babylon the great. The number seven was commonly understood in the ancient world to symbolize completion and derives from the fact that there are seven visible moving heavenly bodies: Sun, Moon, Mercury, Venus, Mars, Jupiter and Saturn.

The Organization of Revelation

Although Revelation seems to be very tightly organized around units of seven, scholars disagree on how, exactly, to understand its structure. The following is one system of organization; it could be far more detailed. This system understands Revelation to be analogous to a dramatic performance.
Read The Revelation of John following the outline below.

The author and his experience:
    1:1–3   Title and introduction
    1:9–20   First vision
The Spirit writes to churches
    2:1–3:22   Letters to Seven churches
Prologue to the Drama
    4:1–11   Vision of the Throne of God
Dramatic Act One
  Scene One
    5:1–8:1   The Seven Seals
  Scene Two
    8:2–11:14   The Seven Trumpets
Dramatic Act Two
  Scene One
    12:1–14:5   The Attack of the Dragon and Beasts
  Scene Two
    14:6–20:15 The Judgment of God
    14:65–20   The Sickles

It needs to be emphasized that the more carefully scholars read Revelation the more they discover that it does not quite fit any one organizational scheme. The author of Revelation is clearly writing in a symbolic fashion. On a few occasions he gives clues to the interpretation of his symbols (1:20, 4:5, 5:6, 17:9–18, 19:8) but they are often obscure. There are discontinuities, variations in the meaning of symbols, and elements that do not seem related to the context in which they appear. Some hypothesize that Revelation was compiled, somewhat crudely, out of a set of originally independent apocalyptic vision texts. Others have composed highly intricate schemes to account for all of Revelation, but no such scheme has been completely accepted.

One widely shared conclusion of scholarship is that Revelation is written partially out of absolute unremitting hatred for the Roman empire and its emperor. Few other New Testament texts share that attitude. Perhaps Revelation was written during a period of the persecution of Christian people by Roman authority and the visions written down by the author are a response to this persecution, or perhaps the persecution was more a matter of Christian perception than of official decree. In any event, the author of Revelation declares that Christians, especially martyrs to persecution, can expect ultimate vengeance and victory. Babylon the great (the Roman Empire) will be overthrown and the beast killed. How do we know Babylon is Rome? Because it is the city of the seven hills (17:5,9). The author knows of seven emperors of whom five have fallen, one reigns and one is to come and reign for but a little while. The beast that once was alive and is alive no longer is an eighth emperor and yet one of the seven. This sounds simple enough, especially when one understands that there was a popular legend that the emperor Nero would come back to life (so he could be the eighth who was one of the seven). Unfortunately, it is possible to identify the sixth emperor (who is alive at the time of the production of Revelation) with Nero, or Vespasian, or Domitian. Scholars have made cases for each of these. It depends on which emperors one counts; some only ruled for a matter of days.

We hear that the number of the beast is 666 (13:18) a number that has been the cause of considerable speculation. The number value is said to be the value of the letters of a man's name. In the ancient world, in all languages, letters were used as numbers. In Rome, for example, D = 500, C = 100, L = 50, X = 10, V = 5, I = 1. If one takes the numerical value of the letters of the name Caesar Nero as written in Hebrew they equate to 666, and that solution to the mystery of 666 is often offered. But it is a cumbersome solution, for one must move from the Greek text to a Hebrew numbering system for a Latin name and title. It's more likely that the letters given above, in order, in Roman numerals, equate to that mystery number for DCLXVI = 666 and so the number of the beast is the numbering system of Rome and so is code for Rome itself.

Readers who wish to investigate the structure and symbolism of Revelation further may turn to any of dozens of published interpretations. There are three principal ways interpreters approach the decoding of the Revelation of John.

First, some believe our evidence sufficient to determine in some detail the author's view of the author's own time and situation. Revelation was written in the latter half of the first century and reflects persecution of Christians by Roman authority. It reflects other social and environmental conditions: famine, earthquake, war and so forth. It contains clues (the seven emperors, the mystery of 666) that may be decipherable.

From this perspective Revelation is not intended to predict events much further in time than a few decades. The author thought that the new heaven and new earth would arrive soon; it did not. But, nevertheless, we can hope to decipher his text in order to understand his date, his circumstances, and his beliefs about what is to happen. Unfortunately, the range of scholarly opinion among those who take this approach is very great and it is unclear whether any single point of view will ever prevail.

But if the political situation of the author, and his date, may not be discoverable for certain, we can certainly make progress in understanding Revelation in reference to other apocalyptic works, canonical and non-canonical, Jewish and Christian. This will allow greater understanding of the author's thought, and the thought of Christians and Jews of his time.

Second, one might believe that Revelation speaks to one's own time. This is not an uncommon approach. For centuries, some Christians have thought that the decoding of Revelation should be done in reference to events taking place in the centuries or decades preceding their own date.

And , from this, they have concluded that the arrival of the new heaven and the new earth would take place in a few years or decades. This has sometimes had pernicious effects; David Koresh, who orchestrated the Waco, Texas disaster of 1993, firmly believed that he had the key to Revelation's decoding. Among his conclusions was that law enforcement officials of the United States were agents of the Beast and that he and his followers would die the death of Revelation's martyrs.

Those who regard Revelation as a prophetic text and believe its code to be directed toward their own time and situation are a bit arrogant. God, they seem to think, did not intend to speak to people one hundred, five hundred, fifteen hundred years ago, or 500 years from now, but meant only to speak to them. Over the centuries hundreds of attempts have been made to decode Revelation in light of the events of the decoder's particular period of time. Each attempt has exactly the same validity as all other attempts, for there is no way to determine which, if any, of all their various interpretations are correct. Therein lies the prime difficulty of Revelations. If there is no way to determine whose decoding of the imagery of Revelation is correct, then anyone may make it mean anything they want and so claim the authority of the word of God for their opinions. In this century various symbols in Revelation have been declared to represent Franklin Delano Roosevelt, Ronald Reagan, popes of the Roman Catholic church, the European Common Market, the leadership of the Soviet Union, victims of the AIDS epidemic, the United States Alcohol, Tobacco and Firearms authorities, and dozens of other groups and individuals. No one can prove these identifications are correct. Political prejudices and ideologies can be made to look Christian by such misreadings of Revelation, for, where no rules apply, anything goes.

Third, one may say in all candor and honesty that Revelation's symbolism cannot be understood in significant detail. We do not have enough evidence to go on and what evidence we have is too ambiguous. But still, leaving aside the effort to decode Revelation, we must acknowledge that this text has had profound influence on poets and artists through the ages. Today too, novelists and filmmakers show their indebtedness to the imagery of Revelation. Revelation is an interesting piece of writing and should be understood as such. It can tell us much about the apocalyptic mentality of early Christian and Jewish thinkers. But efforts to decode it in historical detail or in light of present circumstances are not time well spent.

Bibliography

Barrett, C. K. *The Pastoral Epistles*. New Clarendon Bible Commentary. Oxford: Clarendon Press, 1963.

Brown, Raymond E. *The Epistles of John*. Anchor Bible Commentary, vol. 30. Garden City, NY: Doubleday, 1982.

Collins, Raymond F. *Letters That Paul Did Not Write*. Collegeville: Michael Glazier, 1988.

Debelius, Martin, and Heinrich Greeven. *A Commentary on the Epistle of James*. Hermeneia Commentary. Philadelphia: Fortress Press, 1976.

Ford, J. Massyngberde. *The Apocalypse of John*. Anchor Bible vol. 38. Garden City, NY: Doubleday, 1975. (This book contains the argument that Revelation primarily derives from John the Baptist and his followers.)

Fuller, Reginald H., et al. *The Letter to the Hebrews, James, 1 and 2 Peter, Jude, Revelation*. Proclamation Commentaries. Philadelphia: Fortress Press, 1977.

Giblin, Charles H. *The Book of Revelation* (Good News Studies). Collegeville: Michael Glazier Books, 1991.

Hewitt, C.M. Kempton. "Guidelines to the Interpretation of Daniel and Revelation," in Armerding and Gasque Eds., *A Guide to Biblical Prophecy*. Peabody, MA: Hendrickson, 1989.

Kelly, John N. D. *A Commentary on the Pastoral Epistles: I Timothy, II Timothy, Titus*. Harper's New Testament Commentary. New York: Harper & Row, 1963.

Minnear, Paul. *I Saw A New Earth*. Washington: Corpus Books, 1968.

Reicke, Bo. *The Epistles of James, Peter and Jude*. Anchor Bible Commentary, vol. 37. Garden City, NY: Doubleday, 1964.

Sanders, James A. *Canon and Community: A Guide to Canonical Criticism*. Philadelphia: Fortress Press, 1984.

Schüssler-Fiorenza, Elizabeth. *Revelation: Vision of a Just World* (Proclamation Commentaries). Minneapolis: Fortress Press, 1991.

Smith, D. Moody. *First, Second, and Third John* (Interpretation Commentaries). Louisville: Westminster/John Knox Press, 1991.

Exercises

Analytical Study of the New Testament

1. Select an interesting passage from one of the four Gospels. With the aid of the tools discussed at the end of this chapter, write an essay on the context and meaning of that passage.

2. A Gospel is a document written to explain the importance of Jesus which takes the general form of a biography. Write a Gospel of at least five pages. You may glance at the New Testament Gospels to refresh your memory, but do not copy out passages word for word. You may invent stories and sayings if you wish. If you believe Jesus had no particular importance, your Gospel should reflect that point of view.

3. Skim through the Gospel of Luke to see the variety of events and discussions a New Testament Gospel contains. As you will be expected to read it carefully later, a general overview will be sufficient for the present.

   Analyze one of the Gospels written for the exercise above—own or another's. What features are absent? What is stressed most strongly? For example, is the birth story stressed? Does Jesus appear to his followers after his resurrection? Are his sayings prominent? Is the Jewish Law mentioned? What view of the disciples do you find? Compare at least one saying or story in the Gospel you read with a corresponding version in a New Testament Gospel.

   What do you now know about the kinds of choices and decisions a Gospel writer must make? What sources does a Gospel writer have? How much freedom of interpretation does a Gospel writer have?

4. To show the changes that can result from oral transmission of sayings, several people should be asked to write down the parable of the prodigal son (or another commonly known parable) as best they can remember it. At the outset those people who declare they know nothing of the parable should be given an opportunity to read it, while those who declare they have some knowledge of it (however slight) should not read it. Compare the versions written with the original. What expansions, deletions, explanatory commentaries, or additional material appear in the various versions?

5. Take a map of your region and a map of Palestine at the time of Jesus. If possible try and obtain maps where the "scale of miles" is the same [this is relatively easy if you have access to a reducing/enlarging photo-

229

copier]. Take a compass and draw circles around your location and around Nazareth (or Jerusalem) at, say, twenty mile intervals. There's no better way to get a feel for the distances involved in stories of Jesus.

Judaism and the Roman Empire

1. Assume you have chosen to follow all the Torah laws. Read Leviticus 11:1–47. Write a two-page letter to inform people what should no longer be prepared for meals when you are there. Do not mention foods you would not eat anyway. Use specific citations from Leviticus in your letter. Citations are number references to the text (example: Lev. 11:34–35), not written quotations from the text.
2. Read Luke 5:1—6:11. Identify the social groups mentioned or implied in that section of the Gospel. What arguments about Torah Law take place? What positions does Jesus take regarding the Law?
3. A wide variety of accusations are made against Pharisees in chapter 23 of the Gospel of Matthew. From the perspective of a Pharisee, write a defense of Pharisees against some of the accusations. Use common sense.
4. There are cultural "food laws" in America. For example, large four-legged creatures may be eaten but thou shalt not eat six-legged creatures. Identify other such laws or customs and describe your emotional response to the idea of eating "impure" foods. How, for example, would you feel if you observed someone eating a bowl of worms?

Gospel Sources

Miracles sources

1. Read 2 Kings 4:1–44, especially the end, 4:42–44, and compare the story there with Mark 6:30–44, Mark 8:1–9, and John 6:1–13. Some scholars believe the miracle of the loaves and fishes is derived from the account of Elisha's similar miracle. Do you agree? Or do you find there are such substantial differences the two are only coincidentally similar?
2. Read each of the miracles stories contained in the sources and make careful note of what actions Jesus performs. What does he do, what words does he use? Why do you think the more detailed stories are original or that the details were added?

Q source

1. Read the book of Jonah in the Hebrew Scriptures and references to it in Luke 11:29–32 and its parallel, Matthew 12:38–42. Determine as best you can the basic message the book of Jonah seeks to communicate.

The Q passage refers to the book of Jonah; what do you believe the passage means by "the sign of Jonah"? Does the version of the saying in Luke or the version in Matthew seem most likely to be original? The reference to the Queen of the South is to the Queen of Sheba mentioned in 1 Kings 10:1–10.

2. Read Proverbs 22:1—23:29. These are sayings written down before the time of Jesus but well known at that time. What similarities of style and content exist between these sayings and Jesus' sayings in Q? What differences are there?

3. Find references in Q to the Son of Man, and, from those references, describe the Q people's view of the Son of Man. Is Jesus Son of Man in the sense of God's agent in the final days? Do the versions of Q found in Matthew and Luke lead to different conclusions on this question? Use as evidence only the Q sayings you have located and not other New Testament passages.

4. There are three ancient versions of the parable of the wedding feast. Two come from Q, one from the Gospel of Thomas. Those in Q are found in Luke 14:16–24 and Matthew 22:1–14. The version in Thomas is saying 64:

> Someone was giving a big dinner and invited many guests. At the dinner hour the host sent his slave to tell the guests: "Come, it's ready now." But one by one they all began to make excuses. The first said to him, "I just bought a farm, and I have to go and inspect it; please excuse me." And another said, "I just bought five pairs of oxen, and I'm on my way to check them out; please excuse me." And another said, "I just got married, and so I cannot attend." So the slave came back and reported these ⟨excuses⟩ to his master. Then the master of the house got angry and instructed his slave: "Quick! Go out into the streets and alleys of the town, and usher in the poor, and crippled, the blind, and the lame."
>
> And the slave said, "Sir, your orders have been carried out, and there's still room."
>
> And the master said to the slave, "Then go out into the roads and the country lanes, and force people to come in so my house will be filled. Believe you me, not one of those who were given invitations will taste my dinner."

Possibly one or more of these stories refers to a passage in Deuteronomy (20:5–8) allowing certain excuses. Which version of the parable has a superior claim to being the original version? What kinds of decisions did you make in selecting one (for example, the shorter is better, the longer is better, the ones with explanations are better, the one most closely related to the Deuteronomy passage is better)?

Paul

1. Carefully read Galatians 3:1–18 once again. Paul's argument repeatedly refers to the Hebrew Scriptures. Look up each reference and determine how Paul uses the passages given below to construct his argument.

   Galatians 3:6   Genesis 15:6
   Galatians 3:8   Genesis 12:3 and 18:18
   Galatians 3:10   Deuteronomy 27:26
   Galatians 3:11   Habbakuk 2:4
   Galatians 3:12   Leviticus 18:5
   Galatians 3:13   Deuteronomy 21:23
   Galatians 3:16   Genesis 12:7; 13:15; 17:7; 24:7
   Galatians 3:17   Exodus 12:40

2. In Galatians 4 Paul makes an allegorical argument based on the story of Abraham. Read Genesis 16:1–22:19 and judge to what extent Paul's interpretation of the story is valid.

3. Either through careful reading or the use of a concordance locate the passages in Galatians speaking of Jesus as the Son of God or of Christians as sons or children of God. Using those passages, and referring to their context, write an essay on the concept of the Son of God in Galatians.

4. Read 1 Corinthians from chapter 11 to the end. This section contains many crucial and interesting passages, including Paul's version of the Lord's Supper. Write a description of a communion meeting of the church in Corinth featuring some of the difficulties Paul wrote to correct.

5. Read 1 Thessalonians and compare the eschatological ideas you find there with those in Q. To what extent are they saying the same thing? Are there significant differences? Read 2 Thessalonians and compare the ideas there to those in 1 Thessalonians. Would you conclude Paul wrote 2 Thessalonians?

Mark

1. Read in the Hebrew Scriptures Daniel 7:1–8:27. Chapter 13 of Mark is probably influenced by a passage in the book of Daniel (7:13) referring to "one like a son of man," which is also translated "one like a man." Many early Christians believed this being who is "like a son of man," was Jesus, the Son of Man. Reread Mark's chapter 13. How might it be argued the statements about the Son of Man in Mark 13:26 and 14:62 are derived from the passage in Daniel?

2. Compare Mark 10:1–12 with Matthew 5:31–32, 19:3–12, Luke 16:18, and Paul's 1 Corinthians 7:10–11. Is divorce permitted according to these passages? If so, under what circumstances? Is remarriage after divorce permitted? Why or why not?

3. It is possible the story in Mark 5:1–20 is not a miracle story at all but an allegory. In the allegory the man possessed by demons could signify the nation of Israel occupied by Romans. Pigs might signify Gentiles, for Gentiles ate pork while Jews regarded it as forbidden. The word *Legion* is a Latin word for an army division. Does this make sense in the context of the Roman occupation of Israel, or is it reading too much into the story? Locate Gerasa on a map of ancient Palestine. What does its location on the map and its implied location in the story tell us of Mark's knowledge of Palestinian geography? Why do you suppose here, as almost nowhere else, Jesus forbids a person to follow him, does not order silence, and commands the person to go and announce what happened?

4. Reread Mark 12:38–44. Write an argument either that the poor widow is an example of proper piety in giving her money to the temple treasury, or that she is an example of someone misled by the "doctors of the law" who "eat up the property of widows."

Matthew

1 The following are passages from the birth story and the prophecies to which they apparently refer.

Matthew 1:22	Isaiah 7:14
Matthew 2:6	Micah 5:2 and 2 Samuel 5:2
Matthew 2:15	Hosea 11:1
Matthew 2:18	Jeremiah 31:15
Matthew 2:23	Isaiah 11:1
Matthew 3:3	Isaiah 40:3

Read three of these passages in their own context in the Hebrew Scriptures and refer to standard commentaries on the Hebrew Scriptures for information about their historical settings. Prepare arguments for or against the idea that Matthew's interpretations are justified.

2. Use a copy of *Gospel Parallels* and locate a passage or set of passages showing changes made by Matthew when he revised the Gospel of Mark. Make intelligent guesses as to Matthew's motivations in making such changes and write an essay discussing these motivations and your reasons for ascribing them to Matthew. Your guesses should reflect your understanding of Matthew's overall perspective as given in his Gospel.

3. Read the first two chapters of Matthew and the first two chapters of Luke. These are the New Testament's only two accounts of Jesus' birth. Locate common features. List features you think are significantly different. What special interests do you discover Matthew had that Luke did not have?

4. You have read Paul's letter to the Galatians. Assume that Matthew, passing through Galatia on a vacation trip to the Black Sea, stops in the home serving as the Christian church in Galatia and is shown a copy of Paul's letter. Write a response, in the form of a letter, from Matthew to Paul.

The Gospel of Luke and the Acts of the Apostles

1. In the book of Acts several passages refer to psalms of the Hebrew Scriptures. The psalms are traditionally said to have been written by the King David (ca. 1000 B.C.E.), and Luke accepts that attribution, although no scholars do so today. Read the Psalms 2, 16, 69, 109, 110, and 132. To what extent do you believe they are interpreted correctly in Acts 1:16–22, 2:22–36, 4:25–27, 13:32–41, and why?

2. Read the accounts of the women who come to Jesus' tomb and discover it to be empty. These are found in Matthew 27:55–28:10, Mark 15:40–16:8, Luke 23:49–24:11, John 19:38–20:18. Make a list of the common features and of the features you think are significantly different. Write an essay giving your opinion as to why certain of these differences exist.

3. Use a copy of Gospel parallels and locate a passage or set of passages showing changes made by Luke when he revised the Gospel of Mark. Make intelligent guesses as to Luke's motivations for making such changes and write an essay discussing those motivations and your reasons for ascribing them to Luke. Such guesses should reflect your understanding of Luke's overall perspective as given in his Gospel.

4. Read Paul's Letter to the Romans, chapters 1 and 2. In those chapters he is discussing the place of Gentiles in God's plan. This he also does in the speech in Acts 17:22–31. Construct an argument either to show the two discussions are saying essentially the same thing or to show they are saying different things.

5. Read the "we passages" in the book of Acts: 16:10–18, 20:4–21:18, 27:1–28:16. Write an essay defending either the point of view that these were invented by Luke to add interest to the book of Acts or that they were eyewitness accounts Luke used in the writing of Acts, or, indeed, that they are evidence that Luke traveled with Paul.

The Gospel of John

1. John refers to Exodus 16:1–17:7, where "bread from heaven" and miraculous water are given by God. Read these passages in the Hebrew Scriptures and compare them to John's chapter 4, where "living water" is mentioned, and his chapter 3, where "bread from heaven" is discussed. What interpretations of the Exodus passage does John make?

2. Read Proverbs, chapters 8 and 9. Write an essay, comparing the concepts of Wisdom in those chapters with the concepts of Logos in the opening poem of the Gospel of John. Specify elements of difference as well as similarity.

3. Six versions of the miraculous multiplication of loaves and fishes appear in the New Testament: John 6:1–44; Mark 6:30–44, Mark 8:1–10; Matthew 14:13–21, Matthew 15:32–39; and Luke 9:10–17. Matthew's and Luke's versions are revised versions of Mark's. List the differences in the six stories. Assume there once was a single version of the story; write an account you think might have been the original, using elements from any or all of the six. What decisions did you make in order to complete the exercise?

4. Reread the miracle story of the man born blind, John 9:1–41. What interpretations are made of the miracle and of blindness by those sympathetic and those not sympathetic to Jesus? How does Jesus, in John's account, interpret this miracle?

5. Locate the stories of Jesus' resurrection appearances to his followers in the Gospels of Matthew, Mark (use the passages following 16:8), Luke, and John. They are different. What common features can you discover? What conclusions can be drawn from those common features? What differences do the stories contain? What conclusions can be drawn from the stories' differences?

Concluding Letters

1. Reread 2 Timothy. Can you find reasons why analytical scholars came to the conclusion that the author of Romans and Galatians did not write it?

2. Reread Jude and compare it carefully to 2 Peter. Note the changes or deletions made in Jude by the author of 2 Peter. What motivated the author of 2 Peter to make these alterations?

3. Reread the letter of James. Write an essay to defend the position that this letter resembles Matthew's perspective on Law more than Paul's, or more of Paul's perspective on Law than of Matthew's. Be sure carefully to reread Galatians from chapter 5:13 to the end before making a judgment, for the answer is not obvious.

4. Write a commentary in which you decode as best you can one section of the Revelation to John chosen from chapter 4 to the end in terms of the events of the past century. Don't take your results too seriously. Conclude your commentary with a discussion of the kinds of decision you had to make in the process of decoding.

Appendix

The Gospel of Thomas

These are the secret sayings that the living Jesus spoke and Didymos Judas Thomas recorded.

1 ¹And he said, "Whoever discovers the interpretation of these sayings will not taste death."

2 ¹Jesus said, "Those who seek should not stop seeking until they find. ²When they find, they will be disturbed. ³When they are disturbed, they will marvel, ⁴and will reign over all."

3 ¹Jesus said, "If your leaders say to you, 'Look, the kingdom is in the sky,' then the birds of the sky will precede you. ²If they say to you, 'It is in the sea,' then the fish will precede you. ³Rather, the kingdom is within you and it is outside you. ⁴When you know yourselves, then you will be known, and you will understand that you are children of the living Father. ⁵But if you do not know yourselves, then you live in poverty, and you are the poverty."

4 ¹Jesus said, "The person old in days won't hesitate to ask a little child seven days old about the place of life, and that person will live. ²For many of the first will be last, ³and will become a single one."

5 ¹Jesus said, "Know what is in front of your face, and what is hidden from you will be disclosed to you. ²For there is nothing hidden that will not be revealed. [³And there is nothing buried that will not be raised."]

6 ¹His disciples asked him and said to him, "Do you want us to fast? How should we pray? Should we give to charity? What diet should we observe?"

²Jesus said, "Don't lie, ³and don't do what you hate, ⁴because all things are disclosed before heaven. ⁵After all, there is nothing hidden that will not be revealed, ⁶and there is nothing covered up that will remain undisclosed."

7 ¹Jesus said, "Lucky is the lion that the human will eat, so that the lion becomes human. ²And foul is the human that the lion will eat, and the lion still will become human."

8 ¹And he said,

The human one is like a wise fisherman who cast his net into the sea and drew it up from the sea full of little fish. ²Among them the wise fisherman discovered a fine large fish. ³He threw all the little fish back into the sea, and easily chose the large fish. [4]Anyone here with two good ears had better listen!

9 [1]Jesus said,

Look, the sower went out, took a handful (of seeds), and scattered (them). [2]Some fell on the road, and the birds came and gathered them. [3]Others fell on rock, and they didn't take root in the soil and didn't produce heads of grain. [4]Others fell on thorns, and they choked the seeds and worms ate them. [5]And others fell on good soil, and it produced a good crop: it yielded sixty per measure and one hundred twenty per measure.

10 [1]Jesus said, "I have cast fire upon the world, and look, I'm guarding it until it blazes."

11 [1]Jesus said, "This heaven will pass away, and the one above it will pass away. [2]The dead are not alive, and the living will not die. [3]During the days when you ate what is dead, you made it come alive. When you are in the light, what will you do? [4]On the day when you were one, you became two. But when you become two, what will you do?"

12 [1]The disciples said to Jesus, "We know that you are going to leave us. Who will be our leader?"

[2]Jesus said to them, "No matter where you are, you are to go to James the Just, for whose sake heaven and earth came into being."

13 [1]Jesus said to his disciples, "Compare me to something and tell me what I am like."

[2]Simon Peter said to him, "You are like a just angel."

[3]Matthew said to him, "You are like a wise philosopher."

[4]Thomas said to him, "Teacher, my mouth is utterly unable to say what you are like."

[5]Jesus said, "I am not your teacher. Because you have drunk, you have become intoxicated from the bubbling spring that I have tended."

[6]And he took him, and withdrew, and spoke three sayings to him.

[7]When Thomas came back to his friends, they asked him, "What did Jesus say to you?"

[8]Thomas said to them, "If I tell you one of the sayings he spoke to me, you will pick up rocks and stone me, and fire will come from the rocks and devour you."

14 [1]Jesus said to them, "If you fast, you will bring sin upon yourselves, [2]and if you pray, you will be condemned, [3]and if you give to charity, you will harm your spirits. [4]When you go into any region and walk about in the countryside, when people take you in, eat what they serve you and heal the sick among them. [5]After all, what goes into your mouth will not defile you; rather, it's what comes out of your mouth that will defile you."

15 ¹Jesus said, "When you see one who was not born of woman, fall on your faces and worship. That one is your Father."

16 ¹Jesus said, "Perhaps people think that I have come to cast peace upon the world. ²They do not know that I have come to cast conflicts upon the earth: fire, sword, war. ³For there will be five in a house: there'll be three against two and two against three, father against son and son against father, ⁴and they will stand alone."

17 ¹Jesus said, "I will give you what no eye has seen, what no ear has heard, what no hand has touched, what has not arisen in the human heart."

18 ¹The disciples said to Jesus, "Tell us, how will our end come?"

²Jesus said, "Have you found the beginning, then, that you are looking for the end? You see, the end will be where the beginning is. ³Congratulations to the one who stands at the beginning: that one will know the end and will not taste death."

19 ¹Jesus said, "Congratulations to the one who came into being before coming into being. ²If you become my disciples and pay attention to my sayings, these stones will serve you. ³For there are five trees in Paradise for you; they do not change, summer or winter, and their leaves do not fall. ⁴Whoever knows them will not taste death."

20 ¹The disciples said to Jesus, "Tell us what the kingdom of heaven* is like."

²He said to them,

It's like a mustard seed. ³ ⟨It's⟩ the smallest of all seeds, ⁴but when it falls on prepared soil, it produces a large plant and becomes a shelter for birds of the sky.

21 ¹Mary said to Jesus, "What are your disciples like?"
²He said,

They are like little children living in a field that is not theirs. ³When the owners of the field come, they will say, "Give us back our field." ⁴They take off their clothes in front of them in order to give it back to them, and they return their field to them. ⁵For this reason I say, if the owners of a house know that a thief is coming, they will be on guard before the thief arrives, and will not let the thief break into their house (their domain) and steal their possessions. ⁶As for you, then, be on guard against the world. ⁷Prepare yourselves with great strength, so the robbers can't find a way to get to you, for the trouble you expect will come.

* The translation of the Gospel of Thomas is the Scholars Version, except where the author has substituted the traditional translation "kingdom, kingdom of heaven, the Father's kingdom."

⁸Let there be among you a person who understands. ⁹When the crop ripened, he came quickly carrying a sickle and harvested it. ¹⁰Anyone here with two good ears had better listen!

22 ¹Jesus saw some babies nursing. ²He said to his disciples, "These nursing babies are like those who enter the kingdom."

³They said to him, "Then shall we enter the kingdom as babies?"

⁴Jesus said to them, "When you make the two into one, and when you make the inner like the outer and the outer like the inner, and the upper like the lower, ⁵and when you make male and female into a single one, so that the male will not be male nor the female be female, ⁶when you make eyes in place of an eye, a hand in place of a hand, a foot in place of a foot, an image in place of an image, ⁷then you will enter [the kingdom]."

23 ¹Jesus said, "I shall choose you, one from a thousand and two from ten thousand, ²and they will stand as a single one."

24 ¹His disciples said, "Show us the place where you are, for we must seek it."

²He said to them, "Anyone here with two ears had better listen! ³There is light within a person of light, and it shines on the whole world. If it does not shine, it is dark."

25 ¹Jesus said, "Love your friends like your own soul, ²protect them like the pupil of your eye."

26 ¹Jesus said, "You see the sliver in your friend's eye, but you don't see the timber in your own eye. ²When you take the timber out of your own eye, then you will see well enough to remove the sliver from your friend's eye."

27 ¹"If you do not fast from the world, you will not find the kingdom. ²If you do not observe the sabbath as a sabbath, you will not see the Father."

28 ¹Jesus said, "I took my stand in the midst of the world, and in flesh I appeared to them. ²I found them all drunk, and I did not find any of them thirsty. ³My soul ached for the children of humanity, because they are blind in their hearts and do not see, for they came into the world empty, and they also seek to depart from the world empty. ⁴But meanwhile they are drunk. When they shake off their wine, then they will change their ways."

29 ¹Jesus said, "If the flesh came into being because of spirit, that is a marvel, ²but if spirit came into being because of the body, that is a marvel of marvels. ³Yet I marvel at how this great wealth has come to dwell in this poverty."

30 ¹Jesus said, "Where there are three deities, they are divine. ²Where there are two or one, I am with that one."

31 ¹Jesus said, "No prophet is welcome on his home turf; ²doctors don't cure those who know them."

32 ¹Jesus said, "A city built on a high hill and fortified cannot fall, nor can it be hidden."

33 ¹Jesus said, "What you will hear in your ear, in the other ear proclaim from your rooftops. ²After all, no one lights a lamp and puts it under a basket, nor does one put it in a hidden place. ³Rather, one puts it on a lampstand so that all who come and go will see its light."

34 ¹Jesus said, "If a blind person leads a blind person, both of them will fall into a hole."

35 ¹Jesus said, "One can't enter a strong person's house and take it by force without tying his hands. ²Then one can loot his house."

36 ¹Jesus said, "Do not fret, from morning to evening and from evening to morning, [about your food—what you're going to eat, or about your clothing—] what you are going to wear. [²You're much better than the lilies, which neither card nor spin. ³As for you, when you have no garment, what will you put on? ⁴Who might add to your stature? That very one will give you your garment.]"

37 ¹His disciples said, "When will you appear to us, and when will we see you?"

²Jesus said, "When you strip without being ashamed, and you take your clothes and put them under your feet like little children and trample them, ³then [you] will see the son of the living one and you will not be afraid."

38 ¹Jesus said, "Often you have desired to hear these sayings that I am speaking to you, and you have no one else from whom to hear them. ²There will be days when you will seek me and you will not find me."

39 ¹Jesus said, "The Pharisees and the scholars have taken the keys of knowledge and have hidden them. ²They have not entered, nor have they allowed those who want to enter to do so. ³As for you, be as sly as snakes and as simple as doves."

40 ¹Jesus said, "A grapevine has been planted apart from the Father. ²Since it is not strong, it will be pulled up by its root and will perish."

41 ¹Jesus said, "Whoever has something in hand will be given more, ²and whoever has nothing will be deprived of even the little they have."

42 ¹Jesus said, "Be passersby."

43 ¹His disciples said to him, "Who are you to say these things to us?"

²"You don't understand who I am from what I say to you. ³Rather, you have become like the Judeans, for they love the tree but hate its fruit, or they love the fruit but hate the tree."

44 ¹Jesus said, "Whoever blasphemes against the Father will be forgiven, ²and whoever blasphemes against the son will be forgiven, ³but whoever blasphemes against the holy spirit will not be forgiven, either on earth or in heaven."

45 ¹Jesus said, "Grapes are not harvested from thorn trees, nor are figs gathered from thistles, for they yield no fruit. ²Good persons produce good from what they've stored up; ³bad persons produce evil from the wickedness they've stored up in their hearts, and say evil things. ⁴For from the overflow of the heart they produce evil."

46 ¹Jesus said, "From Adam to John the Baptist, among those born of women, no one is so much greater than John the Baptist that his eyes should not be averted. ²But I have said that whoever among you becomes a child will recognize the kingdom and will become greater than John."

47 ¹Jesus said, "A person cannot mount two horses or bend two bows. ²And a slave cannot serve two masters, otherwise that slave will honor the one and offend the other.

³"Nobody drinks aged wine and immediately wants to drink young wine. ⁴Young wine is not poured into old wineskins, or they might break, and aged wine is not poured into a new wineskin, or it might spoil. ⁵An old patch is not sewn onto a new garment, since it would create a tear."

48 ¹Jesus said, "If two make peace with each other in a single house, they will say to the mountain, 'Move from here!' and it will move."

49 ¹Jesus said, "Congratulations to those who are alone and chosen, for you will find the kingdom. For you have come from it, and you will return there again."

50 ¹Jesus said, "If they say to you, 'Where have you come from?' say to them, 'We have come from the light, from the place where the light came into being by itself, established [itself], and appeared in their image.' ²If they say to you, 'Is it you?' say, 'We are its children, and we are the chosen of the living Father.' ³If they ask you, 'What is the evidence of your Father in you?' say to them, 'It is motion and rest.'"

51 ¹His disciples said to him, "When will the rest for the dead take place, and when will the new world come?"

²He said to them, "What you are looking forward to has come, but you don't know it."

52 ¹His disciples said to him, "Twenty-four prophets have spoken in Israel, and they all spoke of you."

²He said to them, "You have disregarded the living one who is in your presence, and have spoken of the dead."

53 ¹His disciples said to him, "Is circumcision useful or not?"

²He said to them, "If it were useful, their father would produce children already circumcised from their mother. ³Rather, the true circumcision in spirit has become profitable in every respect."

54 ¹Jesus said, "Congratulations to the poor, for to you belongs the kingdom of heaven."

55 ¹Jesus said, "Whoever does not hate father and mother cannot be my disciple, ²and whoever does not hate brothers and sisters, and carry the cross as I do, will not be worthy of me."

56 ¹Jesus said, "Whoever has come to know the world has discovered a carcass, ²and whoever has discovered a carcass, of that person the world is not worthy."

57 ¹Jesus said,

The kingdom of the Father is like a person who had [good] seed. ²His enemy came during the night and sowed weeds among the good seed. ³The person did not let the workers pull up the weeds, but said to them, "No, otherwise you might go to pull up the weeds and pull up the wheat along with them." ⁴For on the day of the harvest the weeds will be conspicuous, and will be pulled up and burned.

58 ¹Jesus said, "Congratulations to the person who has toiled and has found life."

59 ¹Jesus said, "Look to the living one as long as you live, otherwise you might die and then try to see the living one, and you will be unable to see."

60 ¹⟨He saw⟩ a Samaritan carrying a lamb and going to Judea. ²He said to his disciples, "⟨...⟩ that person ⟨...⟩ around the lamb."

³They said to him, "So that he may kill it and eat it." ⁴He said to them, "He will not eat it while it is alive, but only after he has killed it and it has become a carcass."

⁵They said, "Otherwise he can't do it."

⁶He said to them, "So also with you, seek for yourselves a place for rest, or you might become a carcass and be eaten."

61 ¹Jesus said, "Two will recline on a couch; one will die, one will live."

²Salome said, "Who are you, mister? You have climbed onto my couch and eaten from my table as if you are from someone."

³Jesus said to her, "I am the one who comes from what is whole. I was granted from the things of my Father."

⁴"I am your disciple."

⁵"For this reason I say, if one is ⟨whole⟩, one will be filled with light, but if one is divided, one will be filled with darkness."

62 ¹Jesus said, "I disclose my mysteries to those [who are worthy] of [my] mysteries. ²Do not let your left hand know what your right hand is doing."

63 ¹Jesus said,

There was a rich person who had a great deal of money. ²He said, "I shall invest my money so that I may sow, reap, plant, and fill my storehouses with produce, that I may lack nothing." ³These were the things he was thinking in his heart, but that very night he died. ⁴Anyone here with two ears had better listen!

64 ¹Jesus said,

A person was receiving guests. When he had prepared the dinner, he sent his slave to invite the guests. ²The slave went to the first and said to that one, "My master invites you." ³That one said, "Some merchants owe me money; they are coming to me tonight. I have to go and give them instructions. Please excuse me from dinner." ⁴The slave went to another and said to that one, "My master has invited you." ⁵That one said to the slave, "I have bought a house, and I have been called away for a day. I shall have no time." ⁶The slave went to another and said to that one, "My master invites you." ⁷That one said to the slave, "My friend is to be married, and I am to arrange the banquet. I shall not be able to come. Please excuse me from dinner." ⁸The slave went to another and said to that one, "My master invites you." ⁹That one said to the slave, "I have bought an estate, and I am going to collect the rent. I shall not be able to come. Please excuse me." ¹⁰The slave returned and said to his master, "Those whom you invited to dinner have asked to be excused." ¹¹The master said to his slave, "Go out on the streets and bring back whomever you find to have dinner."

¹²Buyers and merchants [will] not enter the places of my Father.

65 ¹He said,

A [. . .] person owned a vineyard and rented it to some farmers, so they could work it and he could collect its crop from them. ²He sent his slave so the farmers would give him the vineyard's crop. ³They grabbed him, beat him, and almost killed him, and the slave returned and told his master. ⁴His master said, "Perhaps he didn't know them." ⁵He sent another slave, and the farmers beat that one as well. ⁶Then the master sent his son and said, "Perhaps they'll show my son some respect." ⁷Because the farmers knew that he was the heir to the vineyard, they grabbed him and killed him. ⁸Anyone here with two ears had better listen!

66 ¹Jesus said, "Show me the stone that the builders rejected: that is the keystone."

67 ¹Jesus said, "Those who know all, but are lacking in themselves, are utterly lacking."

68 ¹Jesus said, "Congratulations to you when you are hated and persecuted; ²and no place will be found, wherever you have been persecuted."

69 ¹Jesus said, "Congratulations to those who have been persecuted in their hearts: they are the ones who have truly come to know the Father.

²Congratulations to those who go hungry, so the stomach of the one in want may be filled."

70 ¹Jesus said, "If you bring forth what is within you, what you have will save you. ²If you do not have that within you, what you do not have within you [will] kill you."

71 ¹Jesus said, "I will destroy [this] house, and no one will be able to build it [. . .]."

72 ¹A [person said] to him, "Tell my brothers to divide my father's possessions with me."

²He said to the person, "Mister, who made me a divider?"

³He turned to his disciples and said to them, "I'm not a divider, am I?"

73 ¹Jesus said, "The crop is huge but the workers are few, so beg the harvest boss to dispatch workers to the fields."

74 ¹He said, "Lord, there are many around the drinking trough, but there is nothing in the well."

75 ¹Jesus said, "There are many standing at the door, but those who are alone will enter the bridal suite."

76 ¹Jesus said,

The kingdom of the Father is like a merchant who had a supply of merchandise and then found a pearl. ²That merchant was prudent; he sold the merchandise and bought the single pearl for himself.

"³So also with you, seek his treasure that is unfailing, that is enduring, where no moth comes to eat and no worm destroys."

77 ¹Jesus said, "I am the light that is over all things. I am all: from me all came forth, and to me all attained. ²Split a piece of wood; I am there. ³Lift up the stone, and you will find me there."

78 ¹Jesus said, "Why have you come out to the countryside? To see a reed shaken by the wind? ²And to see a person dressed in soft clothes, [like your] rulers and your powerful ones? ³They are dressed in soft clothes, and they cannot understand truth."

79 ¹A woman in the crowd said to him, "Lucky are the womb that bore you and the breasts that fed you."

²He said to [her], "Lucky are those who have heard the word of the Father and have truly kept it. ³For there will be days when you will say, 'Lucky are the womb that has not conceived and the breasts that have not given milk.'"

80 ¹Jesus said, "Whoever has come to know the world has discovered the body, ²and whoever has discovered the body, of that one the world is not worthy."

81 ¹Jesus said, "Let one who has become wealthy reign, ²and let one who has power renounce ⟨it⟩."

82 ¹Jesus said, "Whoever is near me is near the fire, ²and whoever is far from me is far from the kingdom."

83 ¹Jesus said, "Images are visible to people, but the light within them is hidden in the image of the Father's light. ²He will be disclosed, but his image is hidden by his light."

84 ¹Jesus said, "When you see your likeness, you are happy. ²But when you see your images that came into being before you and that neither die nor become visible, how much you will have to bear!"

85 ¹Jesus said, "Adam came from great power and great wealth, but he was not worthy of you. ²For had he been worthy, [he would] not [have tasted] death."

86 ¹Jesus said, "[Foxes have] their dens and birds have their nests, ²but human beings have no place to lay down and rest."

87 ¹Jesus said, "How miserable is the body that depends on a body, ²and how miserable is the soul that depends on these two."

88 ¹Jesus said, "The messengers and the prophets will come to you and give you what belongs to you. ²You, in turn, give them what you have, and say to yourselves, 'When will they come and take what belongs to them?'"

89 ¹Jesus said, "Why do you wash the outside of the cup? ²Don't you understand that the one who made the inside is also the one who made the outside?"

90 ¹Jesus said, "Come to me, for my yoke is comfortable and my lordship is gentle, ²and you will find rest for yourselves."

91 ¹They said to him, "Tell us who you are so that we may believe in you."

²He said to them, "You examine the face of heaven and earth, but you have not come to know the one who is in your presence, and you do not know how to examine the present moment."

92 ¹Jesus said, "Seek and you will find. ²In the past, however, I did not tell you the things about which you asked me then. Now I am willing to tell them, but you are not seeking them."

93 ¹"Don't give what is holy to dogs, for they might throw them upon the manure pile. ²Don't throw pearls [to] pigs, or they might . . . it [. . .]."

94 ¹Jesus [said], "One who seeks will find, ²and for [one who knocks] it will be opened."

95 ¹[Jesus said], "If you have money, don't lend it at interest. ²Rather, give [it] to someone from whom you won't get it back."

96 ¹Jesus [said],

The kingdom of the Father is like [a] woman. ²She took a little leaven, [hid] it in dough, and made it into large loaves of bread. ³Anyone here with two ears had better listen!

97 ¹Jesus said,

The kingdom of the [Father] is like a woman who was carrying a [jar] full of meal. ²While she was walking along [a] distant road, the handle of the jar broke and the meal spilled behind her [along] the road. ³She didn't know it; she hadn't noticed a problem. ⁴When she reached her house, she put the jar down and discovered that it was empty.

98 ¹Jesus said,

The kingdom of the Father is like a person who wanted to kill someone powerful. ²While still at home he drew his sword and thrust it into the wall to find out whether his hand would go in. ³Then he killed the powerful one.

99 ¹The disciples said to him, "Your brothers and your mother are standing outside."

²He said to them, "Those here who do what my Father wants are my brothers and my mother. ³They are the ones who will enter the kingdom of my Father."

100 ¹They showed Jesus a gold coin and said to him, "The Roman emperor's people demand taxes from us."

²He said to them, "Give the emperor what belongs to the emperor, ³give God what belongs to God, ⁴and give me what is mine."

101 ¹"Whoever does not hate [father] and mother as I do cannot be my [disciple], ²and whoever does [not] love [father and] mother as I do cannot be my [disciple]. ³For my mother [. . .], but my true [mother] gave me life."

102 ¹Jesus said, "Damn the Pharisees! They are like a dog sleeping in the cattle manger: the dog neither eats nor [lets] the cattle eat."

103 ¹Jesus said, "Congratulations to those who know where the rebels are going to attack. [They] can get going, collect their imperial resources, and be prepared before the rebels arrive."

104 ¹They said to Jesus, "Come, let us pray today, and let us fast."

²Jesus said, "What sin have I committed, or how have I been undone? ³Rather, when the groom leaves the bridal suite, then let people fast and pray."

105 ¹Jesus said, "Whoever knows the father and the mother will be called the child of a whore."

106 ¹Jesus said, "When you make the two into one, you will become children of Adam, ²and when you say, 'Mountain, move from here!' it will move."

107 ¹Jesus said,

The kingdom is like a shepherd who had a hundred sheep. ²One of them, the largest, went astray. He left the ninety-nine and looked for the one until he found it. ³After he had toiled, he said to the sheep, 'I love you more than the ninety-nine.'

108 ¹Jesus said, "Whoever drinks from my mouth will become like me; ²I myself shall become that person, ³and the hidden things will be revealed to him."

109 ¹Jesus said, ·

The kingdom is like a person who had a treasure hidden in his field but did not know it. ²And [when] he died he left it to his [son]. The son [did] not know ⟨about it either⟩. He took over the field and sold it. ³The buyer went plowing, [discovered] the treasure, and began to lend money at interest to whomever he wished.

110 ¹Jesus said, "Let one who has found the world, and has become wealthy, renounce the world."

111 ¹Jesus said, "The heavens and the earth will roll up in your presence, ²and whoever is living from the living one will not see death." ³Does not Jesus say, "Those who have found themselves, of them the world is not worthy"?

112 ¹Jesus said, "Damn the flesh that depends on the soul. ²Damn the soul that depends on the flesh."

113 ¹His disciples said to him, "When will the kingdom of the Father come?"

²"It will not come by watching for it. ³It will not be said, 'Look, here!' or 'Look, there!' ⁴Rather, the kingdom of the Father is spread out upon the earth, and people don't see it."

114 ¹Simon Peter said to them, "Make Mary leave us, for females don't deserve life."

²Jesus said, "Look, I will guide her to make her male, so that she too may become a living spirit resembling you males. ³For every female who makes herself male will enter the kingdom of heaven."

Thomas' Synoptic Parallels

Thomas	Matthew	Mark	Luke
4a	11:25	Q*	10:21
4b	19:30	10:31	13:30
5//6b	10:26	4:22	8:17; 12:2
6a	6:1–8, 16–18		
8	13:47–50		
9	13:3–9	4:3–9	8:5–8
10			12:49
11a	24:35	13:31	21:33
13	16:13–17	8:27–30	9:18–21
14b	10:8	Q*	10:8–9
14c	15:11, 17–18	7:15–20	
16	10:34–35	Q*	12:51–53
20	13:31–32	4:30–32	13:18–19
21b	24:43–44	Q*	12:37–40
21c			12:35
21d		4:29	
21e	13:9	4:9	8:8
22a	18:1–3	10:15	18:16–17
25	22:39	12:31	10:27
26	7:3–5	Q*	6:41–42
31	13:57–58	6:4–6	4:24
32	5:14		
33a	10:27	Q*	12:3
33b	5:15	4:21	8:16; 11:33
34	15:14	Q*	6:39
35	12:29	3:27	11:21–22
36	6:25	Q*	12:22
39a	23:13	Q*	11:52
39b	10:16b		
40	15:13		
41	13:12; 25:29	4:25	8:18; 19:26
44	12:3–32	3:28–29	12:10
45	7:16, 12:34–35	Q*	6:44–45
46a	11:11a	Q*	7:28
46b	18:3	10:15	18:17
47b	6:24	Q*	16:13
47c			5:39
47d	9:17	2:22	5:37
47e	9:16	2:21	5:36
48	17:20; 21:21	11:22–23	17:6

Thomas	Matthew	Mark	Luke
54	5:3	Q*	6:20
55a	10:37–38	Q*	14:26–27
55b	16:24	8:34	9:23
57	13:24–30		
61a	24:40	Q*	17:34
62a	13:11	4:11	8:10
62b	6:3		
63			12:16–21
64	22:1–10	Q*	14:15–24
65	21:33–39	12:1–8	20:9–15
66	21:42	12:10	20:17
68//69a	5:11	Q*	6:22
69b	5:6	Q*	6:21
71	26:61	14:58	
72			12:13–14
73	9:37–38	Q*	10:2
76a	13:44–46		
76b	6:20	Q*	12:33
78	11:7–8	Q*	7:24–25
79a			11:27–28
79b			23:29
86	8:20	Q*	9:58
89	23:25–26	Q*	11:39–40
90	11:28–30		
91	16:1–3	Q*	12:56
92a//94	7:7–8	Q*	11:9–10
95	5:42	Q*	6:34–35
96	13:33	Q*	13:20–21
99	12:47,49	3:32–34	8:20–21
100	22:16–21	12:14–17	20:21–25
101//55a	10:37–38	Q*	14:26–27
102//39a	23:13	Q*	11:52
103//21b	24:43–44	Q*	12:37–40
104	9:14–15	2:18–20	5:33–35
106//48	21:21	11:23	17:6
107	18:12–13	Q*	15:4–6
109	13:44		
111a//11a	24:35	13:31	21:33
113	17:20–21		

* Because these sayings are found in both Matthew and Luke but not in Mark they are frequently assumed to derive from a written list of sayings used by Matthew and Luke as a source document. That document is known in scholarship as "Q."